THE MENTAL GAME OF
TRADING

ALSO BY JARED TENDLER

The Mental Game of Poker

The Mental Game of Poker 2

THE MENTAL GAME OF
TRADING

A System for Solving Problems with
Greed, Fear, Anger, Confidence, and Disipline

JARED TENDLER, M.S.

JT PRESS

Published by Jared Tendler, LLC
www.jaredtendler.com

ISBN-13: 978-1-7340309-1-4

Cover design by Laura Duffy
Book design by Karen Minster
Author photo by Amanda Laster

PRINTED IN THE UNITED STATES

CONTENTS

THE MENTAL GAME OF
TRADING

CHAPTER 1

A SYSTEM TO FIX MENTAL GAME PROBLEMS

"We cannot solve our problems with the same
thinking we used when we created them."

—Albert Einstein

Your goal is to make money. But something is getting in your way. You lose money when you shouldn't, or even if you consistently make money, you leave profits on the table. The question is why.

For the answer, you'll most likely look at your technical skills first. That's obviously a critical step. You analyze trades, tighten your rules, learn new techniques, develop your system, do more research, and test new strategies. Despite all of that work, the bleeding continues. You try again and again, but you still don't get anywhere because the answer doesn't lie in what you know about trading. The answer comes from the mental and emotional side of the game—your mental game, and you're not effectively working on it.

That's not to say trading is all about psychology. It's not. Even a perfect mental game—emotionally balanced, always focused, consistently in the zone—won't make you profitable long term if you don't have an edge in the market. But if you *have* an edge, yet aren't making what you should, or are struggling with greed, fear, anger, confidence or discipline, your mental game may be costing you more than you realize.

Think about your most costly errors in execution. Do they include any of the following?

- Forcing mediocre trade setups
- Hesitating on entries

- Exiting trades too early
- Chasing the market price up and down
- Moving a stop too soon
- Moving your profit target before it hits
- Talking yourself out of a good trade

Often when these mistakes occur, you're unable to stop yourself from making them. Your emotions get in the way, and they have the power to force your worst impulses.

Don't beat yourself up over this. Part of the reason you haven't eliminated your execution errors is that you didn't know what you were up against. Just like trading follows a basic set of rules, so too does the mental game. For example, the part of your brain where you actively make decisions can access only a limited amount of information at any given time. What's more, emotions have the power to reduce and even shut down your decision-making process entirely. If you don't understand these and other rules of the mental game, you can't reliably correct your mistakes.

That's why I like the term "mental game" to describe the mental and emotional side of trading. The word "game" automatically infers rules and strategy for how you improve vs. a one-and-done solution. Terms like trading mindset, trading mentality, or trading psychology all imply something static. As if finding the right advice is all you need to have the perfect mind for trading. This, my friends, is a myth.

Many of you have been looking for silver bullets, when what you need is a strategy or system. In this book, you'll learn a practical, step-by-step system for correcting the most common emotional issues in trading: greed, fear, anger, overconfidence, and low confidence. These issues are causing the errors in execution you've been unable to stop. I'll not only show you how to solve them, I'll also show you how to address the discipline issues that interfere with your focus, routines, habits, and execution. And I'll highlight some straightforward ways to make lasting progress.

This system is the culmination of 15 years of work. Clients from around the world at the highest levels of competition in golf, poker, esports, and trading have used this system with tremendous results. What makes it so effective is that it's designed to find and correct the root of the problem. You can't kill a weed unless you get the roots out. Stomping on it, or chopping off what grows above ground, only yields a temporary result. This is likely what's happened with your most common trading mistakes. Whatever you've done hasn't finished the job.

To be clear, you're not going to learn how to execute trades, come up with trade ideas, read charts, or recognize fundamentals here. The traders who are successful using my system are already skilled enough in these areas to be clear about where their real problems lie.

Throughout the book you'll read some of their stories; their experiences may provide some of your most important lessons. At the time of this writing, they were working the system and continuing to make progress every day. This is exactly what I would expect, because there's no magic to this system. You're not going to get some secret tip that will eliminate your greedy attempts to make money, your fearful hesitation to enter trades that fit your system, or your angry impulse to make up for a loss by quickly taking another trade.

What you *will* get is a system that gives you the foundation to address those problems. A system that enables you to solve current and future mental game problems by giving you a deeper understanding of what causes them in the first place. A system that methodically walks you through the steps to recognize and correct them in a lasting way.

You'll learn how to identify the signals that indicate a problem is likely to emerge, much like you get an alert of a potential trade setup that requires your attention. This system is accessible, logical, practical, and repeatable. If you take the time to learn it and do the work that I suggest, you're likely to make significant strides toward improving your mental game.

Before we get more deeply into the system and how it works, let's do a little more myth-busting around a topic at the heart of it all that's widely misunderstood—emotion.

EMOTIONS AREN'T EVIL— THEY'RE SIGNALS TO USE AND LEARN FROM

The way many of you have been battling your trading errors is completely ass-backwards—what you think is the problem is not actually the problem. If you're going to have any chance at solving issues like greed, fear of losing, or hatred of mistakes, you must first have an accurate understanding of what you're up against. That begins with changing your perspective on the role that emotion plays in causing your trading errors.

One of the fundamental differences between this book and the advice commonly found in other trading psychology resources is how to view emotion. Conventional wisdom says that emotions are the problem, and gives advice that mainly focuses on reducing, controlling, and releasing emotion. You can certainly make short-term improvements this way, but these strategies can only take you so far. Why?

Because you aren't addressing the real problem. Instead, you're spending time and effort fighting what you *think* is the problem—the emotion generated from trading. You call emotions irrational, try to trick your mind, or work to rationalize, deny, avoid, ignore, deflect, project, distract, numb, or desensitize them. You might even use healthy options like meditation, yoga, and exercise, among the other—less healthy—options to blow off steam or release stress from the day. But you're not solving the problem.

Or, instead of ignoring or rationalizing emotions, you're very aware of them and have created your own "solutions" that are really just ways of managing them. You exit early to lock up profit and avoid a potential blowup if the trade turns against you. You stop trading on days your emotions are too high, until you can get your head on straight. You also may do the following:

- Move a stop to breakeven
- Walk away from an active trade so you don't interfere with it
- Quit a session early to ensure a profitable day
- Review sticky notes on your monitor before entering a trade
- Talk to yourself to stay disciplined and motivated
- Constantly remind yourself of basic concepts, like "losses will happen; don't let it affect you"
- Take extended time off from trading

The problem with these work-arounds is that you've minimized your profitability as well as your ability to adapt and improve as a trader. Trading smaller, exiting earlier, and booking a profitable day all in an effort to keep your emotions in check is not how you ultimately want to play this game. Yes, they can be good short-term strategies, but they're best used like training wheels. And until you lose the training wheels, your upside potential as a trader is significantly limited.

Let's dig in a bit deeper. It's a myth that emotions such as anger, greed, and fear are the problem causing your trading errors. Rather, these emotions are actually *signals*. This is a critical change in perspective. Don't fight your emotional state. Instead, treat emotions as signals and get curious about what they're trying to tell you. We do this all the time when it comes to physical ailments. And, like our emotions, sometimes the real cause is not always obvious.

For example, let's say you've been getting headaches at the end of the trading day. At first you think they're caused by the stress from trading. Family and friends agree with you, but you still get them on the weekend and even after a weeklong vacation. You go to the doctor fearing it's something worse, yet everything checks out. You've been taking over-the-counter meds for a few months now, trying to manage your headaches, but you still haven't found the cause. Then, as you finish up your trade journal at the end of a trading day, you notice yourself squinting and decide to get your eyes checked. Turns out, your vision has progressively worsened over the past six months and eye strain is causing your headaches. Change your eyeglass prescription, problem solved. Headaches weren't the problem—they were a signal, and it was your job to interpret what that signal meant.

Similarly, negative emotions are signals pointing you to a problem you're not addressing. If you follow those signals to identify and correct the underlying cause, you'll automatically stop:

- Moving your profit target out of a greedy attempt to make a killing
- Chasing the market from a fear of missing out
- Overtrading out of anger to make up for losses or mistakes
- Thinking you can outsmart the market because of overconfidence
- Sticking with a losing trade too long because your confidence can't handle another loss

Just as you stop taking medication when your headaches go away, you don't need to spend time and energy trying to manage or control these emotions, because they stop getting triggered. That's the power of this mental game system. When you identify and solve the real problem, you don't have to fight for control or rely on training wheels for protection. The emotional reactions disappear and you're freed up to focus on trading.

Think of your emotions like the indicators you follow in the market. As a trader you use signals all the time and, based on your level of expertise, you are more or less skilled in leveraging those signals to deploy your edge. In the mental game, negative emotions are signals of the hidden flaws that undermine your trading. For some of you, these hidden flaws cause subtle problems. They're like computer programs running in the background but not open on your desktop. They dull your sense of the market, reduce clarity in your thinking, and slow your reaction time.

For others, the hidden problems are the cause of a barrage of error messages and blue screens. You make trades you know you shouldn't, but you can't stop. You stare at a textbook trade but can't pull the trigger. You know you should close, but fear or greed blinds you. You know the right way to react, but can't stop yourself from overreacting. Regardless of how much these flaws impact your trading, they must be identified and corrected to consistently trade at the level you expect or aspire to.

Emotion Fuels Performance

With all of this focus on how emotions interfere with your performance, it's tempting to write them off as bad. Emotions, however, are key to reaching your peak. They are an essential source of energy to fuel your performance. In this regard, an emotion is neither good nor bad.

Even emotions typically seen as negative are not always bad. For example, anger can be a phenomenal source of energy. Michael Jordan used anger as motivation, most notably from being cut from his high school basketball team, to become one of the greatest basketball players of all time. Some traders are at their best when they're pissed off. Others when their back is against the wall and under a ton of pressure. Thinking of emotions as being inherently bad doesn't make any sense and the results prove otherwise.

The downside of using anger or fear for optimal performance is that most people lack the ability to control them. Jordan, and other elite performers like him, have a mastery of their emotions. They have figured out how to maintain the right mixture of emotion, energy, or fuel to consistently perform at the top of their game. In the hands of a novice, anger and fear can be extremely volatile.

Having the right mixture of emotion is key, but stability of those emotions counts a lot for the long term. Imagine being on a small boat in choppy seas and trying to board another boat that has pulled alongside. The unpredictable nature of the waves makes it difficult, if not impossible, to correctly anticipate when you should jump from one boat to the other.

That's what it's like trying to get into the zone when your emotions are volatile. You can do it, but the odds are low and big mistakes are likely. On the other hand, when the seas are calm, or your emotions are stable, reaching the zone consistently is much easier.

WHY YOU NEED A SYSTEM

By using my system, you'll learn how to clear out the mental and emotional volatility caused by your underlying performance flaws. What automatically emerges is an intense drive, but with greater stability. You get the benefit of the Jordan-like anger without the turmoil. The process to reach the zone becomes easier and more straightforward. And in the long term, you will enjoy your work more, reduce the odds of burnout, and strengthen your ability to produce higher returns.

You can correct all the specific problems covered in this book—greed, fear, anger, overconfidence, lack of confidence, and poor discipline—using the same core strategies. No matter who you are, the basic rules of the mental game are the same. We are all bound by these constraints. When solving any mental game issue, you must work within them. However, you can easily mold the system to your style of trading, regardless of your strategy, time frame, trade frequency, or number of markets you trade. It doesn't matter if you trade equities, options, futures, forex, cryptocurrencies, or bonds, or whether you make three trades an hour or three trades a month. Once you have a good idea of how the system works, you'll be able to mold it in a way that's optimal for you.

You're learning a system that will not only help you to fix your current mental game problems but future ones as well. Using this system will become a skill in itself that enables you to continually refine your mental game when new issues pop up. For instance, a fear of losing may be the issue you're looking to solve now, while later on, greed or overconfidence might become a problem.

As humans, we'll never achieve lasting perfection, especially in an industry as competitive and dynamic as trading. Even though future problems may be less severe, you'll always have something to work on in your mental game, and you can come back to this system again and again.

How My System Helps with Common Performance Flaws

Helping you to identify and correct the performance flaws that affect your trading is the focus of this book. But what do I really mean by performance flaws? Here are two examples: high expectations and confirmation bias.

To be clear, high expectations aren't inherently bad. Many successful people have incredibly high expectations of themselves and the people around them, and these expectations have been an important driver of their success. And yet . . . high expectations can be like a double-edged sword, causing self-inflicted damage, often subtle, to performance. You may get intensely angry when you fail to meet those expectations, most often after you make a mistake, close out a big losing trade, or fall farther into drawdown or from your equity highs. Or you may get incredibly nervous, and resort to comfortable trades with very little risk.

For others, it's a nasty cycle where anger turns into fear, which damages confidence, which further weakens the ability to perform, which makes it even harder to achieve your expectations, which leaves you angrier, more anxious, and more down about your prospects. Amazingly, you can often tolerate all that while still performing at a comparatively high level. But the internal chaos and damage that high expectations can inflict make it impossible to realize your potential.

Another common performance flaw is confirmation bias. For those who are unfamiliar, confirmation bias basically means you seek out information that confirms your preexisting belief and ignores or rejects information that opposes that belief. You get married to a position, setup, or sector, but then it falls out of favor, and you're slow to respond because of how much money you made. A position immediately validates your entry as it races toward your target, but when it retraces and stops you out, you're quick to reenter, trying to prove you were right. Or you see another trader making money. Your bias is that you'll definitely make money by following them, but, instead, you end up behind the curve.

There are people who believe biases like these can't be changed. That the best we can do is to be aware of them and try to limit their damage. While that may be true in some cases, clients of mine have made significant improvement by identifying the performance flaws driving their confirmation bias. For example, it can come from a weakness in confidence. As a trader you can believe anything you want, but the market dishes out cold truth. Yet, traders with this bias will often, unknowingly, ignore this reality, trying to prove what they *believe* to be true vs. trying to figure out what is *actually* true, in order to protect their confidence.

These are two of the many performance flaws that will be discussed throughout the book. You'll learn to find your flaws by using your emotions as signals. Emotions provide data on how we operate, for better or worse, at an unconscious level. They provide information on a host of things, including our underlying belief systems, biases, goals, perspectives, flaws, ingrained habits, wishes, and illusions. This is important, because what happens at the unconscious level has a direct impact on your thoughts, actions, and trading decisions.

Now, I'll bet that when some of you see the words "unconscious level," you think I'm referring to Freud, or how we need to analyze your childhood or wade into psychobabble type stuff. That's not my style, and that's not required to produce the outcomes we're after. The fact is, the unconscious contains everything from simple habits, like how to brush your teeth, and how to input an order, to beliefs that affect your perception of risk, as well as other performance flaws that are common among people operating in highly intense and competitive industries.

As you work through this book, you'll become aware of the flaws, illusions, and biases affecting your trading. Then, through practical and actionable steps, you'll understand how to correct them, so they cease to undermine your execution.

How This System Elevates Your Entire Game (A-game, B-game, and C-game)

When it comes to execution, everyone has their own performance range, both mentally and tactically. You're likely aware, intuitively, that you have one too. It's easy to tell the difference between when you're trading at your absolute best from when you're trading at your absolute worst. But have you ever stopped to think deeply about the different levels of your performance in a precise way? Most haven't. For simplicity in discussing the concept here, I'll stick with calling these levels your A-, B-, and C-games.

When performing at an A-game level, your emotions are clear and stable. You're in the zone, or close to it, so you make high quality decisions because there's no negative emotional interference with your process. Any mistakes you make at this level are caused by something technical—for example, knowledge you haven't yet gained or a recent change in the market you haven't identified yet.

Frankly, to call these "mistakes" is a bit of stretch. You wouldn't say a toddler was making a mistake when they fall soon after taking their first steps. Your attempts to take your A-game higher are no different. These "learning mistakes" can't be prevented. They're an inherent part of the process.

On the flip side, your C-game is chock full of emotional volatility, and that's the primary cause of your poor performance. You make mistakes that are so obviously wrong, you know it seconds afterward. At this level, there's nothing new for you to learn tactically. You know what you should have done, and it's why you're so quick to recognize it was a mistake. In that moment, you lacked access to the knowledge and skills you typically rely on, either because excess emotion caused your mind to malfunction, or you lacked sufficient energy to think properly.

Some traders don't make big, obvious mistakes. Their mental game has advanced to a point where their C-game consists of more subtle mistakes. For example, you might have a tendency to read too much into price action, and force trades that lack a strong indication of edge within your strategy. Whether the mistakes are big or small, C-game is where your performance flaws live. Those flaws create emotional chaos, cause your perspective to be out of sync, and result in mistakes that are basic, relative to your range.

The nature of your B-game is more complicated. In your B-game you're likely making some marginal tactical errors—things that you need to improve but aren't super obvious. If it were obvious, that would make it a C-game error. You'll find some emotions holding you back from being in your A-game, but not enough to pull you down into your C-game.

From a mental and emotional standpoint, one of the biggest differentiators between B- and C-game is that, in B-game, you have the impulse or thought to make a C-game mistake, like forcing a trade or closing one too early, but instead you retain the presence of mind, mental energy, and emotional control to avoid it. In C-game, your emotions are too strong, and you can't stop yourself from forcing or getting out too early. While in A-game, the impulse or thought doesn't happen, or it's so small you barely notice.

The graphic below summarizes the points I've just made and labels the types of mistakes that show up in each level of your game.

C-GAME	B-GAME	A-GAME
OBVIOUS MISTAKES	MARGINAL MISTAKES	LEARNING MISTAKES
CAUSE: Mental or emotional flaws caused your emotions to be too intense, or your energy was too low	CAUSE: A blend of weakness in your tactical decision-making and mental or emotional flaws	CAUSE: Unavoidable weakness in your tactical decision-making

The key to unlocking the backend of your game and eliminating your most common errors in execution is correcting the performance flaws that cause your C-game. Even if you're a seasoned trader with 20-plus years of experience, some performance flaws still cause your worst mistakes. This is true regardless of whether your mistakes are significantly less awful than the mistakes junior traders make. Every trader has performance flaws, no matter how experienced or skilled.

You can't escape the gravitational force of your C-game by focusing solely on improving your trading knowledge and skill. If you improve only on the technical mistakes that exist in your C-game, your performance flaws will continue to generate the same level of excess emotion. You'll make different, but still obvious, mistakes.

That strategy isn't wrong; it's just inefficient. You'll continue to go through unnecessary ups and down in your execution, and your performance will continue to lag. To move your entire game forward, you must move your C-game forward. And to do that, you must prioritize fixing the flaws causing your C-game. That's where my system comes in.

Before you can prioritize fixing those flaws, however, we've got to bust one more myth. That's the idea that controlling your emotions is a solution to the problems in your mental game. Not true. Control is not the answer.

Emotional Control Is Not a Solution—RESOLUTION Is

In any game, we develop a strategy to help us accomplish the goals we set. When it comes to the mental game, traders have set their sights too low. They think their best strategy is to control their emotions. But this common aspiration is not an end game; it's a permanent job.

If controlling your emotions is your only tactic, you're going to be constantly fighting a barrage of emotional reactions. Trading is hard enough without devoting mental energy to fight to control your emotions. It's draining, and in the long term, makes it impossible to reach your potential as a trader.

The end goal to strive for is resolution. Resolution means you have corrected the performance flaws causing your trading errors, permanently. Automatically, the things that would have triggered anger, greed, fear, etc., simply don't anymore. You no longer need to manage, control, or work around your emotional reactions, because they are gone.

What does your trading look like once your emotions have been resolved? Your emotions aren't gone in the sense that you're void of them, like a robot. Quite the opposite. You'll be:

- Full of emotion, but the good kind—energized, confident, focused, and motivated
- More patient and able to let the market come to you, rather than chasing it

- Focused more on execution than PnL
- Able to handle losses
- Decisive and rapid in your execution

Not only will your emotions be stable and positive, but the common trading mistakes you make when you're blinded by greed, tilt, or fear will be gone as well. Why? Those emotions were the primary cause of your mistakes. This doesn't mean you won't make mistakes—no trader is perfect—but now your mistakes will be smaller comparatively.

The concept of resolution may not make complete sense yet, but you've seen and experienced it before. Perhaps you just didn't realize it. Here's a non-trading example to help make it clear: Imagine being pissed off at a friend who acted like an ass the last time you hung out. Normally you'd let it go, but something about the way he acted was different this time. You don't say anything, and while it doesn't stop you from having fun the next few times you see him, it's not the same as it was before. There's clearly tension between the two of you, noticeable enough for another friend to mention something to you.

After a month, you finally say something. He barely remembers, gets defensive, and denies he would ever act like that. The conversation gets heated and he leaves. But 20 minutes later he comes back and apologizes. You agree it was wrong to leave things unsaid like that for so long. If the issue is truly resolved, the frustration and tension are gone, and never again show up related to that incident. That's resolution, and that's what you want for your performance flaws.

My system for reaching resolution has distinct stages, each of which has different steps and strategies embedded within it:

1. **Map Your Pattern:** You need to identify an overall macro view of your emotional volatility in order to have a clear idea of what you will face on any given day. You also need a detailed map of what those emotional reactions look like at a micro level, so that in real time you can quickly spot them and minimize the damage. You'll learn this mapping process in chapter 2.

2. **Identify the Roots of Your Problem:** To get to the real reason behind your problems, you need to uncover the hidden flaws, biases, and illusions, including errors in learning that can either prevent you from progressing or create significant ups and downs in your progress. You'll be introduced to this process in chapter 3. In chapters 4 to 8, you'll identify the specific flaws that apply to you.

3. **Correct Your Problem:** This is where you tackle the problem head-on, by consistently applying the correction. In chapter 9, you'll learn a straightforward way to stop your reactions in real time, and minimize your mistakes.

The outcome of this system is resolution of the performance flaws causing your problems. The importance of resolution can't be overstated. Imagine not having greed, fear, tilt, confidence, or discipline problems. At all. That's an outcome worth the hard work required to get there. And if you work the system, you can get there.

Now, let's get started.

CHAPTER 2

MAP YOUR PATTERN

"The unseen enemy is always the most fearsome."

—George R. R. Martin,
A Clash of Kings

You can't stop what you can't see. Many of you don't realize that your attempts to correct or control your emotions are mistimed so badly, they're almost guaranteed to fail.

Let that sink in.

They're almost guaranteed to fail.

If you want to keep your emotions from affecting your decision-making, you must be able to recognize they're rising in real time and take action before they cause your mind to malfunction.

Mapping your pattern is the key to recognizing the escalation of emotion. While that may seem like something you should already be able to do, you can't, because you haven't done the work yet. Many traders are blind to the patterns in their mental game, much like they couldn't spot patterns in the market earlier in their career.

Recognition is a skill like any other. But from a mental and emotional standpoint, it's often overlooked as something that can be improved. You *can* get better at recognizing not only escalating emotions but also the patterns behind that escalation.

Right now, many of you are just realizing how much emotions are part of the equation. But the essence of this first step, recognizing and mapping your emotional patterns, is no different than what you do every day as a trader. You look at information and parse through noise to identify when the signals and indicators tell you to buy, sell, or hold. To everyday investors your skills look like wizardry or luck. They either have god-like reverence for what you do or think it's complete BS.

What we do, in fact, is very similar (and I experience BS-like skepticism too). While you look at market signals to find opportunity, I use emotions, thoughts, and actions to see causality where others don't. You've already proven to have a strong ability to read signals, and I'll train you to use that skill to better understand your emotions and mental game.

The goal of this step is to recognize the patterns associated with the most common trading errors that impact your performance. You may think these mistakes happen randomly, but they don't. They repeat, over and over again, allowing you to map the signals that indicate a rise in emotion, so you can stop your mistakes from happening.

Imagine driving down a road that leads you to consistent returns, a strong feel for the market, and the ability to follow your trading strategy without hesitation. Now, imagine that a thick fog rolls in, you can't see a thing, and you take a wrong turn without realizing it. To make matters worse, farther down this road a bridge has washed out and you're about to drive off a cliff. With a map of your patterns, you create an internal GPS that alerts you when you've taken a wrong turn, so you can quickly make a U-turn and get back on the road to profitability.

Some of you aren't aware a mistake is coming until it's too late and the car is in midair, flying over the edge—you've just doubled down on a dog. Or your issues are relatively smaller. You're not at risk of driving off a cliff, but the longer you head down the wrong road, the more you unnecessarily burn money, time, and opportunity. Regardless of the scale of your problems, the better you map your pattern, the easier it is to gain control of your emotions and get back on track.

UNDERSTANDING EMOTIONS AS SIGNALS

Emotions, thoughts, actions, and even trading decisions provide data on how we operate at an unconscious or instinctual level. In a way, by following the trail of clues, you're taking on the role of a forensic detective. The detonated "bomb" you're analyzing is the chaos from an overactive emotional system. The clues to identifying the cause of your emotional reactions lie in the details of what blew out of that bomb.

This examination can completely change your perspective about the emotional event, because looking at it provides invaluable insights into what led up to it and what flaws were behind it. Both are key to resolving the problem so you can prevent future explosions.

Start looking closely at the specific emotions, thoughts, actions, and decisions that are automatically triggered while you're trading. They're the data that will help you understand the full scope of the problem. Become like a detective, eager to gather up clues and curious to understand what they mean.

Typically, traders throw those clues out. By choosing to blow off steam, or trying to forget what happened and move on, they essentially delete the clues that can solve the problem. Using those tactics is understandable when you lacked a system that could help you make sense of your reactions. That's not the case anymore. These clues are essential details to map your mental game problems.

Two Causes of Emotion

Viewing emotion as a clue or signal is a shift in perspective, but it doesn't explain where the emotions come from and why they so often catch you by surprise. One reason is that you often don't even recognize what's happening. The emotion comes up as an immediate reaction, or reflex, to a trigger, such as quickly getting stopped out in a trade, triggering anger, an amazing setup, triggering excitement and nervousness, or hearing about how much money other traders are making in a trade you missed, triggering a fear of missing out (FOMO).

Think about this initial emotion like a reflex. It's the equivalent of a doctor hitting your knee with a rubber mallet or your instinct to catch a ball thrown at your face. It's a split-second reaction. There's no conscious thinking involved. A snap of the fingers, and boom, emotions spike.

Traders often misinterpret the trigger as being the problem. The trigger is simply the detonator. The underlying flaw is the bomb. The trigger could be a mistake, taking a loss, being stopped out by two ticks, only to reverse and take off, or an offhanded comment you thought was disrespectful. This point can cause some confusion, so let's look at an example—booking a big loss. Many traders get furious, break things, and force additional trades without proper entry signals.

But this doesn't happen to all traders, which means that a big loss doesn't invariably cause anger. If it did, then every trader would have the exact same reaction. Instead, some traders handle big losses easily, because they instinctively know these outliers are distinct possibilities. Figuring out what triggers the problems you want to fix is a key part of mapping your pattern.

As you begin mapping, keep in mind that, in many instances, the initial trigger only generates a small amount of emotion. In fact, it may be so tiny that it barely registers consciously. You're simply not aware of the effect it has on your emotional stability. And yet, at the same time, automatic or habitual thoughts, actions, and decisions have already begun changing how you're interacting with the market.

For instance, two hours into a trading day that started poorly, the possibility of an entry comes up and triggers a mixture of tension, excitement, and stress. You may also think, *Don't mess this up!* You immediately lean closer to your screen and second-guess the validity of what you're seeing. Instantly, your thoughts, emotions, and physical state have changed.

Then comes your response. If your next thought is, *Relax, I've got this,* you're fighting the reaction. If it works, it will reduce your emotions and improve execution.

If, however, your next thought is, *Don't mess this up,* or *I can't lose money here again,* those thoughts produce **secondary emotions** that can lead to a downward spiral. You start making basic errors trying to compensate for the mistakes you just made. Then comes disbelief and self-criticism for making those basic errors: *What the hell is wrong with* *me? Why can't I do it? It's so simple!* And boom, your emotions are spiraling out of control.

The common mistake traders make is to interpret the thought *Don't mess this up* as the trigger *and* the cause. If you believe the problem is thinking negatively, you battle to control and change your thoughts. You listen to advice that implies the problem is simply a result of negative thinking: *Don't think so negatively. Just keep your emotions in check.* No. *Don't mess this up* isn't a conscious thought—it pops into your mind automatically.

To be clear, secondary emotion is produced as you become aware of, or respond to, the emotions, thoughts, and actions that were initially triggered. When you become aware of anxiety, anger, or boredom, the mind can amplify that emotion. You get more anxious because you're already anxious; you become angrier because you recognize that you're angry; your boredom increases because you're aware of how bored you are. When this happens, it's accurate to say that thoughts cause emotions.

In day-to-day life, people don't differentiate emotions in this way. But distinguishing between the immediate reflex and the secondary cause of emotion is critical. If you don't identify the source of the reflex, you can't map your pattern or correct the problem.

Triggers will continue to create more and more emotion that you'll either have to control or work around. If there's a leak in your ceiling, you want to get to the source of the problem. No one wants to endlessly dump out buckets of water, or patch something that keeps breaking. Fix the damn problem and move on.

As you map your emotional patterns, be aware of both the initial reaction and the secondary emotion. Why? Because taken together, these are the starting points for digging into deeper flaws. In the next chapter, I'll show you how to uncover and correct the flaws causing your problems. First, though, you need to create a map of your pattern and understand one more key element about emotions.

Emotions, as you have probably already noticed, can build on top of other emotions. I call this **accumulated emotion**.

Accumulated Emotion

Now you understand that emotions are signals of deeper flaws and can intensify as you become aware of your reaction. But do you know what the rise in emotion looks like? This is critical, since catching the rise early is your primary defense.

The reality is, emotions are messy. They build up in both the short term and the long term. And while the brain has a natural digestion process for emotion, sometimes there's residual emotion left over—this is **accumulated emotion**. Despite trying to put the previous day's losses and emotional chaos behind you, by perhaps telling yourself, "Today is a new day," you aren't really starting fresh. You don't have a reset button or a clean slate to work from. Lurking beneath your optimism, emotions are accumulating, day over day.

To make matters worse, over weeks, months, and even years, underlying flaws (and remember, we all have them) can collect emotion and hide it, like an enemy stockpiling ammunition while lying in wait. *Good times.*

Let's look closer at this short-term accumulation first. Emotions are consistently going up and down within the trading day. Imagine tracking their movement like the price action on a chart. On some days, emotions are stable and only go up or down by a tick or two. On other days, there are huge swings throughout.

Let's say, for example, that you book a big loss in the first half of a session that triggers anger, and for the remainder of the session you struggle to get the loss out of your head. But once the session is over, the built-up frustration starts to dissipate. For some traders, all of that frustration could be gone within minutes, or on a really tough day, it could take a few hours, along with a workout at the gym.

Either way, once the emotion is released, the next time you sit down to trade, the frustration from the day before is gone. Like it never happened. You're truly reset and ready to trade with the emotional clarity and balance you ideally want.

Of course, on some days when your performance or results are particularly positive or negative, several problems can occur:

1. Not only do you lose control during the trading day, but afterwards your emotions continue to rise as you celebrate, or you become more angrier, more fearful, or down. You continue to experience the emotional ups and downs as if you were trading after hours.

2. You controlled your emotions during the trading day, but they came out afterwards and caused problems of a different sort. This is akin to market-making news that hits in the middle of the trading day, but you're unable to fully process it until after the close.

From a performance standpoint, you care less about the emotions released after the trading day ends, since they have no bearing on your results that day. However, you care very much about the emotion that carries over and impacts your performance the following day. If your baseline emotion doesn't reset completely, and you start with, say, 10% more emotion, your map needs to account for this in your pre-market warmup.

An extra 10% may not seem like much, but it's enough to prevent you from reaching your optimal level of performance. More consequentially, it's enough to force you to work harder to maintain control—increasing the odds you'll fail.

Or maybe the extra emotion doesn't affect you the following day because the market conditions and your results didn't trigger additional emotion. But imagine if, over the next few days, your results continue to slump or rise at an outsized pace. Your emotions can continue to build and build.

Now you don't just have an extra 10% hanging around; instead, it's 40% more. You start the day already on edge and disorganized in your thinking, so you overreact to price action, sell too quickly, and make a host of other errors. That produces more after-hours emotion, so you have trouble being present with friends and family, lack motivation to hit the gym, and overeat, drink alcohol, and don't sleep well. You wake up early with thoughts swirling in your mind, trying to figure out how to get out of the drawdown, or imagining what you'll do with all the money.

Regardless of when the emotion gets created, whether it's during the trading day or after, it's critical that you be aware of your emotional state at the start of the next trading day. If you're not aware of that extra 10% (or whatever the excess percentage is that day), you'll be unprepared to handle your emotions in the right way.

Accumulated emotion was a particular problem for Frantz, a Canadian trader who left a 15-year career in academia to scalp E-mini futures. He and his wife shared a dream to travel the world. He became a trader to fund that dream, and because it let him be his own boss. But a swirling cocktail of emotions came up on a daily basis, preventing him from executing his strategy consistently. As months turned into years, the pressure was mounting to reach a level of financial success that would enable him to realize the dream.

To hit his financial target, Frantz only needs to take one A+ setup per day. There were plenty of days when his mind was calm, and he could see the action clearly, make quick decisions, and take only those trades. Other days, however, the mental strain of waiting for an A+ setup would lead him to force a trade outside that narrow parameter.

Here's a typical scenario for how it would play out. If the forced trade loses, Frantz immediately starts criticizing himself, while simultaneously trying to convince himself he's done the right thing. Now, a new reversal setup is playing out. He's tempted, but able to stay away. Waiting and waiting, frustration grows from being on the sidelines, and he ends the day with no A+ opportunities and that one mistake.

Unbeknownst to Frantz, he arrives the following day feeling more of an urge to correct his mistake and get an A+ trade. Right out of the gate, he sees a potential trade, but it has some congestion to it, so he stays away initially. When the price takes off, he knows not to chase it, but the urge is too strong. He gets in and loses. Hope arises in his mind that the next trade will cancel the pain from the loss and his mistake.

As he waits, his mind won't relent. The self-criticism builds momentum, "You know the setup was no good. You shouldn't be losing. You know better." He wants to fight back, and he looks at every candle for a clue that there's a setup to take. He sees one and jumps in without processing all the criteria. To make matters worse, Frantz doesn't even notice his analysis has degraded. The trade loses, his anger explodes, and he takes several more trades before finally standing up and walking away.

The rest of the day he tries to clear his mind and spend time with his wife and son, but his mistakes eat at him. He worries that his dream may just be that, and he might never succeed. The next day, he's resolved to improve his execution, but he doesn't realize how frustrated he already is. Tempers flare during his morning routine with the family, fanning the flames and causing him to miss the start of the trading day and an A+ setup. As he sees what was missed, his brain shuts off. Without even waiting for the next candle to close, he enters in a terrible place.

Despite knowing that all he needs to do is be patient and wait for the right spots, cycles like these were common for Frantz. I'll pick up the story later in the book to show how he was able to break out of this cycle.

The buildup of emotion isn't always as clear and sequential as you saw with Frantz. And it can actually happen in a couple of different ways. One is where the emotion builds up around a specific issue, but doesn't show up right away. The second way happens when a change in circumstances intensifies what had been just a minor problem.

In the first scenario, **emotion can accumulate over weeks, months, and years around a particular issue, but not show up consistently.** You'll have days or weeks where there's no recent buildup, but when the trigger comes, you'll feel it with an incredible intensity that seems like it's coming out of nowhere.

Consider a trader who has a pretty high tolerance for losing. But when his PnL drops quickly, by over 10%, it creates a severe drop in confidence, because he fears he'll bust his account and go broke.

It seems illogical to think that way, since it hasn't happened since the early days of his career, but nine years later that fear still lurks in the back of his mind. He vividly remembers having to eat ramen every night, letting the utility bills roll for a few months, and negotiating with the landlord to avoid eviction. Hanging on by a thread took a severe toll on him emotionally. When he finally climbed out, he promised himself it would never get that bad again. And it never did.

But that old emotion gets triggered whenever he unconsciously senses that he might be in danger of going down that road again. Once he goes back to winning and the issue subsides, it's easy to think the problem has once again been solved. But the underlying emotion wasn't corrected, months or even years later. The buildup of emotion can come out anytime there's a perceived threat of going bust—it's stockpiling emotion and it waits for the trigger.

In the second scenario, **you have a flaw that's causing such minor emotional reactions that you don't even pay attention to it.** You can ignore it for a while—until a change in your life, priorities, or goals makes that minor problem into a noteworthy one.

For example, while high expectations have caused short-term emotional volatility and some accumulated emotion over the years, you've managed to perform pretty well. You never considered it a problem. Every year you kept making more and more money. Hit your goals, and then hit them again the next year. Then you have your biggest day ever, and surprisingly, the victory doesn't taste as sweet. Instead of feeling exhilarated as you had before, it just feels like the goal posts have simply moved again. You wonder if you'll ever feel satisfied.

At a macro level you start looking at your career and thinking, *Is this it?* At a micro level you feel trapped by your own success. Your best day ever doesn't excite you like it used to, yet big losses hurt even more. You become more irritable during the trading day. It's not as fun as it used to be, and that carries home with you. You're slowly becoming aware that you're not happy, and start to wonder if you're burned out.

The short-term emotion that normally would be digested is now accumulating, and makes trading to your usual standard more difficult. You always had high expectations, but they didn't cause your emotions to accumulate until you started having larger questions about your career.

Regardless of how the emotion accumulates, identifying whether or not it's impacting your performance is a critical part of mapping your pattern. If you answer yes to any of the following questions, it's likely that accumulated emotion is a factor for you.

- Is your reaction to certain events disproportionate and out of line with what you think is reasonable?
- Are you making mistakes that are so basic, it's inexplicable how you could make those errors?
- Do you find it harder and harder to settle down and truly relax at the end of the day?
- Are you having trouble falling asleep at night, or are you waking during the night with thoughts swirling?
- Do you have a shorter fuse than usual, tending to overreact more easily?

When accumulated emotion is a significant factor, traders typically know exactly what they need to do, but they can't get themselves to do it. The refrain that I hear from my trading clients over and over again is the disconnect of "How is it possible that I can be thinking X and continue to keep doing Y, even when I know better?" They have so much built-up emotional crap, their thoughts can't translate into proper execution. This causes confusion and a further decline in performance.

Accumulated emotion, or as some call it, "emotional baggage," is one of the toughest parts of the mental game to improve. You have to contend with both the emotion created today and the accumulation of emotion built up over time. You must work outside of trading hours to reduce accumulated emotion.

Helping you to develop a strategy that balances the short-term need to release emotion with the long-term goal of correcting your problems is covered in chapters 3 and 9. In the meantime, continuing to manage your reactions with after-work strategies like sports, exercise, going out with friends, etc., is fine. These aren't bad strategies when the alternative is losing your mind. Just make sure you gather up the clues to create your map; otherwise, you'll never truly correct the problems long term.

CREATING THE MAP

So how do you actually track your emotions to map them? By noticing, examining, and writing down what's going on before, after, and during each of your trading mistakes. Here are some of the things you might capture:

- Triggers
- Thoughts
- Emotions
- Behaviors
- Actions
- Changes to your decision-making
- Changes to your perception of the market, opportunities, or current positions
- Trading mistakes

Shine a spotlight on the period of time when these errors take place and analyze all of these details that show up before and after them.

At the beginning you may be able to only recognize a few signals. For example, with FOMO, you might spot:

- An antsy, nervous sensation in your stomach
- The thought, *Don't miss another one!*
- A change to a one-minute chart

Your starting point is what it is. By continuing to pay close attention, over time you'll be able to see more and more of these signals. Here's an example of what you want to map:

- **Trigger:** Trading options intraday
- **Thoughts:** *I can't believe this is happening. I'm not letting the market stop me—I'm going to get this trade right!*

- **Emotions:** I want revenge when any trade I know has an edge doesn't pay off
- **Behaviors:** I'm hyper-focused on one position
- **Actions:** I'm constantly looking at PnL
- **Change in decision-making:** I'm focused on getting revenge and getting my money back
- **Change in market perception:** I'm reading too much into price action, convinced I can predict price movement
- **Mistake:** I'm taking the same trade over and over, until it's clear I'm wrong or getting nowhere

Before the next time you trade, think back to previous instances where the errors happened, and start writing out those details as best you can. This way you can immediately avoid repeating some of these mistakes.

When beginning this process, many traders can't yet spot the signals that occur before their execution breaks down. For example, they don't realize they're angry until they slam their mouse after closing a position they should never have been in, and saying out loud, "Are you kidding me? How the hell could I do that again?" If that's all you can currently map, then the next time you make a mistake like this, be ready to capture the preceding details.

The moments after making mistakes provide a tremendous opportunity to identify how you actually got to that point. What compelled or triggered you to get in that trade? Was it preceded by a series of losing trades, after closing out a big winner, or seeing others making money in a trade you missed? What thoughts, behaviors, actions, emotions, or changes to your perceptions of the market and decision-making, and things you say out loud appeared at that time? When your mind explodes, it's a great time to become a detective and gather clues. Plus, the act of writing things down can actually help to defuse the emotion.

Your job gathering clues doesn't end until you have a complete map of your pattern, including the initial trigger. Achieving that level of detail is your goal for this first step of the system. To get there, this can't be a task you do once and never again.

Recognition is a skill, and like any other skill, you'll develop it through an iterative process. Until you identify the initial trigger, continue to map the pattern as best you can and review it as part of your pre-market warmup. That will enhance your ability to see existing and new signals while you trade.

During the trading session, keep a working document nearby to capture new details so you don't forget them. Afterward, review and consolidate your notes so you're better prepared for the next session. Work like this every day for one to two weeks. It won't be the only thing you do, but make sure you invest the time to keep it on your radar to ensure you nail this step.

High-volume day traders will find intraday note taking nearly impossible, since they don't have the bandwidth to take detailed notes. Instead, quickly jot down what you can, and expand on your notes at the end of the day. Those of you who make fewer trades per day could spend more time taking notes during the day, but I still suggest keeping your analysis to a minimum. Don't abuse the luxury of having more time and have it cause distractions. The last thing you want is your note taking to cost you money.

As you begin this process, you may feel like you're not really accomplishing much, since your mistakes continue to happen and your emotions remain intense. Remember, the ultimate goal is to permanently solve your problems, not temporarily pacify them.

Tips for Creating Your Map

Think of this step like gathering the pieces to a puzzle that doesn't come in a nice prepackaged box with a picture on it. Instead, the pieces are scattered and you don't know what the completed puzzle looks like. Mapping your pattern is how you gather up all the pieces and form a coherent picture of the problem. Then you can begin solving it.

Here are some additional ideas to help you create a map.

Look for earlier signals. Once you can spot the details immediately surrounding your trading mistakes, look for signals that occur prior to each. Look closer for the initial trigger and the emotions, thoughts, behaviors, and actions that happen automatically in response to it. Perhaps you can identify smaller missteps, or notice subtle changes in your perception of the market or your decision-making process; for example, reading too much into price action or taking a trade even though it only meets four of your five criteria.

Examine how secondary emotion is created. What thoughts, actions, decisions, etc., pile on top? Or, if you can't yet spot the initial reaction, use the signals you can see to get closer to it.

Set an alarm. Some traders get so caught up in the market, they have difficulty recognizing the internal signals of emotional volatility. If that's the case for you, try setting a timer to go off at some regular frequency that isn't too disruptive (i.e., every 15, 30, or 60 minutes). At that time, take a moment to be aware of your thought process, examine how you're feeling, and see if there are any signs of a problem. If so, quickly write down those details. Yes, this is disruptive in the short term, but you only have to do it until you build up enough skill to recognize the problem without the timer.

Consider meditation or mindfulness training. While these are by no means a requirement, some of my clients have found meditation or mindfulness training to be a great tool for building greater levels of awareness. With better awareness they're able to recognize additional details that they previously couldn't see.

Understand the intensification of emotion. Traders often don't realize the names of emotions are simply describing greater intensity, not a separate emotion. For example, you may think anger and frustration are two different emotions, but anger is just a larger amount of frustration.

This is important because when you're looking for the precursors to anger, watch for when you begin to feel frustrated or irritated—that will build up and eventually turn into anger. Similarly, uncertainty, doubt, and worry are the common descriptions of small amounts of anxiety.

Understanding how emotion intensifies can help you recognize the details of your pattern, including the initial trigger.

Recognition Doesn't Equal Control

While mapping allows you to see your emotions in real time more clearly, that doesn't mean you can control them. For some of you that can be hard to comprehend—how can you see something and not be able to stop it? But the emotions behind your mistakes are intense. They're fueled by a well-worn pattern that has a momentum all to itself and, once triggered, the most likely outcome at this point is that it will continue to the typical conclusion.

This can be difficult to accept, but it's critical that you do. If you expect yourself to be in control, your emotional reaction will be even worse.

Some of you, however, will experience a placebo-like effect that will make it seem as though you're in control of your emotions. The reality is, this control comes from being inspired by the newness of the strategy or knowledge of your pattern. But control is not a correction. You're only stopping the pattern through the power of your recognition, not by correcting the underlying performance flaw.

Only a small percentage of traders can rapidly go from recognition to correction like that. For most of you, the newness fades, market conditions change, you take a four-day weekend, or you lose momentum for another reason, and this placebo-like control disappears.

The reality for most is that your problems are too complex to be solved just with a map. The real power in my system lies in the next chapter, where you uncover the real cause of your emotional reactions.

CHAPTER 3

FIND THE ROOT OF YOUR PROBLEM

"Truth—more precisely, an accurate understanding of reality—
is the essential foundation for producing good outcomes."

—Ray Dalio

Have you already tried to fix your mental game problems? If so, you're like many of my clients. You've likely read books, talked with other traders, and tried a number of things to stop emotions from interfering with your trading. And despite your best effort, you've been unsuccessful.

Here's an analogy that may help explain why you're still struggling. If you had a toothache that wouldn't go away, you wouldn't think the solution was to just keep brushing your teeth. You'd go to a dentist and get an X-ray, so you'd know what was really going on. Only once you knew what was really going on, based on the examination and the X-ray, would you know how to fix the problem—you need a root canal.

It's essentially the same with solving your mental game problems. At this point, you've learned that emotions are signals of hidden flaws. You've also learned how to map the pattern in which those flaws appear. But we haven't yet examined the root of the problem. What's more, we also need to look deeply into how you've been trying to improve as a trader. Put another way, it's not just that you have a toothache; the way you've been brushing your teeth is a problem. That's what's led to the need for a root canal.

My mental game system uses some unique approaches to X-ray what's going on so you can fix the problems at the root. First, we look at your day-to-day learning process to find the inefficiencies that may be causing emotion volatility. Ineffective learning is the cause, or partially to blame, for a huge number of mental game problems—regardless of your level of expertise. This content tends to surprise my clients, but once they dig into it, they find it invaluable.

You're going to realize that the ways you've been learning can improve with a more reliable structure and a core concept—the "Inchworm." This concept gives you a visual representation of the learning process, so you can test how well you're learning and identify flaws holding you back.

When it comes to actually how to learn, there's a wide variation in the organization and approach traders use and how effective they are. Regardless of where you sit in that range, by taking a more organized and dynamic approach to how you learn, you can:

- Maximize the efficiency of your learning process by avoiding the most common pitfalls
- Become more emotionally stable
- Develop greater consistency through the ups and downs in your results
- Create new ways of evaluating progress and performance that go beyond PnL
- Reach the zone more consistently
- Become more adaptive to a rapidly changing competitive environment
- Maintain interest and enthusiasm, which prevents plateaus, boredom, and burnout

To close out the chapter, you'll learn how to use a tool my clients find essential to their progress—the Mental Hand History. This tool helps you to develop a new perspective for problem solving, and streamlines your efforts to identify the root problem and determine a correction to it.

Let's kick the chapter off with some of the unexpected, yet common, learning flaws that undermine emotional stability and consistency in your trading.

COMMON LEARNING PITFALLS

In the course of your lifetime, you've learned everything from how to walk and talk to the requisite trading expertise, such as interpreting a variety of indicators or fundamentals. You had to learn all of it. But how often do you consider the role of learning as it relates to your mental game? If you're like most traders, not often.

Yet, flaws in how you've been learning are a likely contributor to emotional instability. This is a critical concept. When traders know what to truly expect of themselves, they stop fighting against what they think is true, and can instead work within the reality of what's actually true.

Inefficiencies in learning can be hard to spot. Take the common scenario that many traders go through at some point: transitioning from a demo account or paper trading to the live market. This is an important step that typically happens at the beginning of a career, but it can also occur for some traders when they adapt a discretionary strategy or experiment with a new system.

Many traders have had the experience of being a star in a demo account, only to struggle in the live market. They can't execute with the same calm and precision. There's hesitation, uncertainty, and overthinking that didn't exist in the simulator because those results didn't actually matter. It can be easy to misinterpret those signals as fear, when the simpler explanation is a learning error—failing to understand how to make the transition to the live market.

This common error in learning happens in many performance arenas. The golfer who doesn't play as well in a tournament as in a practice round. Or the new actor who kills it in rehearsals but can't deliver on stage. Like many golfers and actors, if you believe the sim and the live market are the same, there's a fundamental flaw in your understanding of performance. "I'm making the same trades; it should be no different," is a common refrain that highlights this flaw. While the trades may be the same, you are not.

In the live market your results actually matter. Your money is on the line, among other things, like your reputation, confidence, and future. That's not the case trading a simulated market. The truth is, there's a gap. And no matter how much you tell yourself to treat the sim like the live market, they're not the same and never will be.

Amped-up nerves are an inherent part of competing in an intense environment with a great deal on the line and where you have a lot to learn or prove. This is how the nervous system responds to such situations, and having your nerves dialed up helps you learn. Your ability to sense and perceive the environment is heightened, thanks to your nervous system.

You absorb more data than normal, and this helps to fuel the zone and high-level intuition. Pressure and nerves are a vital part of transition. If, however, you believe they're inherently a problem, or that you can't handle the pressure, secondary anxiety will accumulate and that will cause a drop in performance.

The flaw here is not that you feel some pressure or nerves; it's expecting your body to respond to the learning process without them.

To give you a few other examples of learning flaws, let's say you're a seasoned trader who has been trading index futures and recently started trading options. When you make what you assume to be a stupid, basic mistake, like sizing too large, you get extremely frustrated with yourself. You're a seasoned trader and should know better.

But, really, the mistake could be evidence that your knowledge from trading futures doesn't entirely translate to options. There's still a transition to make, and you have to complete the learning process.

Or, perhaps you didn't realize that high levels of competence can be a buffer against underlying emotional flaws. For example, you sized too large because a series of losing trades triggered anger. This hadn't been a problem for a long time, but the newness of trading options exposed an old emotional flaw. Either way, trading a different market made a basic mistake more likely, but if interpreted the right way, the mistake can be corrected quickly.

Or, maybe you tend to overconsume data by trying to learn more and more without fully absorbing it. You may not realize this flaw can cause your performance to have big ups and downs. Sometimes your sense of the market is spot on, but that happens infrequently. More often you have varying degrees of confusion, overthinking, and second-guessing your moves. There are too many ideas or angles in your head to make sense of. You get frustrated, stressed, and assume the best thing is to take a few days to clear your head. That might work in the short term, but this problem keeps resurfacing again and again.

The obvious problem is the secondary frustration and stress, so you assume it's a mental game problem. But it could simply be a basic error in how you're consuming and processing information.

Finally, when correcting your problems with greed, anger, fear, confidence, or discipline, you must go through a learning process. Too often traders believe these problems have quick fixes, but just as you can't become a competent trader overnight, you need to go through a learning process to eliminate a mental game problem.

When you think of correcting emotional issues as a learning process, you'll be able to recognize progress and make the necessary adjustments. If you don't take this strategic approach, your expectations are automatically out of sync with reality. Not only are you dealing with the original problem, but you also create secondary layers of anger, fear, low confidence, etc., as you attempt to correct your issues.

You become angry that you haven't yet corrected your anger or lapses in discipline. You worry that your fear isn't getting better fast enough. You lose confidence that you can regain your confidence. Without understanding the learning process, you misread or ignore signs of improvement, causing you to abandon a strategy that's actually working, just not in a visible way to an untrained eye.

Many of you fall into this category of having unsuccessfully tried to fix your trading problems. Understanding the learning process removes this layer of complexity and allows you to correctly identify whether your mental game strategy is working or not.

In the next section you'll learn about a concept that I created early in my career as I was thinking about how to communicate the learning process to poker players. The Inchworm Concept forms the foundation of an organized and logical structure for learning. For the seasoned traders out there, this theory may be obvious in practice. But many of my clients have found that it illustrates their existing efforts to improve, and this, in turn, helps them become more efficient at developing their expertise.

THE INCHWORM CONCEPT

The Inchworm Concept is literally based on the inchworm, a caterpillar that moves in a distinct way. If you've never seen the way an inchworm moves, it starts by stretching its body straight, anchoring the front "feet," and then lifting up from the backend. It then bends at the middle to bring the two ends closer together, anchors the back feet, and then stretches its body straight again to take another step forward. An inchworm looks like a bell curve that moves.

As it relates to trading performance, a bell curve can show the natural variation that exists in your decision-making. Think for a moment about the quality of your trading decisions over the last 6 to 12 months, or longer if you only make a small number of trading decisions per month. To illustrate a point, let's say you were able to accurately rate the quality of all of these decisions on a scale of 1 to 100, where 1 represents your worst decisions and 100 are your best, and then plotted them on a graph. What you'd see is a bell curve showing the variation in your performance from best to worst, and everything in between.

This defines your current range of decision-making. All the knowledge and skills that you're currently learning exist within that range. Every day you show up to trade, you're bound by your range. There's a limit to how bad your decisions can be, and there's a cap on how good your decisions can be as well.

As a trader with 10 years of experience, it's no longer possible, under any circumstance, for you to think about a trade as rudimentarily as you did when you were six months in. From a performance standpoint, there's a proverbial stop-loss limiting how bad a decision you can make.

And on the flip side, when you were a trader with six months' experience, you couldn't wake up one day and suddenly think about a trade as well as a trader with 10 years' experience. Sure, you could execute the same trade, but the decision-making process to get there would be significantly different. The capacity to shrink nine and a half years of experience into one day doesn't exist.

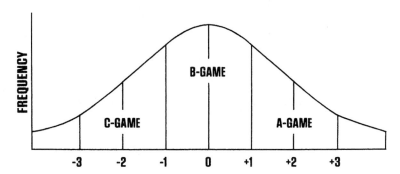

In chapter 1, I talked about your A-game, B-game, and C-game. The bell curve illustrates how each level looks on a graph, and the Inchworm Concept helps you see, track, and improve performance over time.

The concept of Inchworm comes in when you look at how improvement happens over time. A bell curve is a static snapshot of your performance over a defined period of time and shows how frequently you were trading well, at average, or poorly. Improvement is the forward movement of a bell curve over time—something an actual inchworm illustrates perfectly in the way it moves.

Consistent improvement happens by taking one step forward from the front of your bell curve, where your A-game becomes even better, followed by another step forward from the back, where your C-game becomes less terrible.

Over time, that improvement from both sides of your range moves your entire bell curve further to the right on the graph. At that point your old C-game disappears and your stop-loss for poor decision-making has moved forward. It's no longer possible for you to make the trading errors or to think about a trade as you did at that previous level. Your old B-game becomes your new C-game, your new B-game is now at the level of your old A-game, and you have created the opportunity to find a higher level of performance that becomes your new A-game.

If you focus only on frontend improvement, as many traders mistakenly do, your range gets wider. As a result, a host of problems develop, including wild swings in execution, plateauing, burnout, and the inability to maintain high levels of focus. Contrary to what many traders implicitly believe, your backend doesn't automatically move forward because the frontend did.

To counter this, you must consistently focus on backend improvement, especially when you reach a new peak in your ability. Some traders instinctively try to fly too close to the sun, and they push the frontend as far as they can. They end up looking greedy and getting burned by a big drawdown.

These huge missteps can be avoided by understanding how backend weaknesses trip you up. Instead of continuing to push higher and higher, focus on correcting your current greatest weaknesses. Consistently. That moves the backend of your bell curve forward and allows you to take a further step forward from the front, without increasing your risk of blowing up.

Everyone wants to be at their best more often and improve faster. The Inchworm Concept helps you to get honest and clear about your weak points in an organized way. When you're well prepared, you can guarantee improvement every day. Your capacity for learning, the key to fast improvement, will be at its peak.

The Cause of Variation

As long as you're trading, you'll always have aspects of your performance that represent the peak of your ability and the flip side, your worst. Always. Perfection isn't possible over a large number of trades, because the definition of perfection continues to evolve.

There are times when your sense of the market is spot on and you make phenomenal decisions, and other times you don't. Trading is a dynamic profession that's constantly becoming more competitive. This means that the definition of perfection, or even just solid performance, is a moving target.

As long as your performance evolves, that means you're learning. And if you're learning, there will always be a range in the quality of your decision-making.

Variation also exists because, as humans, we're highly dynamic, and there are a large number of variables that impact us—including whether we got enough sleep, exercised, ate right, felt physically healthy and emotionally stable, etc. Now add to that the complexity of the financial markets. Not only are you continually figuring out how to best play the game, but the game can change at any moment. Each individual area causes variability. The key is to solve for as many of those variables as you possibly can and reduce the amount of variation in your performance.

Inchworm forces you to define the different levels of your range and identify the variables that influence your performance in explicit and detailed terms. For example, those traders who take physical health as seriously as other professional performers, such as athletes, can more consistently stabilize their performance. Their Inchworm becomes narrower.

By identifying causality, you gain control over distinct variables that were previously beyond your scope. This book is intended to do that from an emotional standpoint—narrowing the variation that exists within your emotional ups and downs.

For the more statistically minded, I want to point out that the discussion of the bell curve is meant to be illustrative and not perfectly accurate. Depending on the data set, your bell curve could easily be skewed to the right by a higher frequency of peak-level decision-making, or to the left from a large sample of poorer decisions. If you're killing it for six months in a row, the average would skew right, and there would be a flatter tail to the left.

But the flip side can also be true. When you're in a prolonged slump and performing poorly, the curve would skew left, toward your C-game. Even though your curve may be skewed, the concept still applies.

Define Your Range with the A- to C-game Analysis

Imagine being given a superpower that allows you to see where, exactly, the line is between variance and your skill. It's not one they'd ever make a movie about, but as a trader it would be pretty valuable. Suddenly you'd have the ability to always know your real edge.

A power like that would take a lot of the uncertainty out of trading and make your confidence much more stable. On days when you got crushed, but upon reflection wouldn't change your decisions, you wouldn't feel as bad as you do normally. On the flip side, on days where you make an insane amount of money, but they resulted from a series of errors you made that happened to work out, you wouldn't feel as good.

Obviously, no one has this power. But the idea of having a more objective way of evaluating your skill is appealing, isn't it? When you have a clearer way of knowing how you're trading, in real time and day to day, you can focus less on PnL and more on process and execution. You can tolerate short-term ups and downs a lot better, especially in a drawdown or a rush, and your emotions will be more stable. The A- to C-game Analysis is one of the centerpieces of my system, because it delivers those benefits.

The tool is straightforward and can use the details you gathered mapping your problems. Essentially, you identify the key descriptions of each level—A-game, B-game, and C-game—and separate your mental game from your tactical skill. Here's a sample to give you an idea of what it looks like:

A- TO C- GAME ANALYSIS

MENTAL GAME

C-GAME	B-GAME	A-GAME
Distracted	Overthinking	Very relaxed
Risk averse (hesitating)	Attention on wrong market	Decisive
Forcing trades to overcome hesitance	Losing focus	Patient
No patience	Missing obvious trades	Confident
Negative self-talk	Looking at PnL	Trusting gut
Self-doubt	Reacting slower	
Trading PnL	Going against gut	

TACTICAL SKILL

C-GAME	B-GAME	A-GAME
Keep chasing price	Worse understanding of context, correlation, or location	Clear understanding of context of the market as a whole
Keep fading directional moves	Scalping for a few ticks, but no big trades	Clear understanding of correlations with NA, ES and DOW
Cutting trades too soon because I want to get paid	Not aware enough to sit out or pick my spots	Clear understanding of location, price levels, and where we are on the chart
Didn't follow loss limit rules	Cutting trades too soon and not giving it enough room	Letting price come to me
Making impulsive trades because I'm overreacting to one element	Too much attention to depth	Seeing trapped traders
Scaling without planning for price going against me	No good read on volatility	

Much like you've done before, take time to think about this before and after a trading session. As you become aware of information during the session, note it down to add later, when you gather up the pieces. For those of you who might find this more difficult, start with what's most obvious. Create a draft and revise it.

You'll know you have a solid polished first version when you stop seeing any new things for at least three trading days. Once this is solid, you can then use it as your measuring stick, both during and at the conclusion of each day.

You can also review it as part of your warmup to remind you of the mental and tactical improvements to make, as well as the signals that your level has dropped. Don't change it within each month. That sample size is too small to properly evaluate the solidness of your improvements. Just take notes on the side, and update it in the future when you have sufficient proof that your game has changed.

If you want to take this a step further, you can also identify the levels behind your current C-game. This tends to be more important tactically, as they reflect the strengths in your knowledge base or decision-making that always show up, regardless of how fearful, angry, or tired you are. One of the ways to identify these strengths is by analyzing the solid parts of your game when you reach these points, or whenever you're at your worst. This stabilizes confidence by creating a stop-loss, in a sense, for how bad you get, and makes it easier to see what's still in the learning process.

One word of caution is to not use the A- to C-game Analysis as a crutch. While it's an important and helpful evaluation tool, when you completely ignore your results in favor of this new metric, you could use it as an excuse for poor results. Use it, but don't completely disregard your actual real-money results. Simply use the A- to C-game Analysis to improve the accuracy of your day-to-day evaluation.

When Your Range Is Too Wide

When completing the A- to C-game Analysis, or just thinking about your range if you haven't done the task yet, you may notice a big gap between your best and your worst. This problem can happen for a number of reasons. The primary one is failing to consistently upgrade your C-game.

Consistent improvement as a trader has to include a commitment to eliminating your weaknesses. Otherwise, you'll succumb to one of the most common problems I see: a wide range. The solution to that is a narrow range, which is achieved by maintaining a consistent focus on correcting the flaws in your C-game. This steady focus is a trait that elite performers in any industry share, including traders. They understand that the power to compete at the highest level comes first from the strength of the weakest part of their game, both technically and mentally.

The old adage that a team is only as strong as its weakest link also applies to individuals. It's weak to not know your weak points, and even weaker to not want to know them. Your C-game has the power to hold you back, and if you don't work on it consistently, the instability caused by that wide range will ripple through every aspect of your trading.

The idea of working on weaknesses is nothing new. There's a plethora of fantastic advice out there about the value of failure and weaknesses, and yet many traders still have a hard time embracing them, especially when emotions are involved. This indicates the presence of a performance flaw. Maybe you don't understand how your strengths and weaknesses are linked, as shown on the bell curve, and you have the one-dimensional "play to your strengths" mentality. The reality is that no matter how good you are, you always have weaknesses to improve. Even areas of strength have relative weakness.

Perhaps you didn't have a solution to the emotional chaos causing your big mistakes, so it was better to ignore them and focus on what you could improve. Maybe you harbor the old-school mentality that it's weak to be weak, so suck it up and stop being a baby.

Others are actively trying to work on their weaknesses but don't realize they're not fully embracing them. Here's a list of often surprising examples that can prove you're ignoring parts of your C-game:

- Working really hard, and seeing progress in many ways, but randomly having big blowup days where it feels like you forgot everything and all of your efforts were wasted
- Constantly jumping around looking for the next thing to learn, especially when in a drawdown
- Rationalizing bad days by saying "that's so unlike me" and moving on without much thought about why it happened
- Continually coming up with new trading strategies, and with each big insight you think, *Now I've found it!*, implying that from now on you'll be printing money
- Being consumed by healthy activities that are believed to be the "answer" to never showing weakness, such as meditation, exercise, sports, a new diet, etc.
- Lacking trust in your trading, feeling like you're your own worst enemy
- Being unable to stay in the zone for long or even reach it very often
- Secretly believing it's possible to always be at your best

Regardless of the flaw causing these problems, if you ignore, avoid, or deny your C-game, you're unknowingly sucking the life out of your trading. Continually correcting the flaws in your C-game is an essential part of your growth. Inchworm provides a practical way to understand the learning process and the value of embracing weaknesses and mistakes. You'll be able to more clearly focus on the precise reasons these setbacks, failures, or mistakes happen, and how to prevent them in the future.

With all this talk about weaknesses, I want to make one thing clear. My goal is not to make you accept your weaknesses, feel good about them, and that's it. Since you'll always have them, why not have a constant desire to eliminate the weak points in your trading? It's actually pretty simple when you think about it. Your job is to suck less.

The key to moving your Inchworm forward is sucking less in key moments when your C-game is likely. You must take advantage of these opportunities because it can transform your trading.

Those moments are challenging. Emotions often run high, and it's easy to lose sight of the long-term reality. The more you succumb to those mistakes, the better you get at making them. Learning is never neutral. Plus, there's a direct relationship and connection between your peak and the strength of the backend of your Inchworm. By sucking less in those moments, you make it easier to get in the zone.

That simple idea of sucking less was significant for Brian, a futures trader from Canada who had been trading full-time for about five years. Along with the visual of the Inchworm, he was able to solve a majority of his problems with greed and fear almost immediately. That's because his emotional problems weren't deeply rooted. Instead, problems with focus, procrastination, and a lack of structure were the real culprits.

Throughout the trading day, Brian was constantly envisioning a future with a lot of money, where he was trading from the Caribbean and living an island lifestyle. This dream was a persistent distraction that took away the focus and urgency he needed each day to materialize that vision. He'd skip out on his pre- and post-market routines and avoid watching videos to expand his trading acumen. During the trading day, he'd get distracted and then just walk away and do something unrelated to trading.

The emotions came in seemingly random fashion. There would be periods where greed would kick in. Brian would feel on top of the world, and he'd take position sizes that were too big, assuming they would never lose. At other times, he was so fearful of losing or making a mistake, he would only take perfect setups and therefore missed a lot of opportunities.

Once he was in a trade, he'd be too focused on PnL, rather than price action, and couldn't let the trade play out. He'd either quickly take profit or panic-sell once it retraced, because he didn't want to lose. Or those missed opportunities would spark FOMO and he'd try to pick its top or bottom, only to get stopped out for going against momentum.

The combination of greed and fear, along with focus problems and procrastination, crippled his ability to trade. He worried about failing, going broke, and embarrassing himself. But as severe as all this sounds, greed and fear were actually a result of the fact that his big aspirations and high expectations lacked a framework and the discipline to achieve his dream.

In our first session, the Inchworm Concept immediately resonated, and Brian realized that he was stalled out because he wasn't actively trying to move forward. "It's really hard to go forward if you are stretched out flat," he noted. That led us to create weekly goals that were achievable, with daily benchmarks to measure progress. This allowed him to break out of the need to make money now, and focus instead on a daily process of sucking less.

For Brian, the concept of not having to be perfect, to just be 10% less bad, clicked, and reduced the severity of his procrastination. Previously he'd skip his routine entirely if he couldn't do it perfectly. Now, he understands the definition of perfection rises over time and that he needed to suck less to be more perfect.

He laid out an approach for the day and the markets, which has benefited him significantly. He's taking more trades, has a higher win/loss ratio, and is more profitable—his R-factor increased from around 1.25 to 2.25. He's able to stay in trades longer, let them play out, and trust the process. All the things he knew he needed to do, but couldn't. That doesn't mean he has all the answers now, but he has a framework that explains why he was struggling, and that gives him the direction and stability to make continual progress.

Truth be told, the Inchworm Concept and the corrections I've mentioned here didn't fully correct his discipline problems. He needed to deal with focus and procrastination differently, and I'll pick up his story again in chapter 8, where I discuss those problems.

Like Brian, for your game to grow stronger, you need a bigger and stronger foundation on which to build it. Your C-game is the crack in that foundation. Even if you take nothing else from this section, carefully consider the following advice, as it can have a valuable impact on your ability to learn. Avoiding C-game mistakes takes some organization and preparation. But even focusing on it for one minute a day can create enough momentum to help you suck less.

If you're unsure of what to work on in your trading, improving your C-game will be the most beneficial and rewarding place to start. It's also the simplest. Learning can be overwhelming, daunting, and complex at times. Knowing you can always focus on the three or four worst errors you make gives you a reliable and easy starting point.

UNCOVERING WHAT'S CAUSING YOUR BACKEND PROBLEMS

For many of you, the key to moving the backend of your Inchworm forward is correcting the emotional problems that hold your backend in place. But to correct those problems, you must first accurately identify what's causing them. To simplify the way to find the root cause, I developed the following problem-solving process.

Originally developed for my poker clients, it's called the Mental Hand History. I chose the name to encourage poker players to approach the mental game in the same structured and logical way they correct technical mistakes, which involves reviewing "hand histories" of their play. The Mental Hand History helps you to analyze the information you've gathered while mapping your reactions, and it helps you find the faulty patterning at the heart of the issue.

For some of you, using this tool will fundamentally rewire how you solve problems. The five steps are:

STEP 1: Describe the problem in detail.
STEP 2: Explain why it makes sense that you have this problem, or why you think, feel, or react that way.
STEP 3: Explain why the logic in Step 2 is flawed.
STEP 4: Come up with a correction to that flawed logic.
STEP 5: Explain why that correction is correct.

Completing these steps can be challenging. With that in mind I organized the content in the next five chapters to make it easier to spot your problems, identify the details that characterize your struggle, and fill out your Mental Hand History. You can also pull in content, advice, and ideas from other resources. There's a lot of good material out there; it's often just not used in the most effective way.

Now that you have a system, fit in whatever you believe will help get the job done. Be sure to write down your answers as you go along. Otherwise you'll have too much going on in your mind to get deep enough into the flawed logic to come up with a detailed understanding of the problem and solution. You also may need several days and multiple attempts to complete all five steps. Writing allows that iterative process to move faster. Here are some instructions and examples to get you started.

Below is a simple example of a Mental Hand History to give you an idea of how it looks. On the surface, the answers may seem obvious. But when you go through the process and complete each step with personalized answers, you develop a deeper understanding of the cause and correction to your problem.

Then, I'll give you some advice on how to complete each step. I'll show you a more complex example at the end of the section, and you'll see additional examples throughout the book.

1. **Describe the problem in detail:** I can't accept big losses.
2. **Explain why it makes sense that you have this problem, or why you think, feel, or react that way:** My strategy is profitable when I follow it.
3. **Explain why the logic in Step 2 is flawed:** By saying that my strategy is profitable, I'm implying that I will never incur big losses, whether or not I perfectly execute my strategy.
4. **Come up with a correction to that flawed logic:** I must learn how to take a loss. Take the punch. Embrace the feeling—losses taken with good execution are part of the deal.
5. **Explain why that correction is correct:** A profitable strategy will incur losses, sometimes big ones. My edge accounts for that. The bigger problem is allowing a big loss to cost more than it should.

Unpacking the Steps to Complete Your Mental Hand History

The Mental Hand History is an important tool for resolving the backend problems that brought you to this book. The following advice will help you better understand how to complete each step, and avoid the common missteps traders make when trying to complete it.

STEP 1: Describe the problem in detail. To begin, write down what you would say if you were describing the problem in your mental game to me. If you've already been building a detailed map of the problem and the clues surrounding it, use this step to clearly articulate the problem.

You may also want to add in some details about the history of the problem, as context can be important for completing the next few steps. For example, if this problem started six months ago, after you had a significant life change—like getting divorced or having a child. That would indicate something different vs. if being unable to accept big losses had been a problem throughout your professional career.

STEP 2: Explain why it makes sense that you have this problem, or why you think, feel, or react that way. Clients often have trouble with this step, and they think the answer is, "I'm just being irrational or illogical." That is another way of saying that *you* are the problem. But then, is the solution to fix you? What does that even mean? It doesn't make sense. You're not the problem. The flaws, biases, and illusions are the cause of problem, and this step is critical to nailing down precisely what that is.

Mental game problems happen for logical reasons. While that logic is clearly flawed in some way, since it's creating a problem, the cause and effect makes sense when you have the full picture. Once you know the reason, it's a lot easier to know what's wrong with it.

This step can be hard. Explaining why there's a gap between what you know is true and how you're reacting can be difficult. Avoid using answers like, "I'm stupid," or "The market screwed me," because they stop your analysis. Neither you nor the market is the problem.

Take some time to capture the logic behind the problem. Your answer is flawed or incomplete, but you still had a reason that made sense on some level. Ask yourself, "Why do I have this problem? Why does it make sense that I feel this way? Why am I reacting this way?" Your answers will get the hamster wheel in your head turning differently. This happens a lot with my clients, and in doing so, they gained access to knowledge they previously ignored, because the problem was assumed to be illogical.

Lastly, complex problems often have several pieces, or layers. If you identify more than one reason while completing this step, follow Steps 3 to 5 for each individual reason.

STEP 3: Explain why the logic in Step 2 is flawed. Throughout this book I have been reiterating that underlying performance flaws are the cause of the emotional reactions. Now, you get to identify the flaw.

If you try to complete this step without having a good answer in Step 2, you're blindly throwing darts at a dartboard. If you've done a good job at articulating your reasons in Step 2, finding what's flawed is much easier. But again, don't worry if this seems daunting. The next five chapters will help you figure out why the logic or reason you found in Step 2 is flawed, incomplete, or inaccurate.

Lastly—and this is critical—the biggest mistake clients make in this step is thinking that it's a flaw to feel fear or another emotion. Emotion is never the flaw. Emotion is the signal. Thinking otherwise is like saying a fever is the cause of the flu.

STEP 4: Come up with a correction to that flawed logic. Now, we get to the meat of what's going to help you resolve this problem. Taking into account Steps 2 and 3, define a straightforward and logical correction to the flaw that's causing your mental game problem.

Sometimes the correction is simply incorporating a concept or idea about trading, like variance, which you already know well, but haven't applied in the right way. Err on the side of training these ideas first, before getting more complex, because:

- These are important ideas and you need to master them anyway

- They may be enough to solve the issues you're facing right now
- If they're not enough, you get a closer look at what's actually flawed

STEP 5: Explain why that correction is correct. This step is a bit of a bonus. But for some traders it can add repetition, clarity, and detail to the new logic, which more firmly roots it in their mind.

Here's another example so you can see how all five steps work together:

1. **Describe the problem in detail:** I lose faith in a trading strategy when I'm unsuccessful, and jump from one methodology to another before mastering the technique in all market conditions. I think there must be a more consistent, profitable technique and doubt my ability to make the current strategy work for me.

2. **Explain why it makes sense that you have this problem, or why you think, feel, or react that way:** If I'm unsuccessful, I should find a strategy that actually works for me. Life has taught me that there's always a better way—it's just a matter of finding the right one for me. I don't have time to waste on techniques that have proven fallible.

3. **Explain why the logic in Step 2 is flawed:** If I jump from one strategy to another whenever the market changes, or when I am unwilling to adapt, I will never master a strategy. I will continue to be stuck at the beginning stage and never achieve my goal of trading for a living.

4. **Come up with a correction to that flawed logic:** A beginner can explore the landscape and test new ideas, but to be a professional, I need to commit to a methodology, and learn to adapt it, and myself, to the changing market. I need to trust a strategy and do everything possible to understand its strengths and weakness in all market types.

5. **Explain why that correction is correct:** When I've found a viable strategy that's well suited for me, continuing to explore other opportunities increases the likelihood that I'll fail. If I commit to the strategy, do the necessary work, and trust in the evidence, I give myself a greater chance at success.

Looking at the typical approach to problem solving in comparison to the Mental Hand History, traders were basically jumping from Step 1 to Step 4. In this way you arrive at corrections that sound good in theory but don't get to the root of the issue. Understanding this process and using it going forward will help you enormously as you work through the rest of this book.

Moving the Backend Forward

I strongly advise that you read at least the beginning sections of the next five chapters, which go into detail about the most common mental and emotional problems in trading. That information will help you identify the real problems affecting your trading.

Correctly determining them can be difficult—even seasoned traders often get it wrong at first. I see it all the time. Greed was thought to be the main problem, when it was actually anger. A presumed discipline problem was really overconfidence. Anger seemed to be the obvious issue, but it turned out that fear was the driver. If you're only looking at the surface, and not digging down to the roots, you risk getting it wrong.

For instance, you can't look solely at the trading mistakes that you make and accurately conclude the emotions or issues behind them. Take a look at this list:

- Forcing mediocre trade setups
- Hesitating on entries
- Exiting trades too early
- Chasing the market price up and down
- Moving a stop too soon

- Moving your profit target before it hits
- Talking yourself out of a good trade

All of these common trading mistakes can be caused by greed, fear, anger, overconfidence, lack of confidence, or a discipline problem. In and of themselves, they don't tell us anything about the underlying issues that cause these errors in execution. You can't say you exited a trade too early out of fear, unless you have cataloged the details that prove it's fear. Anger, a lack of confidence, or discipline could just as easily be the culprit. You simply don't know just by looking at the error.

The key is to use your errors in execution as a starting point to begin mapping the surrounding details—thoughts, emotions, actions, triggers, and changes to your perception of the market and decision-making. Then match what you find with the descriptions in chapters 4 through 8.

That's often the beginning in figuring out the underlying reason that you're compelled to make that trading mistake. There's such a high priority on getting it right, because once you do, as you'll see in chapter 9, you can develop both a day-to-day and real-time strategy to correct it once and for all.

The first problem to tackle is greed—and right away you'll learn the truth that greed is not a problem in the way you think it is.

CHAPTER 4

GREED

"Greed is a basic part of animal nature.
Being against it is like being against breathing or eating."
—Ben Stein

There's a lot of confusion in the trading world about greed, including about how to solve it. The solution isn't just to be less greedy—that's like saying be less ambitious. Here's the truth: What makes solving greed so challenging is that there are actually no flaws unique to this emotion. Instead, you'll find the roots of greed lie in the flaws, biases, and illusions that cause fear, anger, overconfidence, and lack of confidence. Most often, they lie in overconfidence.

Overconfidence is that feeling of invincibility, thinking you can turn a trade into a winner, and that you'll make money with ease. Carelessness. A "fuck it" mentality. Blind faith, and being blind to risk. Excess ambition in this way is overconfidence in both your ability to make money and in the way you'll make it.

On the flip side, if greed comes from a lack of confidence, you feel like nothing is ever good enough, no matter how much you make. Your greedy drive is that constant push for more money, based on the false idea it will yield lasting satisfaction, pride, or confidence. Or a drawdown triggers questions about your competence, and you get greedy to quickly eviscerate any doubt about your ability to make money.

Anger is a common co-conspirator. Revenge trading is epitomized by the intensity that follows a string of unlucky losses—the trades that stop you out by a tick, only to race to your profit target without you. That emotion may seem like greed, but it's anger. You double your next position and it quickly stops you out. Now you're pissed because you know you're making mistakes, and you force another trade trying to make up for it.

To a lesser degree, fear can lurk behind greedy impulses. FOMO is the most common problem. You don't want to miss a big move and you greedily get in too late, just in case the trend continues. There's a panicky feeling that happens when you see other traders making money and you want to do so, as well. You end up chasing price, and justify a worse price because the opportunity still "feels right." Aside from FOMO, the fear of loss, mistakes, and failure can all drive actions that appear greedy.

While the whole point of trading is to make money, greed actually *costs* you money. Your unrestrained desire to make more forces you into decisions that, in the long term, make you less successful. The market punishes your attempts to squeeze out every penny and make the maximum return from every trade. Of course, that's not always the case— sometimes greed is rewarded with massive winners or perfect exits. But you wouldn't be reading this if you didn't think greed was a problem.

There are a lot of theories and debates out there about the positive or negative role that greed plays in society at large. That debate is beyond the scope of this book. My focus is simply on improving your execution and performance as a trader. And, for many of you, that means curbing the damage that greed does to your profitability.

That may seem counterintuitive to the generations who grew up on Gordon Gekko's famous "Greed is good" speech in the movie *Wall Street*. Only we must remember the full quote. Gekko's actual words are, "The point is, ladies and gentlemen, that greed, for lack of a better word, is good." "For lack of a better word" is the point of distinction. *Ambition* is the better word.

THE NATURE OF GREED

In trying to understand the nature of greed, it's helpful to look at Merriam Webster's definition: "a selfish and excessive desire for more of something (such as money) than is needed." Since we're discussing this from a performance standpoint, and not from a societal one, we can remove the beginning and end of the definition. That leaves the phrase "an excessive desire for more," which perfectly summarizes the problem. Greed is the emotion that indicates the point where your ambition becomes excessive.

Ambition is the competitive drive to be great, more successful, or earn more. It's what motivates you to read books, like this one, to further hone your craft. Ambition is the drive to win, balanced with the understanding that losses are both inevitable and often helpful in reaching higher levels of success. You wouldn't call the ambitions of Michael Jordan greedy, or for that matter any athlete who strives to win at the highest levels. No, we'd say they have an intense hunger, will, or drive to win. We applaud their relentless effort and outsized dreams. Is that greed? Of course not. Think of yourself like an athlete, and greed becomes simply a performance problem.

Greed exists in every competitive arena. While the aspiration of athletes to win wouldn't be characterized as greedy, that doesn't mean they aren't greedy while competing. But as observers, we can't say with certainty which decisions are greedy or not. Intent matters.

Consider the athlete who tries to make a big play—like a lineman in football attempting to pick up a fumble and run with it, or a baseball player trying to score from second base on a short single to center field, with two outs in the bottom of the ninth of a tied game. Whether or not they're successful, if they assessed the risk as usual, then a healthy ambition and drive to win is likely what drove the decision. If, on the other hand, there is a drive to achieve personal glory above the aims of one's team, or a need to prove to the skeptics that they deserve to be classed as a professional, then it's likely some level of greed has affected the decision.

The excessiveness that characterizes greed is different for everyone, and can't be judged from the outside. There will always be the outliers—those traders who produce massive returns over a long period of time and appear greedy. For them, however, it may not be greed. It just looks that way. You can't know from the outside when someone else has crossed the line from ambition to greed. Remove the comparisons and focus on yourself.

Where is that line for you, where ambition turns into greed? You likely already know. It's when you just can't stop yourself. The common advice sounds simple enough. Don't let greed get the best of you. You can't build an account in a single trade. Stick to your trading plan, be disciplined and patient. But in the heat of the moment, your drive to make money supersedes that logic, and it's difficult to know when, and when not, to curb that drive.

Ultimately, that's not even how you want to be trading—having to constantly be on the lookout for greed and reining in those impulses. Like a thoroughbred in a horse race, you run faster when you're free to run as fast as you can, not when the jockey is constantly pulling on the reins.

In a business where fortunes can be made and lost in a flash, you can't rely on having to quickly decipher if greed has hijacked your decisions. The goal is to correct the underlying flaws, illusions, or biases that turn your ambition into greed. Then you can drive yourself as hard as possible, knowing that you'll automatically make decisions within your strategy, because you know that's how to make the most money, long term.

COMMON SIGNS OF GREED

When ambition reaches a point where decision-making becomes compromised, that's greed. You start focusing more on the money and your account balance, rather than the percentage or price action. You feel like you need to be making money, and so you race into a trade. As it intensifies, your judgment becomes even more clouded. You miss a clear exit point and think about the killing you're about to make, reveling in your own brilliance.

Then what happens? You end up making decisions you know are wrong in the long term, but you can't help yourself. You're driven to get the best possible entry and exit, make massive returns, and profit from every single trade. There's an unquenchable thirst for more that's never satisfied. It needs money now, and that intensity blinds you to risk.

Greed ignores risks and seeks to earn money without regard for edge, strategy, or system. It emerges in a wide variety of situations. There's the blind optimism that things are bound to go your way and keep going up forever. Or you fantasize about some high PnL number that you want to make from a trade, set your target too high, and imagine what you'll do with the profit. You're not assessing the whole situation and determining if it's worth the risk; you're only focused on money, and can't see how you'll lose.

You get overleveraged, oversized, add to winners, open too many positions, and think you can outsmart the market. You don't sell. "Let winners run" is what you're supposed to do, so you move your profit target, thinking you can turn it into a home run. Or maybe you sold, but immediately get back in because it could be a monster, and you'll kick yourself if you were on the sidelines.

For some traders, greed only kicks in during a drawdown or after a string of break-even trades. You feel like you have to make money right now. Money is all you're focused on. You see other traders taking trades and making money, forget there will be more opportunities that fit your style, and greedily go after everything you can. But you get stopped out again, and immediately reenter at twice the size. Maybe you get a little lucky and you're back in the green. Now, you want more, and try to squeeze out every cent and hope it doesn't retrace.

Some of the specific signs of greed may also include bragging about winners, talking about how much you're up in your positions, and making it seem like you have it all figured out. Building positions that are too large or too concentrated, thinking you can't lose. Shortcutting your usual process to race into a trade because you see others piling in. Feeling like you have to be making money all the time. Always wanting more. Never feeling satisfied. And yet, at times, avoiding the hard work and discipline required to do it the right way.

Now, that you have some ideas of the signs of greed to look out for, you're ready to map your pattern.

MAPPING YOUR GREED

In those moments when you cross the line and make decisions that are counter to what you know is correct, you're not making a conscious choice. Greed has taken control, and you're compelled to take the trade, stay in it, add to it, take on more leverage, or squeeze out every tick. Emotions are powerful, especially greed, and to have a chance at correcting them, you need to map the signals that indicate an escalation.

The following steps will help you to create an actual document that will become your map of greed.

Step 1

Over the next few weeks pay close attention to your **pattern of greed**. Examine and capture the signs that greed has become a problem, including:

- Thoughts
- Emotions
- Things you say out loud
- Behaviors
- Actions
- Changes to your decision-making
- Changes to your perception of the market, opportunities, or current positions
- Trading mistakes

Also be sure to spot the things that trigger greed, such as winning, a string of losses, or sensing a monster opportunity. Keep a document open on your computer or a notepad next to you while you trade, and take notes throughout the day. At the end of the trading day, review what you found and add additional details. Be as comprehensive as you can.

When you first take notes, there's a lot of brainstorming. You're not going to identify all the details perfectly the first time you do it. If this is really hard for you at the beginning, don't worry. Everyone has their own starting point. Use what you find and build on it over time. If it takes you three months to get it right, so what? As long as you keep working and thinking about it, you'll learn more and get closer to a complete picture. Here are some questions to help get you started:

- What situations typically cause you to become greedy?
- How does your body react? For example, are you jacked up, ready to fight, or hyper-focused?
- Can you describe the point where ambition becomes excessive and turns into greed?
- What specifically is going through your mind? What thoughts do you have?
- How is your decision-making process different?
- What is the earliest sign that greed has become a problem?

Mapping greed is an iterative process. When you spot new details, even just slight adjustments, be sure to add them. Small details matter, and can make the difference between making progress or not.

Step 2

Now, you're going to organize your notes into a chart that **assigns a level of increasing severity**, using a scale from 1 to 10, to each observation you've made. For instance, ranking something with a 1 would characterize a slight urge to force results, while ranking something a 10 would indicate unrestrained greed. At each level, identify details that clearly distinguish it from the other levels.

As you assign levels of severity, split them into two categories: the mental and emotional side of greed, and the technical side. They sit side by side, so level 1 on the mental and emotional side corresponds to level 1 on the technical side, and so on.

Be sure to base this on *your* personal experience of greed. Everyone has their own range, and if you judge yourself against another trader, you're at risk of over- or underestimating the severity, which will make your strategy less effective.

You also don't need to have details for all 10 levels. Most traders that I work with aren't able to distinguish their pattern to that degree. Complete as many as you can, making sure you complete a minimum of three. Here are some questions to distinguish the differences in each level of greed:

- What triggers the initial urge to force profits at level 1? How does it then increase or accumulate to reach higher levels? For example, after closing your second winning trade of the day, you start thinking about having a career day and ignore your strategy. As a result, you move your profit target on an existing position. When it pays off, you start blindly entering trades, assuming you'll win.
- What are the signs that greed is small and still manageable?
- What are the signs that greed has become uncontrolled, completely disrupting your execution?
- How is your perception of the market, opportunities, or current positions different when your greed level is higher?
- How does your decision-making process differ at level 1 compared to levels 5 and 10?

Then take the details you've categorized and put them into a map like this:

GREED LEVEL .

Describe the thoughts, emotions, things you say, behaviors, and actions that highlight each level of greed. Complete at least 3 levels.

1: Start thinking about the utility of money. Wanting to lock up the gain. I want to have that big trade to secure the profit and achieve better returns to see progress.

2:

3:

4:

5: Wonder if I should move my profit target. Really close, I could secure in now, but I could move the target farther away. If I push the trade further, I'll be secure for longer.

6: Wonder if I should trail my stop; I don't want to give anything back. More irritated with people when they ask about my trading.

7:

8: I give up my trading plan, but maintain a clear stop and profit target so it's still safe. Much more personal; is the market with me or against?

9:

10: I want to make the absolute best return, right now. Give up all control and am only focused on making money right now. No longer-term thinking.

TECHNICAL LEVEL

Describe the quality of your decision-making, perception of the market, opportunities, or current positions at each level of greed.

1: No change.

2:

3:

4:

5: Start feeling emotions in terms of my trading plan; there's an urge to change things.

6:

7:

8: Don't have a plan; it's all based on how I feel the market is moving. Move stop and profit targets. Perception is more about money.

9:

10: Manually manage the trade; looking every single minute to try to get the best price by looking at every single change in the market. Looking at every 5- or 10-min candle vs. 1- to 4-hr candle. (Trades usually last from 1 day to 2 weeks.)

Some of you will assume this step is impossible because your signs of greed are all extreme. The small signs are there; you just can't see them yet. This is an iterative process. Continue to work the process by paying close attention to the buildup. Remember, one of the best times to do this is after an instance where greed got the better of you. Be a detective. Look at why it reached that point, and the signs you could detect next time.

Once complete, you have a solid draft that you can use while you're trading to **recognize your pattern and quickly respond with the correction.** Since these patterns can take a lot of experience and training to correct, don't revise your map until you get consistent evidence that it has permanently changed.

THE REAL CAUSE OF GREED

You may be able to determine some of what was driving you—greed or other emotions—when you do your mapping exercise. But to really assess greed, you need to know what's driving the decision, and that's up to you to determine. What might be a greedy trade for one trader could instead be a well-executed one for another. The key is to clarify what flaws lie below the surface of what you perceive to be greed.

To help make this point, let's look at four stories of traders who each identified prior to coaching that they had a problem with greed. And in each situation, the flaws associated with fear, anger, overconfidence, and a lack of confidence proved instead to be the main drivers.

First up is Alex, a 16-year trading veteran from Germany. He worked for years in a big firm as a market maker for power and natural gas options. Currently he works for an oil trading group, and he's mainly responsible for their algorithmic options trading. He also trades a personal account on the side, which is the main reason he came to me for coaching.

For Alex, greed showed up in a specific way—he felt that he wasn't making enough money on his winning trades. He'd catch himself fantasizing about some high PnL number that he wanted to make, and he was often filled with regret for getting out too early or being talked out of trades that would have made him a ton.

At first glance, Alex's example of greed is minor in comparison to the other stories you're about to read. However, his story is important to highlight because even small instances of mental game problems coded as greed need to be corrected. As you'll read in the continuation of Alex's story in the next chapter, greed was signaling a fear of being wrong that caused him to legitimately underperform in a big way. He had good reason to think about those high PnL numbers, as he was missing out on a lot of potential profits.

Rodrick on the other hand, a trader from the U.S. with a decade of experience trading all the global CME products, U.S. stocks, and forex, had a much more visible version of greed. He's an incredibly hard worker who would react very poorly to a loss or mistake. Immediately, he would force trades, trying to take more than the market was giving him. He would try to recover, but spiral out of control, ultimately losing a lot of money on the day. Conversely, on the days where he made money easily, he would want to make even more. No amount was enough.

When greed showed up for Rodrick, he would attempt to earn without a proper edge or system. He knew this, and initially assumed that worrying about money for life and bills was the problem. He tried putting away all the money that he'd need for an entire year to take care of himself and his family, but that didn't change a thing. "Perhaps it's a gap in knowledge," he speculated. That idea drove him deeper into the markets, trying to gain more and more knowledge, and yet no matter how much more he learned, his greedy attempts to make money continued.

As we began our work, it became quickly apparent that what Rodrick thought was greed was actually anger. He hated to make mistakes, and in his mind, losing *was* a mistake. He expected to make money on every trade, to trade better and make more money, and to never miss an opportunity. Failing to meet any of these expectations meant that he wasn't perfect, which triggered an explosion of anger. In chapter 6, I'll continue Rodrick's story, and you'll see how he was able to fix his unrealistic expectation of perfection.

Next is Max, a forex trader from France. He began trading about five years ago to prove to his friend that he could do it and became hooked. For the last two years he's been able to sustain a full-time income, and eventually wants to get investor funding. To get there, however, he first needs to get control of his emotions, namely greed.

On the surface, Max is happy with his progress, but there's a hidden urge that he constantly fights against. For example, when price is in a great zone, even though he knows to wait for the right entry, the idea that he could make so much money that it could change his month causes him to jump in so as to not miss it. He also wants to make money because it gives him a good feeling, like he's making progress and knows what he's doing.

For Max, greed gets worse after a string of break-even or losing trades. He wants to make the absolute best return right now, and he loses sight of the long-term strategy or the value of having made a plan. He can't wait, and will eagerly take a marginal trade.

Between our first and second sessions, Max worked incredibly hard to map his pattern of greed and was able to distinguish 10 levels. The sample map from the previous section was a draft that he put together prior to our first session. Here's the second version:

GREED LEVEL SECOND VERSION

1: Logging into my brokerage account to have a brief look at the PnL I am currently running in a trade. Feeling good if it's positive, but not negatively impacted if it's a loss.

2: Start thinking about the utility of money. Wanting to lock up the gain. I want to have that big trade to secure the profit and have better returns to see progress.

3: Thinking about how much more % or $ return I need to cover expenses this month and next month. I feel excited about these trades and think this is great, I'm back on the ball.

4: Wonder what other people will think of my trade—other traders, family, investors. I am happy to talk in depth about my position with others instead of being brief and humble. **I want to share and be a show-off about it.**

5: Wonder if I should move my profit target. Really close, I could secure it now, but I could move the target farther away. If I push the trade further, I'll be secure for longer.

6: Wonder if I should trail my stop, I don't want to give anything back. More irritated with people when they ask about my trading. I stay in front of the computer, even if I don't need to monitor how the market is moving.

7: I don't want to lose or give back money to the market, so I keep thinking nonstop about my trade. I am hunched over, looking at my screen and don't do a lot more than stare at live charts. I can't get myself away from them.

8: **Trading feels much more personal, like the market is with me or against me.** I give up my trading plan but maintain a clear stop and profit target, so it's still safe.

9: I think the market is controllable; I think I can understand the flow of the market—whenever it goes higher or lower, I can predict it. Staring at my screen, snapping at people as soon as someone talks to me.

10: I want to make the absolute best return, right now. Give up all control and I'm only focused on making money right now. · No longer-term thinking.

In Max's original map, the first signal of greed was thinking about the utility of money, but now that's at level two, and the first cue is looking at the PnL of an active trade. This is important, because it enables him to correct greed sooner, while the scale is small.

Looking at the deeper emotions fueling his greed, you'll notice the two sentences in bold provide the clues. Greed is fueled by a weakness in confidence. Max has reasonable aspirations, but the deep urgency to prove himself causes him to make decisions outside his strategy. In chapter 7, we'll pick up his story and show how he was able to eliminate greed and make significant progress with his confidence.

Let's look at another trader. When I first met Chris, who is from the U.S., he had been trading full-time for about seven years. He typically day-trades stocks and U.S. index futures, and swing-trades forex and options. For Chris, greed compelled him to ignore preplanned targets and try to hit a home run. More times than not, it hurt him. But he couldn't help it. The threat of regret carried a lot of weight and forced him to push too hard to avoid missing out on what could be a home run.

The roots of his greed were planted before he became a full-time trader, when Chris sold way too soon out of a stock that he had planned to hold. Within a month of selling, the company was acquired and the gains would have been life-changing.

A decade had passed, and yet the pain was still fresh. As we analyzed why, also looking at the reasons why he would cycle through periods of overconfidence and lack of confidence, and the times he would get pissed off and doubt his strategy, all roads led to one place—an expectation of perfection. In chapter 7, you'll see how Chris resolved the pain from selling that stock and removed the emotional volatility that came from his quest for perfection.

You may have noticed that two of these four traders had an expectation of perfection as the underlying cause of greed. This is a topic that I talk about in the fear, anger, and confidence chapters because it's a common cause of emotional instability among highly motivated people. I applaud the aspiration to be perfect and the desire to achieve success at the highest level, but expecting to attain perfection is a different story. Because it's impossible, expecting perfection always causes emotional instability in your mental game.

As you saw in Alex's story, greed can have close ties with fear. Fear of failing, fear of underperforming, fear of ending the day with less money than you started with—trading is associated with a host of fears. In fact, you may be so familiar with fear in trading that you assume the emotion must be there. A certain amount of nervousness is a given, yes. But by drilling down into the specifics of what makes your fear excessive, you can ensure that it doesn't damage profitability. That's exactly what we look at in the next chapter.

CHAPTER 5

FEAR

"We can easily forgive a child who is afraid of the dark;
the real tragedy of life is when men are afraid of the light."

—Plato

Fear in trading is so well known, it may be overblown. This is important because to clearly identify and resolve your issues with fear, you need to be specific. You may have already labeled some of these issues for yourself. Fear of losing. Fear of mistakes. Fear of failing. These are all real fears, and I'll talk about them later in this chapter.

But we also need to address misinterpretations about what fear *really* is, as opposed to what it isn't. Without this distinction, we can't identify and correct the performance flaws causing actual fears.

Misinterpretations are easy to make because trading is far more intense than the typical job. Imagine how much would change in the corporate world if salaried employees were paid based on their day-to-day performance. What if they had money taken out of their paychecks if they underperformed? Considered in those terms, not even professional athletes have the same pressure. Tom Brady doesn't get his pay docked if he throws an interception. Tiger Woods doesn't personally hand over fifty thousand dollars on the first tee to play in a tournament.

Even if you're in a prop firm or an institutional trader, and it's not your money on the line, big mistakes or consistent underperformance will still cut the size of your book, or get you fired. All of this is to say that natural nerves are an inherent part of trading, and it can be easy to mistake them for the anxiety and fear generated by a performance flaw.

Another common source of fear that isn't driven by a performance flaw is having a weak or incomplete trading strategy. Higher amounts of uncertainty are inevitable when you are less clear on how you make money, what trades to take, or whether a loss was due to a mistake or bad luck. This uncertainty can create increasing amounts of nervousness, doubt, and fear, simply because your ability to measure and evaluate your trading is less accurate. On the surface, those emotions can signal a weakness in your strategy.

This was certainly true for Vishal, a trader from the U.K. who began trading about six years ago. He's a trader who uses technical analysis to drive his decisions in the forex and futures markets. There's also a strong discretionary piece to his strategy, where he uses intuition to decide if he's going to take the trade or not. This is where Vishal was experiencing a lot of anxiety.

At the moment of execution, he would hesitate. Vishal's mind would fill with questions, such as "But what about this? And this? And this?" and he would suddenly doubt the setup. If he skipped a trade and it lost, he felt justified, and if it won, he would beat himself up, saying things like "You should be doing better. You knew that it looked good."

At first, we spent time mapping Vishal's fear, and we identified an excessive need to be right. But the turning point came when I pointed out that for him, right now, trading should be 10% mental and 90% technical. That brought him back to the basics, to where he realized the plan he was bringing into battle was not comprehensive enough. He couldn't pull the trigger because he had too many unanswered questions. The doubt and hesitation were signals of weaknesses in his strategy.

He became much more open-minded about his trading. Hesitation and losses, which used to cause a mix of criticism and additional fear, became opportunities to question the technical elements of the trade, refine his strategy, and become more systematic in his approach.

He also reduced the amount of time he spent in front of the screens. Vishal turned them off, and instead worked on his edge until he got an alert. He was able to tighten up his strategy by putting in the time to answer ahead of time many of the questions he would otherwise have at the point of execution.

It has taken painstaking work to make his discretionary decisions more mechanical, while maintaining a quantifiable edge. The payoff is that Vishal has seen a dramatic change emotionally. Today, he relies more heavily on factual data to evaluate trades, and is certain that his technical edge is good enough that it's ok if he misses a few trades.

Most important, at the point of execution, his mind isn't filled with questions because he's answered them. Now they come *afterward*, as he reflects on how to improve. A lot of noise has been removed from the whole process, which has improved his execution, as well as his ability to trust his intuition and learn from it.

I'm not suggesting that a trading plan, or working through the holes in your strategy like this, is an antidote to everyone's fear. But having a trading plan can provide clarity on where the fear is coming from. If you have a plan that's researched and has a proven edge, you have something you either believe in or know works, and that eliminates some uncertainty. Then, if nerves, doubt, worry, pressure, or anxiety prevent you from executing your plan, that's a clear indication that fear is caused by one of the flaws covered later in this chapter.

Ideally the role of anxiety and fear is to highlight that something is wrong or unknown with your read of the market, your positions, or how your strategy lines up with the market. If that's what's happening, it means your mental game is solid and largely free of the flaws, beliefs, or illusions that typically cause fear. For many of you, however, that isn't the case. You may, for example:

- Worry about blowing up
- Consistently size too small, especially in positions that you sense could be home runs
- Stay out of trades, concerned about getting it wrong
- Constantly think about going broke
- Avoid trades that have the potential to be very volatile

To get a clearer look at exactly what you're facing, first rule out that it's not a consequence of the normal competitive nerves or a weak trading plan. Once you've done that, it's time to dive into what may be driving your fear.

THE NATURE OF FEAR

If you're going to resolve the issues causing your fear, you need to first understand where fear in trading comes from. At a basic level, fear can be reduced to uncertainty. Yes, that's overly simplistic. But think about it this way: When you have certainty, you don't have fear. The unknown is taken out of the equation.

Imagine you had a fear of losing, and you were particularly on edge because of a recent drawdown. But a few minutes before the market opens, a magical trading fairy appears on your shoulder and tells you the outcome of the day—you'd know to expect a handful of small losses in the first hour, but two large wins in the afternoon would make the day solidly profitable.

Instantly, the tension, nerves, and fear would disappear. You'd be pumped to have a profitable day, and more importantly, rather than triggering fear and possibly costing you some of the afternoon profits, you'd be confident that those early losses wouldn't affect you.

Of course, there is no trading fairy. Yet some traders can take even heavy losses and not experience fear. How are they able to do that? What they have in common is certainty. They are so certain their strategy will pay off, they simply aren't worried about the short-term losses. They can also be certain in their ability to find a way to make money, adapt if market conditions change, or develop a new strategy.

Certainty is the antidote to fear. I'm not suggesting the end goal is to always have certainty. That's not even practical. Instead, I'm suggesting that certainty and fear can't coexist, and uncertainty is the breeding ground for fear.

Uncertainty is essentially a question you don't have the answer for, or don't have enough experience to prove the answer you already have is correct. When these questions are unanswered or unproven, doubt lingers, worry builds, and eventually that worry accumulates into anxiety. If this goes on long enough, it turns into fear.

As with other emotions, fear exists along a scale, one that begins as a question. You need to dig into your fear and pull out the questions that are unanswered, unproven, unclear, or uncertain, because they indicate what you want to know at a deeper level. The following are examples of common questions traders have:

- Why am I losing money?
- Why did I make that mistake?
- Is this a spot where I can add discretion?
- Is what I'm looking at worthwhile?
- What if I've missed something in my analysis?
- What am I doing wrong?
- When will I start making money again?
- How could I have been so stupid?
- Will I make it as a trader? What will I do if I can't make money from trading?
- Have I lost it? Am I going to be able to figure it out?

Sometimes these are legitimate questions that linger in the back of your mind without being answered, or that can't yet be answered, leading to more uncertainty. Other times they're answered automatically, with responses such as "It's because I'm stupid that I make these mistakes;" "I'm never going to make money again;" or "I'll end up working some soulless corporate job because I'm just not a good enough trader." These answers generate secondary emotions and perpetuate fear.

What's more, flaws often contaminate these questions. Asking "What am I doing wrong?" or "How could I have been so stupid?" presumes that you were wrong and stupid. Asking "When will I start making money again?" presumes you could possibly know that.

Uncertainty is a core element in your profession. You need to embrace that fact so deeply, it's as if it's coded in your DNA. But as a trader struggling to control your fear, simply embracing uncertainty isn't enough. You need to identify and correct the underlying flaws that force you to *need* certainty when you can't have it yet.

COMMON SIGNS OF FEAR

Fear takes your ability to assess risk, think, decide, trust intuition, and make predictions—and turns it against you. Better understanding how and why that happens will help you to uncover the flaws that cause your fear. As you begin to analyze your pattern of fear, think about the presence of the five common signals of fear described below. Avoid the temptation to view them as inherently negative—they simply highlight functions of the mind gone awry.

Risk Aversion

Risk is the reason trading provides an opportunity for profit. So on the surface, it seems counterintuitive that traders would struggle to handle this essential thing. And yet it happens all the time. You'll see traders make mistakes, like not letting a winner run to avoid the risk of it going against them, not building a bigger position when they have a lot of conviction because they fear it will blow up again, or avoiding a trade with a slightly higher risk/reward because it seems like a gamble. As you've learned already, mistakes like these are really signals.

To understand the function that risk aversion serves, we need to look at the reasons behind these actions more objectively. What are you protecting yourself from? What are you trying to avoid? Within the three mistakes listed in the prior paragraph, you can see there's a desire to avoid losing, blowing up, and gambling. Nobody wants those outcomes—and that's basically the point.

Risk aversion is essentially a natural reaction to protect yourself from the pain associated with negative outcomes. It's no different than how you'd instinctively raise your arms to protect yourself if someone tried to punch you in the face. Now instead, if you were about to get punched by a two-year-old child, how likely is it that you would instinctively put your arms up as a defense (except in exaggerated fashion to make the kid laugh)? With no threat of pain, there's nothing to fear. This is important to distinguish, because it's likely that risk aversion doesn't happen on every trade.

Sometimes risk aversion happens for practical reasons, such as when you don't have a good sense of the market and struggle to evaluate the risk. That aversion isn't a problem, but perhaps at previous times like this you've traded poorly and put capital at unnecessary risk of loss. Now you've wised up, and need to make the transition from being overconfident to prudent. However, prudence can feel like fear or being averse to risk, especially if ghosts from your past remind you not to make the same mistakes.

Over time, your aversion to this type of risk will disappear as you prove to yourself that you can make sound decisions when your sense of the market isn't clear. In this case, the real risk you were averse to was the threat that overconfidence posed to your capital, not market risk.

All of the types of fear detailed in this chapter can cause risk aversion. And, in fact, other problems, like greed, tilt, and low confidence, can as well, particularly when those problems are well known but uncontrolled.

By shying away from risk, traders protect themselves by keeping these problems from showing up. They either consciously or unconsciously recognize when the risk of these problems occurring is greater, and they factor that into their risk calculation. If a loss here triggers greed or tilt, it'll lead to a further drawdown, or it'll damage confidence, and they'll bleed EV from not trading well for a few weeks.

Quick Tip: Only once you start to resolve fear, tilt, greed, or a confidence problem does it make sense to correct risk aversion. Otherwise you risk creating more chaos. Once you make progress, risk aversion will either automatically go away or you'll need to push yourself to take more profitable risks. At first, that might take a leap of faith, so consider setting a specific amount of money to invest when pushing yourself to take more risks. Often just knowing that your potential losses are limited helps to free you from any aversion to risk.

Overthinking

When functioning in an optimal state, thinking is controlled. You want to think; you think. You want to think about a particular topic; you think about that topic. Sure, some random ideas may come to mind, or your thoughts may go in unpredictable directions, but when you want to stop thinking, either in general or about a particular topic, you can do that easily.

That isn't the case when your mind is driven by anxiety and fear. Instead, your mind can't settle. The market does something you don't expect and you have what seems like a thousand thoughts all at once. Or, after a string of losers, your mind loops in circles, covering the same territory again and again—"Can I still make money? Is my strategy still viable? Why am I so impulsive?" Each time around doesn't produce any new answers; it just makes focusing on the market and executing your strategy harder.

After you're done for the day, you try to move on and enjoy time with family or friends, but you can't stop thinking about a position you're worried has grown too large. You wonder what will happen if there's a market crash or all your positions move against you at once. You're restless when trying to relax—your mind won't let you. Sleeping is a challenge. Thoughts rip through your mind, and the more tired you get, the more uncontrolled they are.

Overthinking happens because you can't find the answer to your underlying question. If the antidote to fear is certainty, overthinking is your mind's desperate attempt to find certainty. When fear is particularly intense, your mind won't stop thinking until it gets an answer; or you're either exhausted or distracted. One of the reasons this happens is due to a limitation in a part of the brain, called working memory.

Working memory is where you think. It's where the voice in your head lives, and it's like a whiteboard in your mind where you consciously put pieces together and work through problems.

Under normal circumstances you have access to between five and nine pieces of information at one time in your working memory. This part of the brain is already limited, but anxiety and fear shrink that number even further. You struggle to answer the question driving your fear because you lack the space to consider all the relevant data. Imagine trying to complete a 1000-piece puzzle by only looking at three pieces at a time—your mind goes into overdrive in a desperate attempt to find the pieces needed to solve the problem.

Quick Tip: Writing is a great tool to work around the limitations of the mind. As overthinking creates confusion and clutter in your mind, writing helps you to find answers more efficiently. When you recognize that your thinking is getting out of control, whether during the trading day or afterward, write down what you're worried about, and why. Being able to see and read your thoughts can give you a different perspective. It's like being able to see more than three puzzle pieces at once. Sometimes that's all you need to answer the question driving your fear.

Second-Guessing

After making a decision, whether just in your mind or after entering a position, you immediately question whether the decision is correct. Before getting in, you're excessively thorough in your analysis. This is appropriate for a risky trade that has high potential downside. But it's unnecessary for your usual trades, and can cause you to get a worse price or miss an opportunity entirely.

Once you're in the trade, your mind will randomly cycle back and agonize over it. You wonder whether you should close it or hold onto the position. When fear gets involved, there's an excessive desire to avoid making a mistake or losing money. You worry you missed something, question your reasoning, doubt that your sense of the market is accurate, or wonder if you were overconfident. You may even scratch it because the tension is too much to handle.

Second-guessing goes beyond the productive back and forth you go through in your decision-making process. While it can have an overthinking quality to it, overthinking is much broader and could apply to anything: *What is the Fed going to do? What is my boss going to say about my drawdown? Should I be trading another market? Why can't anyone figure out that Batman and Bruce Wayne are the same person?*

Second-guessing, on the other hand, is specific to decisions. Some trades are straightforward, and second-guessing doesn't show up. But when uncertainty is greater, second-guessing is more likely, and you're at risk of changing your mind.

Quick Tip: Write down, in detail, your optimal decision-making process. Then when you start to second-guess a decision, ask if what you're reconsidering needs to be part of that process or whether it's excessive and driven by fear. Second-guessing is worse when there are holes in your decision-making. Clearing up that process makes second-guessing less likely, and then when it does occur, you get a clearer look at the fear that's driving it.

Not Trusting Your Gut

Fear can wreak havoc with your ability to make decisions based on your gut. Even though there's a strong feeling the decision is correct, you can't clearly articulate the rationale for why the idea is right. This lack of certainty makes trusting your gut inherently feel riskier, so you go against it.

How does this play out? Maybe you've become pretty good at recognizing major momentum shifts in the market, but can't get yourself to trade on them. Maybe initially you went with your gut, but you were too early, got stopped out, and didn't get back in before the massive move you saw happened.

One common reason why traders don't trust their gut is that they don't know what the hell it is. Your goals, livelihood, and confidence are on the line, so why would you trust something you don't understand? You wouldn't trust a random stranger to advise you on the right opportunity to short oil futures. If your gut is unfamiliar, trusting it seems dangerous. Fear thrives in this space.

The tension builds between wanting to trust your gut and being uncertain what it is, why it's right, and worrying if it's wrong. Plus, under pressure, you naturally retreat to what you know best: your standard way of making trades. So just like the advice from a stranger, your gut-level decisions are discarded as untrustworthy.

Trusting something unfamiliar is especially tough when there is more downside to getting it wrong than upside to getting it right. Especially if you're making a good-sized bet or need to justify your decision to someone else.

Quick Tip: Your gut is most accurate when you're in the zone or operating at a high level. That doesn't mean that, in that state, it's always right, but when you're in your C-game, your gut is almost certainly wrong or based on some biased view, not on an accurate sense about the potential opportunity. Learn to identify the qualitative differences between this and how you think and feel when your gut tends to be accurate. For example, one client noted that his gut is accurate when it seems like several puzzle pieces come together all at once—there's a feeling of knowing combined with mental clarity. And when it's incorrect, he feels tension in his chest and stomach, and his mind is filled with "what if" type questions. Making this distinction has made it significantly easier to trust his gut.

Negative Future

One of the basic functions of the mind is anticipating and predicting the future. The utility of this ability is obvious when it's functioning correctly. But what isn't obvious for traders who have issues with fear is how their predictions can go awry and create more fear.

If you're evaluating a trade without fear, you can objectively consider the range of possible outcomes and evaluate the risk. When fear gets involved, however, traders will overestimate the likelihood that a negative event will occur, skewing their sense of the risk. Or worse, they make the classic error of being a shitty psychic and become absolutely certain those negative events will occur; for example, envisioning a position going against you before even initiating the trade. Both the overestimation and anticipation of future negative outcomes cause additional fear, and that further compromises the decision-making process.

These prognostications can hide in plain sight. Consider a question like "What if I lose money putting on a trade here?" That question predicts a mistake will happen and you'll look stupid for making it.

"What if" type questions are commonly associated with negative predictions. *What if I lose another $50k? What if I can't turn it around? What if I blow my account again?* These aren't really questions. You aren't legitimately asking yourself what will happen. You've already assumed those negative outcomes will happen. If you're on edge to begin with, that pseudo question triggers secondary fear, making additional mistakes and losses—and the negative future you fear—a more likely reality.

Quick Tip: Rather than allow a "what if" scenario to run wild, treat it as a legitimate question and write down your answer. If that were to happen, what would it mean and what would you do? Playing out the fear like this can clarify what you are actually afraid of, and can help to uncover the hidden flaws contributing to it.

MAPPING YOUR FEAR

The idea of mapping your fear isn't metaphoric; you're actually creating a map. This map is essential to recognizing the escalation of fear in real time, enabling you to quickly correct it, or at least minimize the damage to your execution. Plus, this map helps you to understand the flaws causing your fear. It also helps you to identify the sections of this chapter most relevant for you to work through.

Follow the steps below to create a document that will become the map of your fear.

Step 1

Over the next few weeks, pay close attention to your **pattern of fear**. Examine and capture the signs that fear has become a problem, including:

- Thoughts
- Emotions
- Things you say out loud
- Behaviors
- Actions
- Changes to your decision-making
- Changes to your perception of the market, opportunities, or current positions
- Trading mistakes

Keep a document open on your computer or a notepad next to you while you trade, and take notes throughout the day.

At the end of the trading day, review what you found and add additional details. Be as comprehensive as you can. It's ok to identify things that only happen once in a while.

If this is hard for you, don't worry about it. You're not going to identify all the details perfectly the first time you do it. (And if you're overly worried about making mistakes mapping your fear, then it's likely that a fear of mistakes is a problem you need to correct.)

Everyone has their own starting point. Use what you find and build on it over time. Don't worry if it takes a month to get it right—that's not uncommon. During that time, as long as you keep it on your mind, you'll continually learn more than you knew before. Progress is progress regardless of the speed. Here are some questions to help get you started:

- What situations typically provoke uncertainty, doubt, anxiety, or fear?
- How does your body react when you're nervous? For example, is there heart pounding, sweating, nausea, dry mouth, foot or hand tapping?
- Can you describe the point where nerves go from helping you perform to being excessive and causing problems?
- What specifically is going through your mind? What thoughts do you have? How is your decision-making process different?
- What are the earliest signs that fear has become a problem?

In the previous section I described five *general* signs of fear. To recap, those are risk aversion, overthinking, not trusting your gut, second-guessing, and a negative future. By contrast, here are some *specific* signals of fear that you may experience:

- Can't pull the trigger, out of fear you missed something
- Your heart rate spikes when sizing up, even after trading for many years
- Paralyzed and unable to get out of positions or manage risk properly
- Doubt that you're seeing things correctly
- Looking for opportunities outside of your system, or using indicators or charts that you normally wouldn't
- Talking yourself out of a good trade
- Quickly taking profit to ensure you don't lose money
- Struggle sleeping after bad days
- Focus gets too narrow—tunnel vision blocks out important factors

Be sure to capture as many triggers as you can find, regardless of the amount of uncertainty, anxiety, worry, or doubt they create. If you need help identifying your triggers, look closely at your thoughts and the things you say out loud. Remember, don't judge or criticize what you say or think. Your thoughts are caused by a performance flaw that often directly relates to the trigger. Here are some common triggers:

- Prospect of losing money
- Realizing you made a mistake
- The thought *Don't fuck this up*
- Threat of embarrassment
- Seeing negative PnL for the month
- Seeing a position quickly move red
- Being unable to stop yourself from exiting a winning position

Mapping your fear is an iterative process. When you spot new details, even just slight adjustments, be sure to add them. Small details matter and can make a big difference. Progress in correcting your fear and improving your execution is on the line. It's worth being exhaustive with the details.

Step 2

Once you've gathered a lot of details, organize what you've found by putting them in order of severity. Rank each detail on a scale of 1 to 10, where 1 characterizes a slight doubt or worry, and 10 is what happens under the most intense amount of fear. At each level, identify details that clearly distinguish it from other levels.

As you assign levels of severity, split them into two categories: the mental and emotional side of fear, and the technical side. They sit side by side, so level 1 on the mental and emotional side corresponds to level 1 on the technical side, and so on.

Be sure to base this on *your* experience of fear, and not how other traders deal with it. Everyone has their own range, and if you judge yourself against someone else, you're at risk of over- or underestimating what you're capable of. Doing this will make your strategy less accurate.

You don't need to have details for all 10 levels. Most traders that I work with aren't able to distinguish their pattern of fear to that degree. Do a minimum of three and as many more as you can. Here are some questions to distinguish the differences in each level of fear:

- What triggers the initial worry or doubt at level 1? How does it accumulate or increase to become anxiety or fear? For example, maybe it begins with normal uncertainty related to the market, but then your second loss of the day triggers worry about future losses, which leads to a fear that maybe you can't cut it anymore, so you feel like you *have* to make money in the next trade.
- What details are present when fear is still small and manageable? What details are present when it's a monster, completely disrupting your execution?
- How is your perception of the market different when your fear is higher?
- What specific trading mistakes can you avoid at level 1 but can't stop from happening at level 10?

Take what you've categorized and put them into a map, like the one below:

FEAR LEVEL

Describe the thoughts, emotions, things you say, behaviors, and actions that highlight each level of fear. Complete at least 3 levels.

1: Looking at the charts and asking myself if taking this position was the right decision. Did I do the right thing? Is this going to be a loser?

2:

3: Wondering why is the market going against me? I look at my live trades a lot more often than I need to. Start to worry that I'm going to have to accept the 1% loss.

4:

5: Log on to my brokerage account to see how much I have lost over the last few trades.

6:

7: Urge to move stop to breakeven; really want to avoid another loss.

8: Want to take profit as soon as it's running decently green. I want to secure profits to be able to prove to myself I can still do it, that I am able to make money from my trading.

9:

10: Staring at my charts and not really thinking at this point.

TECHNICAL LEVEL

Describe the quality of your decision-making, perception of the market, opportunities, or current positions at each level of fear.

1: Not seeing things objectively. Clouded judgment that a change in the market means I did something wrong.

2:

3: Emotional thinking about past losses; start to disregard probabilistic thoughts.

4:

5: Become distrusting of my own strategy and need to talk to others, like my mentor, to be reassured of where my edge comes from.

6:

7: Mostly focused on guaranteed profits or breaking even.

8: No longer thinking rationally.

9:

10: No longer thinking at all.

Step 3

You now have a solid draft that you can use while you're trading so you can **recognize your pattern and quickly respond with the correction.** Since these patterns can take a lot of experience and training to correct, don't revise your map until you get consistent evidence that it has permanently changed.

Now, use what you identified in this section to focus on the specific types of fear that are most relevant to your trading. I strongly advise that you start by reading through all of the types. Why? Because you may identify with issues that you didn't realize you had at first glance. And, you may remember additional details to add to your map. Then go back and reread the sections most relevant to you.

FEAR OF MISSING OUT (FOMO)

What signals should you be looking for to see if FOMO is an issue for you?

Here are some typical examples. You can't stay focused on the sectors, symbols, or markets you usually watch. You feel like big moves are happening elsewhere. Adrenaline pumps through your body, you're hyper-focused, and driven to avoid missing another big opportunity. You missed the last one, and the urge to get it right this time is overpowering. You know you shouldn't chase, but you worry that price isn't going to come back down and that you have to get in *now*.

Or maybe you overreact to breaking news. You have a panicky feeling and make a rash decision without completing your analysis. You get stopped out, and as it immediately retraces, you convince yourself that it's fine to get in again because it "feels right."

FOMO can come at a time where the market doesn't move in a way that suits your style. There's a lot of potential, but none of your ideas pan out. You're a trader and you need to trade, so you jump into the next one, convinced it's fine to get in even though it missed your entry by a few ticks. Or maybe the market is so volatile you only get a partial fill, and chase to get the rest. You see other traders making money, ignore the risks and size too big, trying to make up the difference in what you think you should have made.

Regardless of exactly how it pops up for you, FOMO forces you into trades outside of your system that you know you shouldn't take. The most vexing part is often trying to understand why that urge is so hard to control, but you simply don't recognize the buildup of emotion. That's why you can't stop yourself.

Just the normal tension of trading can cause your nerves to increase as, for example, you see price dancing around your zone and wait to get a better price. The longer you wait, the more emotion builds up. Then if you happen to lose or miss out on a few trades, anxiety accumulates even more, and eventually compels you to jump into a trade prematurely, make justifications for why the market is still in a good spot, or look at more markets than you can realistically manage.

Nerves or anxiety also accumulate day over day when you're in a drawdown, have been struggling, or need money. For some of you, trading is like going to an amusement park—you love the thrill of riding the roller coaster. When the market hasn't provided many opportunities, your need for action can become too much to contain.

Either way, it's critical that you become aware of the escalation. When mapping your FOMO, pay close attention both to what triggers the emotion and to what signals an increase in it. That will help you get to the bottom of what's driving it.

Find the Real Cause of FOMO

The term FOMO is used so much in trading that it's become an umbrella term that lacks specificity. I've only found one underlying flaw that is completely unique to FOMO—the assumption that there will never be another opportunity. If this is a problem for you, despite logically knowing there will be more opportunities, you'll find yourself unable to see beyond this trade. Your mind gets so focused, you're convinced that you have to take advantage of this opportunity because there won't be another one.

This tends to happen most often when the market is slow and there are, factually, fewer opportunities, or when you're in a drawdown and pessimistic about your prospects. But the fact remains, there will be more opportunities. You know that when you're in your right state of mind. The key is to remind yourself of that fact in those moments before FOMO has a chance to intensify. That will make it easier to avoid getting involved where you shouldn't.

Beyond that flaw, the main causes of FOMO are related to other types of fear, as well as anger and confidence issues. Like greed, FOMO is real, but to solve it, you need to first identify the flaws, biases, and illusions that fuel it.

If you struggle to dig them out, try something that may sound a bit strange at first: Force yourself to stay on the sidelines to intensify your emotions. The reason to do this is that when your emotions are more intense, the cause of them can be easier to identify.

How might this look in practice? Define a narrower set of criteria for what trades you'll take; for example, by only taking A+ trades for a day, a few days, or a week. Or you might deliberately remove some discretionary-type trades that can lead to FOMO.

Keep a notepad or journal open next to you and, in real time, capture the emotions and thoughts that arise. They will be the clues to help you complete a more precise map, laying the groundwork for you to determine the roots of your FOMO and come up with a correction.

If you find yourself hesitating about the financial impact of this exercise, remember this is research. You're investing in a long-term upgrade to your execution that, if successful, will likely recoup those short-term missed opportunities many times over.

After completing this task, you may recognize that FOMO is driven by what you believe are the *consequences* of missing out. You might jump in early because missing out on profit feels like losing, and you have a fear of losing. Maybe seeing others make money while you aren't sparks a fear of failure, leading you to think that you're not good enough. If you consider missing out to be a mistake and fear mistakes, you could be trying to avoid self-criticism. Ironically, fear of making a mistake compels you to make one.

FOMO can also be driven by an angry need to make back losses. It can come from a type of perfectionism, where you expect to catch every move and make the maximum profit from every trade. FOMO might show up because you lack confidence and jump in when the market starts to move to avoid feeling stupid or embarrassed that you missed out. Or perhaps like Carlos, our next example, your FOMO is actually related to a technical mistake.

Carlos is a full-time forex and futures trader from the U.S. He and I originally worked through some problems with anger around losing and mistakes. After making significant progress with his anger, FOMO stood out as a bigger problem. While FOMO wasn't a new issue, it hadn't affected his trading nearly as much as anger, so it wasn't originally a priority. This is common when making progress in your mental game. Once you fix the first problem, you can move on to the next one.

Throughout our work on his anger, the Mental Hand History was an important tool to help break through and understand the roots of the problem. It motivated him to not just map his emotions but to understand and resolve the cause of them. In one session we came up with the phrase "Don't hide; ask why." Carlos was able to firmly reorient his mind around the idea that emotions are signals to be understood. Having that in the forefront of his mind allowed him to tackle FOMO on his own, and from a new perspective.

One day he recognized FOMO getting triggered in a particular setup that had been giving him problems—a limit entry, where he was waiting for price to knife down into his range, and if it turned there, it could rocket up.

In the past, after getting stopped out of this type of setup when the market would start flying back up, he would think, *Man, I'm going to miss the move that I didn't get in.* He would reenter in self-described gambling mode, because he didn't have a plan for that particular pivot. The next trade would get popped out, causing FOMO to intensify, leading to several more bad trades, which would trigger tilt—he'd triple his position size and lose big.

This time, however, Carlos recognized the nervousness and immediately started writing his thoughts and emotions in his journal and then walked away. This was progress in itself, since he at least avoided an increase in emotion and the poorer execution that would follow. As he walked way away from his screens, Carlos asked himself, "Why am I feeling FOMO? What is it signaling?"

He realized that the five-minute chart didn't allow him to see the market turn, something he needed to see because he was only using a 10-point stop loss. That gave him the idea to zoom down to a 30-second chart at the right area at the right time. He also stopped using limit orders. Now he uses stop-limit orders for entry. So, trades that used to take 15 minutes to develop he can figure out in three to four minutes. The fear is gone and precision on his entries has been really high. As he put it, "There's really no reason for my execution not to be spot on, as I can see the move."

In this case, the FOMO was a signal of a legitimate risk of missing out because Carlos couldn't get a good sense of where the market was within his range to time his entries properly. FOMO was correct, but it wasn't an emotional problem. The fear was highlighting a gap in his execution.

Perhaps your FOMO is signaling an opportunity for you to improve your execution. Even if, like Carlos, you don't formally go through each step of the Mental Hand History, you can still use it to work on the technical side of your map—many of my clients have done this. Start with FOMO as the problem in Step 1, and try to work through the technical side to see what you come up with. And if it's not highlighting a technical problem, work through the emotional side by using the system to identify the root cause, and then devise a correction.

FEAR OF LOSING

The threat of losing is always there. Given that you work in an insanely competitive environment, losing, at times, is inevitable. This is obvious—and yet you fear it. You don't even have to have a losing trade that day to feel the fear. It lurks in the background because every trade has the possibility of loss.

The fear of loss forces you to make decisions that you know are less than optimal. You lock up winners too soon, protecting against a pullback that would make even a winning trade feel like a loser. You add to losing positions, cutting the average price to make it easier to break even or not to lose as much.

In a drawdown, your fear of loss is even greater. You pass on high-quality setups, assuming the trade will go against you. You become more protective. Trade less. When you do get in, you're glued to the screen. You move your stops to protect, but that just leads to more losses. The stress is palpable and affects your sleep.

As the fear gets even bigger, thoughts tumble over each other in your head: *Is my edge gone? How am I going to turn it around? Am I done—what will I do?* You may even get to the point where the threat of loss created so much tension, and kept you on the sidelines for so long, you just can't take it anymore. The fear of losing, not any actual losses, has become so intense, you snap, say, "Fuck it," to yourself, and fire off a trade. You don't care what happens. You just want to stop feeling the fear.

You've tried listening to advice that tells you to understand the realities of trading better, that losses are inevitable, and that you should accept the risk that comes with trading. You're trading money you can afford to lose, but still can't be in a calm state. That advice hasn't eased your fears because it doesn't fully capture what losing means to you.

What's on the Line?

To begin to understand the cause of your fear of losing, start by asking yourself: "What does losing or a loss represent for me?" When I ask my clients this, their first response focuses on the money. But typically, as the conversation continues, it becomes clear that losing is about more than just money. The money represents something else that is also on the line.

The money can represent your ability to support your family, or your aspirations to become a full-time trader and prove the doubters wrong. Losing a series of trades can make you feel like you have taken a step backward toward accomplishing your short- and long-term goals. Losing threatens your sense of competence or your status among peers.

Taking sustained losses can lead you to overreact and lose control, so your fear of loss is really a fear of losing control. Money is basically how you "keep score" in trading and having poorer results can cause you to lose confidence in general as a trader, or specifically in your current system and its ability to profit in the current market. Losses can feel like a waste of time—if you're not making money, what the hell are you doing?

Take some time to think about what's on the line for you. Is it the utility of money? Is it your goals? Confidence? Discipline? Status? Others? Or a combination of multiple factors?

If you have trouble answering this, or if some ideas don't immediately come to mind, the next time you take a loss, go through this list again. Ask yourself some pointed questions:

- What else do you feel like you've lost?
- Are you afraid to tell somebody about the loss?
- Are you worried about your ability to make money?
- Are you worried you're going to make even more mistakes now?
- Does it feel like your progress or goals are less likely to be achieved?

Traders are often surprised by how intensely they can fear losing. Identifying and accepting the full picture of what's on the line for you can normalize your reaction. But for many of you, that won't be enough to solve your fear. Instead you'll make the classic mistake of trying to break through your fear by throwing caution out the window, and the pendulum will swing too far in the other direction. You'll become defiant in the face of fear. While that takes the feeling of fear away, you're now at risk of making different mistakes.

Finding the sweet spot between fear and defiance happens automatically when you correct the flaws that contaminate your perspective on losing. Below are several performance flaws that commonly contribute to the fear of losing. Traders with particularly intense fear often have multiple flaws affecting them. Be sure to work through each one that's relevant to you.

Here's an example of a Mental Hand History highlighting a fear of losing:

1. **What's the problem:** I have a need for a trade to be green right from the beginning. My heart rate jumps once I get into the trade, and it goes through the roof if it's immediately in the red. When it's moving in the wrong direction, I get nervous that it's going to get stopped out.

2. **Why does the problem exist:** Part of me thinks the first second of a trade represents what is going to happen in the trade. If it's green, I relax, which is stupid, but really I just want it to hit. Every loss feels like a step backward—like it's going to take me longer to hit my goals.

3. **What is flawed:** I can't control the outcome of every trade. If I make a good bet, that's all I can control. I'm going to lose a lot. That doesn't mean my goals are at risk. One trade tells me nothing about what the year is going to look like. That's like judging the outcome of a baseball game on the first pitch.

4. **What's the correction:** Stay focused on quality execution. Once I'm in, go look at a snapshot of the trade, so I can evaluate the quality of it without being distracted by the chart. If I made a good bet, take the hit, and look for another opportunity.

5. **What logic confirms that correction:** Quality execution in the short term is how I get what I want in the long run. Losses and drawdowns are part of the game—any game, for that matter. Champions don't fear losing; they do everything they can to win.

Pain of Losing

Losing is painful enough that you can fear the feeling of losing itself. Traders tend to be ultra-competitive. While you know it's not possible to profit from every trade, you don't like losing. Losing money never feels good.

Losing sucks and some traders reflexively try to avoid the pain of it, similar to how they would immediately, instinctively, limp to avoid the pain of a badly sprained ankle. The fear of losing is essentially protection from the pain of losing, and the equivalent of limping is quickly taking profit, sizing smaller, or avoiding higher risk trades.

There are better ways to reduce the pain of losing. But on some level, for people who are highly competitive, the pain will always be there. It will never feel good. And that's fine. The goal then becomes more about how to handle the pain. Since you'll never eliminate the pain of losing entirely, you must learn to push yourself through it by realizing the pain isn't a problem.

Imagine you're a professional marathon runner who, just before a big race, feels a sharp pain in your left foot when you run. As you wait for the doctor to give you the results of an MRI, thoughts circle in your mind about having to pull out of the race or, worse, having an injury that requires surgery and will take months to fully heal. You get good news, though. While the injury does require surgery, you won't make it worse running in this race. You just have to endure the pain.

For you, losing may always be painful, but so what? It's simply a result of your competitiveness and your desire to win. Don't fall into the trap of assuming that pain equals something bad. Sometimes pain is just pain and you have to keep going. You're like a boxer with a weak jaw who hasn't learned how to take a punch yet.

Some of you may lack this toughness because you haven't experienced a lot of losing prior to trading. Maybe you were successful in high school, college, or in other jobs, and got heaps of praise. Or perhaps you already had a successful career prior to trading, and you weren't challenged by it in the same way. Maybe you've experienced your share of losing, but the frequency of it in trading is much greater than you've ever dealt with before.

Regardless, you need to become tougher. Embrace the pain and it becomes more tolerable. You get used to the feeling and build up the strength to handle it. As you do, the fear designed to protect you from pain decreases.

One practical way you can become tougher is to take one minute after a loss to feel the pain and talk yourself through it, like your coach or mentor would. Understand what the loss means—it's likely nothing, and is just one of many that you'll have in your career.

Be clear about the need to avoid mistakes over your next several trades. Dig in and push yourself to execute your strategy. Take the hit. The pain of losing one trade is not worse than the pain you'll feel by making more mistakes to try to avoid pain.

Attached to Unrealized Gains

Another cause of the fear of losing is being overly attached to unrealized gains. Take, for example, the following scenario: You're having the best month of your career, positions are killing it, and you still believe there is more room for them to run. The problem is that some positions are still open, but you start to feel like the unrealized gains are already yours. You get ahead of yourself and can't help it. Then your PnL drops. One position goes from a massive winner to breakeven.

Even though you're still up significantly on the month, it feels like your profits are being taken from you. Fear overrides your ability to think clearly. You overreact and panic sell to lock up profit in other positions that you know still have room to run.

Believing, either consciously or unconsciously, that unrealized gains were yours altered your perspective and caused you to panic. If you avoid getting attached to money that isn't yours, you'll automatically remain clear-minded in the trade. The correction here is less about correcting the *fear* and more about identifying the *reason* why you get attached to money that isn't yet yours.

So why do you? Does it happen as you come out of a drawdown and you're relieved to be out of it? Are you overeager to hit your goals, reach higher, and never want to take steps backward? Are you a newer trader who didn't really understand the difference between realized and unrealized profit?

Whatever the reason, be on the lookout for signs that you've become attached to unrealized gains. That's your opportunity to correct this type of fear. If you correct—or ideally *prevent*—yourself from prematurely locking up that profit in your mind, you automatically avoid fearing a pullback in PnL.

Assuming the Worst

After only a handful of losses, does your mind immediately think of the worst-case scenario—being out on the street, broke, and unable to provide for your family? Do you go into a downward spiral, wondering how you'll explain blowing up your account? Are you suddenly convinced that you can't make it anymore as a trader and need to look for a new line of work? Do you assume all your positions are going to zero?

In the moment, your mind is paralyzed by these swirling thoughts and you can't think clearly. These terrible potential outcomes feel inevitable.

Overreactions like this are often caused by the ghosts of your past failures. For example, if at some point you busted your account, struggled to find a new job and rebuild your finances, the pain of having gone through that can lurk in the background of your mind. At the first sign of a possible return to that hell, you freak out. There's a slippery slope in how quickly your mind can fall apart, and the severity of it differs for each trader. For some, it's so tenuous that just one above-average loss sends them reeling.

Even though numerous things have to go very wrong for you to actually bust your account, accumulated emotion from the past can quickly override your ability to think clearly and makes it feel like a strong possibility. By reducing the pain of the past, you essentially close the trap door. You don't forget the past; you just stop it from haunting you. There's a difference between remembering the experience of busting your account and having that experience still carry real emotion with it.

However, if you're like many traders, instead of learning from the past, you try to forget about it and keep moving forward. But you can't forget about it. Fear won't let you. You must *learn* from the past to lessen that fear, or your risk of failing again is higher than it needs to be.

To correct this problem, write down the reasons why your past failures happened. Use that knowledge to develop a well-thought-out plan to achieve your goals this time around.

Another thing to consider is whether the worst-case scenario is really that bad. Research has shown that people tend to overestimate the duration and severity that tragic events have on our happiness and quality of life.[1] This term was coined the "impact bias," by Dan Gilbert, the author of *Stumbling on Happiness*, and his research partner Tim Wilson.

This bias also applies to tragic events, like the loss of a limb or becoming paraplegic. You would think that compared to winning the lottery, losing a limb or the use of your legs would be much worse on your psyche. But you would be wrong. Their research shows that within a year of those extreme events, most people's level of happiness returned to the level it was prior.[2]

If this resonates with you, use it to reduce your estimate that what you fear is really that bad. Then when you feel your mind slipping into worst-case-scenario type thinking, talk yourself through the reasons why it won't be so bad. Think productively about what you can do right now to move toward your goals. As Gilbert and Wilson say, "People are consummate sense makers who transform novel, emotion-producing events into ones that seem ordinary and mundane. . . ."

In other words, if the worst case were to actually happen, you'll find a way to make sense of it and move forward. Going through it won't be fun, but it also won't be *that* bad. You can't know what's going to happen in the future, positive or negative. However, regardless of what happens, you'll do everything you can to come out better on the other side, just like you've done in the past.

It's also worth noting that catastrophe can lead to innovation and adaptation. Take, for instance, the trader who bombs out and has to temporarily take a different job. In that job a new perspective emerges for the value of emotional stability, and discipline improves. When trading resumes, those improved skills become the catalyst for long-term success. No one predicts that their road to success will wind through disaster, but that may turn out to be what was needed.

FEAR OF MISTAKES

For some traders, mistakes are an integral part of the learning process. So, on one level, fearing mistakes essentially means that you fear learning. No one in their right mind would actually fear something so beneficial. But that's the point: In the moment when the fear of mistakes shows up, you're not in your right mind. The way you react to the potential trade, possible exit, or missed entry indicates an error in how you view the learning process. These errors, or underlying flaws, cause you to fear mistakes.

Often the fear of mistakes is subtle, because on the surface it seems like a fear of losing, so the signs can be hard to spot. Here are a few things to keep an eye out for:

- Constantly wondering if your decisions are wrong
- Rushing to get out of a position to end the agony of uncertainty
- Treating all mistakes equally—anything less than perfection is unacceptable
- Hesitating, overthinking, and second-guessing many of your decisions
- Trying to prevent all mistakes by learning everything you can and working as hard as possible
- Quitting after one mistake
- Doing anything to avoid judgment or looking stupid
- Not closing out a trade when you should, to avoid a mistake

At its simplest, fear is all about anticipation. In general, nervousness, anxiety, and fear can build in anticipation of the trading day, at particular times of day, or when you sense a trade opportunity emerging. But the anticipation of a mistake is particularly challenging from a performance standpoint because it affects your execution and makes what you fear—a mistake—more likely.

It could only be momentary, maybe showing up as hesitation or second-guessing, but that's enough to compromise your execution. In that moment, you may not even be aware that your nerves are jacked up because you fear a mistake. But when you dig into why you're hesitating, second-guessing, or not trusting your gut, you'll find evidence that the fear of a mistake is there.

Every decision carries the possibility of a mistake, but that doesn't mean that every decision causes you to *fear* a mistake. Look for clues that indicate underlying fear. Perhaps a particular type of setup or trade is problematic for you. Maybe you're more mistake-prone in a drawdown, when feeling financial pressure. Or you're more likely to slip up after deciding to size up.

It could also be linked to timing—such as earnings season, or breaking news. For some traders it has to do with the time of day, like periods when they get bored or distracted. Or it could be a bigger indication of a weak point in your trading strategy where, for example, you're struggling to trade the open or close.

Your job is to identify and understand the situations where experiencing fear is more likely. That may lead you to uncover tactical reasons for why you tend to make mistakes—meaning that fear was a signal for that weakness in your strategy, system, or execution. You'll likely also find performance flaws that cause you to unnecessarily fear a mistake. In the absence of something tactically wrong, your fear may seem illogical. But the intense pressure to avoid mistakes isn't created in a single instance. It has grown larger as you reflected on and evaluated your mistakes in a faulty way.

Once you identify the flaws, you have a chance to change the anticipation back to normal. Usually that takes steadily chipping away at the anticipation of a mistake. As it gets smaller and smaller, the overthinking, hesitation, and second-guessing are removed, and you can get back to seamless execution.

What are the faulty ways in which you're evaluating past performance that create this fear? Since the mistakes are intertwined with learning, all of the following flaws are, in some way, related to that topic.

Expecting Perfection

Believing mistakes should never happen is another way of saying you expect perfection. There is a big difference between a desire for perfection that spurs peak level trading and the expectation of perfection.

When you *expect* perfection, the pressure to avoid mistakes can be such a burden that it keeps you on the sidelines and, ironically, still causes mistakes—just a different sort. For example, until you feel like you have enough knowledge or a tight enough strategy where you are certain to avoid mistakes, you won't trade a new symbol or get into a new market sector. Being slow costs you opportunity.

Plus, the fear becomes self-reinforcing. Sometimes you simply can't learn enough from the sidelines. You have to experience the market, with skin in the game. But before diving in, you try preventing mistakes by learning everything you can. This may seem like an ideal way to start, but if you expect perfection, all that knowledge can jam up your decision-making process. You're likely to overthink or second-guess your strategy and hesitate. That spikes your anxiety. You have to get it right, but your brain isn't working. So back to the sidelines you go to learn more and button up your strategy, and the cycle repeats.

Expecting perfection also removes your sense of range in the severity of mistakes—you treat them all as equally bad. This gives you no room to move. The pressure to get it right is incredibly high, because even the smallest missteps are feared as much as the big ones.

While it makes sense to expect to avoid basic mistakes, when you consider even a slight misstep to be on par with a big mistake, trading feels like walking a tightrope, where you can easily fall to your death.

Perhaps your expectation of perfection isn't that black and white. You understand that mistakes can happen, but you expect to never make the same mistake twice. Consequently, when it happens again, it's shocking; you weren't expecting it. Questions swirl around in your mind: *How can this happen? How could I have been so stupid? What more can I possibly do!* You do more work to try and trade better, but you still make the same mistake. Your performance feels out of your control and fear multiplies.

When you make a mistake, your job is to correct it, so that you don't make it again. But traders can expect a mistake to be corrected just by being aware of what they did wrong. Sometimes mistakes are more complex, and without doing some real work to understand the cause, they keep happening again, and again, and again.

To begin making progress here, let's look closer at what expectations imply. An expectation is another word for guarantee. I'm not making a linguistic choice; this is an important distinction. By saying, "I expect myself to be perfect," you are basically saying that perfection will happen. While you expect perfection, the reality is that you truly can only expect or guarantee your worst. While that may sound pathetic, it's still true.

Earlier in the book I outlined the idea of having an A-, B-, and C-game, and mapping yours. The only guarantee is your C-game, because the skills present at that level, for better or worse, have been mastered. They show up easily and automatically.

Your A- and B-game, on the other hand, are earned through your study and back-testing; efforts to be in prime physical, mental, and emotional condition; hours collaborating with other traders; and other work you do to become a better trader. Collectively, they power your ability to escape your C-game each day. And from that perspective, when missteps occur, you must become the detective, examine with curiosity the reasons why you fell short, and find a way to improve.

As the Inchworm Concept shows us, perfection is a moving target that will never be attained consistently. Aspire to perfection; don't expect it. Mistakes are inevitable. The goal is to learn from them faster.

I'm also not implying that you should lower your expectations. That's not the correction. Instead, transform your expectations into aspirations or goals. When you *aim* toward perfection, rather than *expecting* it, you automatically treat mistakes in the correct way—as essential for growth. You expect mistakes to be part of the process, and your goal is to correct them as quickly as possible.

Beaten Dog Syndrome

A fear of mistakes can develop from a long period of being intensely self-critical. Fear is not the starting point of this problem. Rather, self-criticism inflicts sustained pain, and over time you develop fear as a way to avoid it. This is akin to a dog that's regularly beaten by its owner. In that scenario, you'll see the dog become fearful when its owner enters the room. The dog is on edge and nervous that any wrong move may provoke being hit. If you have harsh and negative reactions to mistakes, you're essentially cowering from your self-inflicted beatings.

While you may not view self-criticism as a problem, at some point the fear of it emerged. The solution to Beaten Dog Syndrome doesn't begin by trying to correct your fear. The fear comes from a reasonable desire to avoid self-criticism. Your task is to get to the source of the criticism and correct it.

Self-criticism that's strong enough to inflict pain is typically a form of anger. Think of your tone when you provide feedback. Could it be described as harsh, punishing, or cruel? If so, anger is the emotion behind it. Start with the next chapter about anger and correct your self-criticism. You may find the section Glorifying Self-Criticism particularly helpful, as many of you with this problem at one point thought self-criticism was necessary to achieve your goals.

Then, once you've started to make progress, be patient with the process of removing your fear. If you take a beaten dog away from its owner and put it in the most loving, warm home imaginable, the dog doesn't instantly become happy-go-lucky. The dog needs to learn that the new owner won't cause him pain. In the same way, you need to learn how to react differently to your mistakes before the fear can go away.

After getting a strong handle on the self-criticism side of the problem, you're in position to break through the fear. But unlike the dog, you can't just replace your inner critic (the owner). Breaking through the fear is a two-fold process. First, after making a mistake, you must work to decrease your anger. Second, assuming your anger level was lower, pay extra attention to that progress, and push yourself to trust that you can handle the next mistake better. If you're organized and focused, you can create a cycle that can rapidly build trust.

To be clear, you're not excusing mistakes or trying to feel good about them. But the way you handle mistakes determines the speed in which you learn from them. Reducing self-criticism and handling mistakes better is a matter of efficiency. The more self-criticism and fear that exist around the mistakes, the more likely your learning process slows or stops completely, and you continue to make mistakes. Ultimately you want to handle your mistakes better, so you can correct them faster.

Here's an example of a Mental Hand History highlighting a fear of criticism:

1. **What's the problem:** Mistakes cause anxiety and fear. When I see another opportunity, I doubt that I'm right, and even if I get in, my sizing is a lot smaller. I'm on edge and hesitant until I get a win.

2. **Why does the problem exist:** It is natural to be critical of mistakes. In school, I grew up with the threat of criticism and now I do the same thing to myself.

3. **What is flawed:** It's not working! It's a misguided attempt to get me to do better. Sure, I'm motivated to fix my mistakes, but they keep happening, and way more than they should. It's not helping me to consistently execute. The cycle doesn't stop and is a messy way of trying to get better. Of course I can do better. But if I continue to thrash myself for every misstep, I'm making things a lot worse.

4. **What's the correction:** Self-criticism didn't help me to reach my potential. I was poorly trained. I don't know yet how I should be talking to myself when I mess up, but I'm going to figure it out.

5. **What logic confirms that correction:** Realizing how much I was caught in a never-ending cycle has motivated me to fix the bigger mistake—self-criticism. I'm sure there will be ups and down, but there's no way I'm going back.

Weak Process

Another reason a mistake can cause fear is having weak points in your process; for example, in making decisions, developing your competence as a trader, or adapting your strategy to the changes in the market. Uncertainty is amplified by these holes, even more so when you have poor discipline in your work ethic. You need to make improvements, but in the back of your mind, you know that you're not doing everything you could be.

Either way, you can sense something is off and go into the day worried you're going to screw up. There's a lot of hesitation, and you don't pull the trigger as easily in setups that have been standard. You're quick to lock up profit and feel uneasy even after profitable days.

In chapter 4 we saw that prior to coaching, Alex, the options trader from Germany, was underperforming on big trades. Yet he would never have thought that anything about his process was weak. While it was obvious to him that his mental game needed work, after our first session he uncovered several small process imperfections that culminated in his inability to fully capitalize on big opportunities.

Four to five times per year Alex identified trades where he had high confidence that he should be making a large bet, but the fear of being wrong prevented him from doing it. He was paralyzed by thoughts like *What if I lose a big chunk? I don't want to lose that much. What if I'm wrong? I don't want to crash like that.* He would pay more attention to business news and soliciting opinions from other traders, even when he knew it didn't help.

These trades set up over days, and his mind went into overdrive—overweighting the risk of danger and discounting the value of being right. With 20% of his trades driving 80% of his profits, Alex knew that individual trades could have a huge impact, but he couldn't size these trades at a level commensurate with the opportunity.

In our first session, we found our first piece of the problem. To Alex, the fear of being wrong in these big spots meant that his edge had disappeared. Under normal circumstances he could easily explain his core competency in 60 seconds. But if asked to do that while feeling the pressure of a big trade opportunity, his head would go fuzzy, and he wouldn't be able to articulate his skill set clearly and succinctly.

This was the first gap in his process, and I encouraged him to spend time thinking about his strategy, accomplishments, and capability as a trader, so he could clearly explain why he would be right when he would spot these potential home runs.

The exercise was easy to do, and writing down the numerous ideas flying around in his head added clarity to what constitutes his edge.

Consolidating his knowledge like this created certainty around what he was doing, which automatically shielded him from anxiety.

The clarity he gained from the exercise gave him the idea to experiment with cutting off all external sources of information. The first few days were weird, but then he noticed a big increase in his mental capacity. He was able to focus longer and didn't drift off. This second improvement in his process quickly led to a third.

The absence of external information forced him to focus exclusively on his own opinions and intuition. The latter allowed him to increase his competency around his intuition, so he could tell the difference between it and the voices of doubt that held him back. He described intuition as a moment when several puzzle pieces come together—he knows what will happen next and just needs to wait for the signal.

This experience is in stark contrast to fear, which included overthinking and doubtful questioning, as well as a very physical reaction: tightness in his chest and a knot in his stomach. Having these points written out, side by side, allowed him to see the difference in real time, and act accordingly.

These three improvements to his process, especially the last one, proved to be the keys to getting him over the hurdle. While a huge opportunity didn't come up during our sessions, I checked back in with him, and here's what he had to say: "It was eye opening. I realized what was happening and lay back for a few weeks to wait for the right conditions. Then, when the time was right, I traded with no hesitation. I saw the moment. Everyone was on one side of the boat and I knew the piece that would make it flip. I had already planned it out for the trade size and it was on my sheet—the what, why, and, depending on conditions, what percentage I would put in. When the time came, I just did it."

Not only is Alex sizing larger, he's letting it run longer. Before, he estimated that he was capturing around a third of the potential profit— which was a big trigger for greed. Now, the exits are planned. He scales two-thirds out at the juiciest point, and the last third is what he calls the "let it ride" part, where he assumes breakeven at worst.

At Alex's level, given the demands for precision, these small weaknesses in his process proved to be a much bigger problem than he had realized. They were also an appropriate signal of fear. When gaps exist in your process, you'd have to be overconfident not to feel fear—not an ideal correction. Instead, understand that this fear signal is pointing out the need to improve some aspect of your process.

Assumption of a Mistake

A lack of complete control is the only real certainty of the market, right? But some traders artificially remove that certainty by assuming variance doesn't impact their results. They believe each loss, or failure to profit as much as expected, means they made a mistake.

Intraday, that assumption triggers the tension, nerves, and stress that normally follow an actual mistake, causing you to make real mistakes, like getting a worse price because of hesitation, or sizing too small in a juicy spot. By not accounting for the role of variance, you're basically overestimating your control. You're taking too much responsibility for your results. While I would rather you err on that side of the coin vs. blindly blaming variance, it's still a flaw that causes unnecessary mistakes.

This pattern of overestimating your control usually starts with big wins. You had some trades where you got in and out at the perfect time and made the maximum on the trade. At that time, two things happened:

1. You didn't consider positive variance, and, whether you realized it or not, assumed the outsized results were due solely to your skill as a trader.
2. You started to believe that you should get maximum profit from every trade, or at least think it should happen more often.

Now, when you make less than the maximum, you see it as your having made a mistake, even if you made a decent profit. It may not be that black and white, but the more this happens, the more you start to hesitate and second-guess your entries and exits, risk calculations, or other inputs, because you don't want to "make a mistake like that" again.

This desire for complete control creates a binary way of coding performance: correct or incorrect. And let's be real—this game isn't that simple. There's a lot that's out of your hands and out of your control. But there are ways of gaining more control, and one way is to change the way you code mistakes. The following chart, introduced in chapter 1, is a great alternative to that binary coding because it describes three categories of mistakes.

C-GAME	B-GAME	A-GAME
OBVIOUS MISTAKES	**MARGINAL MISTAKES**	**LEARNING MISTAKES**
CAUSE: Mental or emotional flaws caused your emotions to be too intense, or your energy was too low	CAUSE: A blend of weakness in your tactical decision-making and mental or emotional flaws	CAUSE: Unavoidable weakness in your tactical decision-making

As a reminder, A-game mistakes are caused by something technical—for example, knowledge you haven't yet gained or a recent change in the market you haven't yet identified. These are "learning mistakes" that couldn't have been prevented and are an inherent part of the learning process.

In your B-game, you have some emotional chaos holding you back from your A-game, but not enough to fall back into your C-game. And there's some degree of tactical error—something that you need to learn but may not be super obvious. The errors found in your C-game, however, are so obvious there's nothing for you to learn tactically. Instead, mental and emotional flaws cause these mistakes.

To fix this problem, you need to train yourself to identify and categorize your mistakes this way. Using this chart reduces the likelihood of assuming you've made a mistake when you haven't. If you haven't already completed an A- to C-game Analysis, write down all of the obvious mistakes and all the marginal (slightly less bad) mistakes you tend to make. If you can identify recent learning mistakes as well, great. If not, leave it blank.

Then, the next time you think you've made a mistake, see where it fits on your lists. If it doesn't fit as marginal or obvious, take some time to consider if the loss was a result of something that you didn't understand, or something new that would enhance your current ability. If so, it's likely a learning mistake, and fearing that kind of mistake is the mark of someone who's afraid of learning.

Obvious Mistakes

The fear of an obvious mistake is exactly what it sounds like. You fear that you'll make mistakes that are so obviously wrong, it's inconceivable how they could happen.

Even more vexing are the times when you know what you're doing is wrong, and yet you still do it. The shock and disbelief that you can't stop yourself from making mistakes that you know are wrong causes considerable apprehension and tension. You start the day already on edge, worried that if one thing goes against you, you're going to rapidly lose control and make some big mistakes.

Even working hard to prevent these types of mistakes doesn't ease the fear. You don't want your effort to be wasted and end up right back where you started, with no progress and just more fear.

Your fear of an obvious mistake is appropriate because your ability to stop it from happening is low. But often traders are hyper-focused on the actual mistakes and not the *cause* of them. As I discussed in the previous section, obvious mistakes are the consequence of being so emotionally compromised, you don't have a chance of stopping it. However, traders often fail to account for the mental and emotional factors that caused the mistake, especially with mistakes that are more obvious or basic. When they *do* make an obvious mistake, they don't work on it, because they believe they already have the necessary knowledge to avoid that mistake. They write it off as a fluke, or assume that the mistakes are easy to fix.

To improve, you must understand these mistakes aren't an indictment of your trading prowess. Instead, put a spotlight on the mental and emotional problems causing you to make these obvious mistakes. For example, it could be greed, fear of losing, anger, loss of confidence, or overconfidence. These are the problems forcing you to make an obvious mistake in the first place. Then you developed a fear of obvious mistakes in response to being unable to stop them from happening. Fix the real problem and you'll stop making obvious mistakes and your fear will eventually go away.

To speed up the process, do two things at once: Develop a strategy to fix the cause of your obvious mistakes, and rebuild trust in your performance so your fear can subside. Early on you may still be on edge that these mistakes will happen. That's logical; the risk is still high. It's still a tenuous time. As you improve, you'll know when and why they happen, and how to stop them in real time, and the chance of making an obvious mistake will be low.

FEAR OF FAILURE

Success and failure can be binary. There's only one team that wins the Super Bowl. Only one golfer wins the Masters. From that perspective, the sports world is mostly filled with failure—and that's the nature of competition. How you interpret failure, however, makes all the difference to what happens next.

No competitor strives for failure, but the elite recognize the essential role it has in their pursuit of greatness. Failure highlights weakness, both technical and mental. It can make you realize how badly you want to succeed, amplifying your motivation to invest more time and effort into further building your skills.

Michael Jordan lost in the playoffs six straight years to start his career. Those failures drove him; they didn't stop him. He used what he learned to eventually break through and win six NBA championships.

Those who strive to reach their highest levels don't shy away from failure. They embrace its role in helping them to be better and to level up.

While success in trading can be less binary and more fluid than sports championships, having the right mentality about failure is no less valuable, even when rebuilding your capital or reputation. But if you fear failure, there must be a flaw in the way you interpret the meaning of failure. Whether or not you've actually failed in the past is irrelevant. The problem is how you view it.

Failure means different things to every trader. For some, failure simply means failing to hit their target; for others, failure defines them. The fear of failure is not necessarily a bad thing. It can be an incredible motivator to work hard and do everything you can to succeed, and it can also get reckless traders to properly manage risk.

But for some of you, the drive to avoid failure strains the mind, and causes it to break down. The idea of failing looms so large that you over-think decisions, only trade when you feel perfect, make excuses for undersized bets, and obsess over losses and missed opportunities. You might freeze while a position is crashing, only thinking about damage control and how not to do something stupid, or worse, you panic sell for a loss, only to see it retrace to your target. For traders with this problem, the tragic irony is that the pressure to avoid failing makes failure more likely.

Since this fear is so common within trading, and performance in general, there are a lot of existing recommendations written about this problem. You've all heard advice such as "Seek small wins," "Embrace failure," "Failing is what teaches us to win," and "Learn from it and move on." These are accurate and logical. Nevertheless, they're not wholly helpful if there's an underlying and unidentified flaw behind your fear of failing. The following are the most common of such flaws, which as we've seen, must be unpacked if you're going to conquer them.

High Expectations

The nature of high expectations suggests they're difficult to achieve, so over the years you've consistently fallen short. Failing casts doubt on your ability to perform up to your own standard and eventually can turn into fear.

The flaw here isn't that you aimed too high. Aspire as big as your imagination can take you. The flaw is that you *expected* to reach your highest goals. Aspiration implies a process is required to get there, even if you don't fully understand all the steps you'll take yet. Expectations don't care about the process; they demand the outcome without question.

Let's say you aspire to be the number one trader in your firm, and set milestones, seek feedback and collaboration, review all your trades, and perfect your execution, all in pursuit of that outcome. You work the process every day and are relentless about finding ways to improve. From that perspective, if you fail, it sucks, but you'll learn, and the lessons will be used to chase your goal next year.

If, on the other hand, you expect this outcome to happen, regardless of how hard you work or the market conditions, you'll be downright shocked and view your entire process as a waste. Over time, if this or other failures keep occurring, a fear that you'll fail can develop and compromise the pursuit of your aspirations. While high expectations are often used for motivation, they can also cause self-inflicted damage.

This was a problem for Vlad, a trader and owner of a firm in South Africa that applies algorithmic trading systems to their own portfolios. The systems work well and are extremely effective on their own. Where Vlad struggled was to identify the right moments for human intervention. Too often he meddled with the system at the wrong time. He was allowing his bias of market movement to supplant the system, and there was quantitative proof of the cost for not allowing it to run.

To gain clarity on why these mistakes would occur, he took the fear profile and created a spreadsheet to track his emotions. As a systems guy, he liked being able to make his emotions more quantitative and measurable. This allowed him to visually see where each mistake was happening in real time, flag that error, and then dig into it using the Mental Hand History after market hours. He also tracked his daily routine and how poor sleep or outside emotions affected his emotions in trading, and vice versa.

What he found included a continual desire to prove that he was right. Prior to our sessions, he went through a period of tremendous anxiety. He was always picturing worst-case scenarios, where everyone redeemed their capital and the company lost all its money and blew up. He couldn't sleep and when he did, he dreamed of trading. He described it as having no "off" button. He was in a terrible mood, continually staring at screens, fearing negative outcomes.

While his emotional state had improved significantly by the time he and I started, he had yet to find the root cause of the problem. Fortunately, in the process of completing this Mental Hand History, we discovered it:

1. **What's the problem:** My overarching fear is losing value and relevance with investors. At what point do my investors say "No, thank you"? It's no longer an input/output game where I can look objectively at the results and know that my system is profitable long term. And it turns into an emotional thing because of what people say. I can't lose this amount of money because my clients are shitting themselves. And this feeds into a fear of losing value.

2. **Why does the problem exist:** If I look at the steps that I've taken in my life, it makes no sense, because objectively I haven't failed. However, I have failed at meeting my expectations of being a millionaire by 25. I truly believe that I'll achieve what I want in the long term, but there's an inherent fear of slipping off the path. I don't think I'm a failure, but the slight chance of failure scares the shit out of me.

3. **What is flawed:** My expectations of myself are just too high. I truly believe that I'll achieve what I want in the long term, but expecting to attain those outcomes within arbitrary timeframes has added an unnecessary burden.

4. **What's the correction:** To be much clearer on the value that I provide. I'm great at mitigating the downside risk, creating and

deploying new systems and growing the company as good CEOs need to do.

5. **What logic confirms that correction:** My expectations were blinding my perspective of my value as I overweighted my focus on results to the detriment of developing my expertise, value, and contribution to the growth of the firm.

By looking at the root of his emotional reactions in a logical, structured way, Vlad was able to stop himself from interfering when he shouldn't. He was also able to take what he was learning about his emotions and restructure his role in the company in a more beneficial way.

When he fully understood that he was, as a person, risk-averse and overly reactive to the emotions and expectations of others, he changed his approach to work. He stepped back from company processes like marketing, where he was too heavily involved and controlling, and chose to trust his people to run with it. As he said, "It was like diversifying a model. I stepped out to focus on running my company and it allowed them to perform better. Letting go and just focusing on my own primary output relieved a lot of my anxiety."

Of course, there are no miracles, just hard work. Sure he still has some control issues, but now he can sleep. The quality of his life is greatly improved. And so has his ability to focus at work, now that he's not diluting brainpower by trying to control everything.

In addition to the specific steps that Vlad took, here are some steps you can take to round out the negative side of high expectations. First, you need to turn your expectations into aspirations, as I mentioned in the Fear of Mistakes section about expecting perfection. That allows you to keep your motivation high, by attaching to large aspirations, without the pressure caused by expectations. You also learn from mistakes faster because you accept and embrace them as part of the process.

Converting to this perspective, however, isn't enough. The fear of failure is created in part because of the reverberations of past failures.

To correct that accumulated emotion, you need to go back into your trading history, and possibly your personal history, to examine your past failures. This process can help you do that:

Step 1: List all the things you would consider to be failures, both within trading and outside of it. Take a look at that list and ask yourself which ones you continue to think about. Which ones pop into your mind randomly? As you think about them now, which ones still sting—where you feel the pain of the failure, perhaps even years later?

Step 2: Focus on the ones that stand out the most, or currently feel most negative, and examine why you failed. What were the mistakes you made? What did you fail to understand prior? What did you learn? How has it improved you as a trader, or elsewhere?

Step 3: Consider what it is about the failure that you're so you're hung up on, and why. Do you think how your life would be different had this not happened? Do you have regrets about it? Have you not forgiven yourself yet for the mistakes that led to the failure?

Step 4: Use the Mental Hand History to work through the reasons you're unable to move past this failure, and then correct the flaws embedded in those reasons.

Regularly review what you've written until you get to the point where you at least feel somewhat neutral about your past failures. You might eventually get to the point where you're happy about them because of what you've learned, or how much money you ended up making as result. But the first goal is just to get to a point where it's not as negative.

Undervaluing Your Accomplishments

You might fear failure because the pain of your failures has been amplified by paying more attention to them than to your successes. This pattern is common with high expectations, where success is presumed to happen and doesn't get the attention it deserves. There's a lack of satisfaction, pride, sense of accomplishment, joy, or happiness from what you've accomplished. And when you do experience those positive emotions, they don't last that long—you quickly move on to the next target.

I'm not suggesting that you must revel in your own greatness and risk becoming complacent or overconfident. There simply needs to be balance; otherwise you create a dynamic where failure looms larger than it should. The net result is an imbalance in your perspective created by an overdose of attention on failure.

Here's what you can do to rebalance your perspective on success and failure. Write down a list of your prior successes and look for the ones that have tended to go unacknowledged or have been lesser valued. Do this steadily over a couple of weeks, as it's unlikely that you'll remember them all at once. Why was this accomplishment something to value and appreciate? What made it challenging and not guaranteed to happen? What can you feel good about?

Then go through the list again and understand how you succeeded. What did it take? What did you learn in the process?

The goal is to treat successes and failures in the same way. Learning from failure tends to be easier because it's obvious where we fell short. But learning from success is in some ways more important, both practically and to rebuild your perspective.

Regularly review what you've written to strengthen the knowledge to the point where it eventually becomes automatic for you to think about past success from this new perspective. To be clear, this perspective emphasizes the knowledge, skills, habits, and processes that you've attained, and it forms the competencies to pursue the next goal. That will give you greater emotional clarity with your next goal and lower the fear of failing.

Undervaluing Your Skill

You've already seen how uncertainty provides a breeding ground for fear. In some instances, that uncertainty exists because you've failed to recognize your skills as a trader. Becoming more proficient at seeing your competencies can provide a base of certainty that cuts through the inherent uncertainty in trading and reduces your propensity to experience fear. You're not inventing or making up skills that aren't there. You're simply correcting the flaw in your perspective that's caused you to be unaware of them.

Imagine you're standing on top of a mountain that's so high that you're above the clouds. Everything below you is obscured, so it seems like you're actually standing on a cloud. You've been there so long that you've forgotten that you're standing on a mountain. It feels like there's nothing solid beneath you and at any minute you could slip through the cloud and free-fall back to earth. But just then the cloud dissipates entirely, and you see the huge mountain beneath you. You are, in fact, on solid ground.

The mountain is the base of knowledge that you've acquired as a trader. You've climbed to a high level. (Perhaps not yet as high as you want, but that's ok.) When you ignore your competencies, you feel unstable when there's no need to—you've simply lost sight of the bedrock beneath your feet, and that breeds fear. No matter how high you've climbed on your proverbial mountain, take some time to solidify what knowledge, skills, and experience has gone unrecognized, and you'll improve your ability to handle uncertainty and reduce fear.

Thinking You're a Failure

What does it feel like when you fail? Do the losses and lack of success hit you personally and make you feel like you're a failure? If that's true, there's a lot more on the line than just money when you sit down to trade. Trading becomes an exercise in determining how you feel about your ability as a trader.

To defend against branding yourself a failure, perhaps you've unintentionally reduced the amount of time you spend researching new ideas or working on your strategy. This is one of the unnoticed ways the fear of feeling like a failure shows up—by preventing you from giving it your all. Because if you did give it your all and still failed, it would cement your fate as a failure, and that would be too much to handle.

The underlying flaw here is a belief that failure is a permanent part of your character. If you fail, it defines you—you're the reason. That's who you are and that's how it will always be. When viewed that way, you can't see the possibility of success. At best, you only see success as a temporary escape from your fate. Maybe you hadn't thought about failure this way before. Viewing failure as a character trait is subtle and not something people tend to think about. But when you dig into the fear, and the threat that failing poses, you'll see that, to some degree, you do view it this way.

When you harbor this belief about yourself, it's impossible to embrace the value that failing provides and think about it in a productive way. If you're a failure, there's no point in thinking about it practically. To begin cracking through this fear, you need to correct the illusion that this aspect of your character is permanent. Why do you hold onto that belief so rigidly?

Again, refer back to the Mental Hand History as the tool to organize your thoughts. Here's an example:

1. **What's the problem:** I'm fearful that if I size up and fail, that is it—it's as if I'm standing on the cliff and I will either fly or fall.

2. **Why does the problem exist:** I know I have to size up to achieve my goals and dreams. This is a crucial stage, and if I fail, I will feel like it is final, that I can't do it.

3. **What is flawed:** Sizing up, although crucial to long-term success, is not crucial for my trading performance. If it doesn't work out, it isn't the end, and I have a lot more opportunities. It will not play out as fly or fall; I don't know how it will play out yet, but I know the cliff isn't really there.

4. **What's the correction:** Regardless of the size, every trade is just one opportunity to exercise my advantage. Sizing up is not an absolute; win or lose, the journey continues.

5. **What logic confirms that correction:** This is just the next hurdle. One of many I've already jumped, and there will be many more

after it to come. If I don't clear it this time there will be plenty more opportunities . . . but let's see if I can clear it now!

Choking

Have you ever failed because of a dramatic breakdown in execution, aka "choking," like an athlete on a big stage? This is the trading equivalent of golfer Jim Furyk making a series of abnormally poor shots to blow the lead in the 2012 U.S. Open golf championship with six holes left to play. If you've experienced this, it makes perfect sense why you'd fear failing.

In big moments have you been paralyzed, unable to think, and powerless to execute? The first time it happens you can easily disregard it as a one-off. But then it happens again. There's no clear trigger. You don't know when it will happen and, worse, you don't know why, or how to stop it. Those unknowns breed a fear that constantly lurks in the back of your mind. Perhaps this is why Furyk, despite being one of the best golfers of his generation, never won a major tournament after that event, despite being in contention for several.

In trading, choking is a complicated problem in that it happens in different ways and for different reasons for each person. But the commonality among all of them is the presence of intense emotion, most often fear, that rapidly overwhelms the mind and shuts down the ability to think. To correct it, you need to first identify the accumulated emotions central to the breakdown. They're the reasons you choke.

Most often there are multiple emotions and flaws to contend with, including anger and a loss of confidence. Dissect the problem and work through each part of it. Make sure to scale down your sizing or risk to temporarily lower the amount of emotion triggered from trading. Having less emotion to contend with decreases the likelihood that you'll choke. This will give you some breathing room to correct your emotional reactions in real time.

When too much accumulated emotion is triggered, you don't stand a chance. You'll just get run over, guarantee another failure, and have to contend with a chaotic aftermath. Once you've proven you can make progress at lower levels of emotion, scale back up slowly, like you're rehabbing from an injury. Eventually, choking will become a thing of the past.

As we've seen in this chapter, fear wears many hats and has many underlying causes. Using the Mental Hand History and mapping tool will help you ferret out the roots of fear systematically, so you can improve your mental game more effectively.

Those tools will be, if anything, even more important as we move into our next emotion—tilt, aka anger. Anger may show up in nearly opposite ways of fear, and the feeling itself can complicate digging into its patterns. When you're ticked off, you're less likely to feel like doing the work you need to resolve anger issues. Yet, if you want long-term resolution, you're going to need to peel back the layers. We'll do just that in chapter 6, Tilt.

CHAPTER 6

TILT

"Anger is a bad advisor."

—Czech proverb

For those unfamiliar with the term "tilt," it's commonly used in poker to describe a player who gets steaming mad and plays really poorly as a result. The common refrain is they're "on tilt." There are also some great derivations, like "raging monkey tilt" to describe the poker player who is not only making horrendous decisions and losing a lot of money but is also making a spectacle of themselves. As you can imagine, there's always a line of players waiting to play against an opponent in such a state.

The term "tilt" didn't originate in poker. It actually came from pinball, where players would literally tilt the machine to avoid losing the pinball between the flippers, or to control where they wanted the ball to go. I know some traders already use the term, and I say we go ahead and make it as ubiquitous in trading as it is in poker. It's more fun and descriptive to say "I tilted," rather than "I got angry and made some terrible decisions." After all, if you have an anger problem, you might as well have a bit of fun when talking about it.

Some of you already recognize how anger impacts your performance and are acutely aware of the costs. Anger builds steadily throughout the trading day, or over successive days, until the accumulation reaches a boiling point. You become more prone to take speculative trades, hold on to winners and losers too long, or become overly aggressive. You chase losses and rush into decisions. Explosions come out of nowhere, seemingly without warning.

Perhaps you tilt without realizing it—you're an internal tilter. Your seething frustration and rage lie hidden, even from yourself, because you aren't overtly angry like other traders you see. Your tilt is much less obvious. When you're steaming, you get quieter, tenser. You're like a pressure cooker about to explode.

This could be a result of your style, your personality, or the way you carry yourself. Maybe you've learned to keep it to yourself. Some of you work in environments where that kind of behavior is considered unacceptable, and so you quickly learned to contain it during the trading day.

Tilt can be set off in a number of ways. The frustration can be with your results, the market, or yourself. You never get angry randomly; there's always something specific that triggers it. Maybe the market turned against you and the price action is moving in the opposite of your desired direction. Or when you went to hit the bid and close out the trade, the offer disappeared. Or you're annoyed because a fund is spraying the market with their order and it's moving the market dramatically.

Then in reaction to those tilt triggers, you might:

- Click too many trades out of frustration
- Think *Fuck the market, this is bullshit.*
  You've got to be kidding me! I can't believe my luck!
- Force trades, trying to recoup losses and end the day positive
- Deviate from your strategy (instead of letting things
  come to you)
- Take a bad setup that you know is wrong
- Chase the market, thinking, *It can't go up or down more*
- Believe you know better than the market: *How can they
  buy or sell at this price level? It makes no sense. It will go back
  down/up*
- Take trades, one after the other, without as much thought,
  almost as if the floodgates open once you take one bad one

After having those reactions, you may turn to strategies such as taking deep breaths, taking breaks, quitting, going to the gym, or positive thinking. These strategies are fine for temporarily managing tilt while you work toward resolution, but they're not a permanent solution. **Remember, anger is the signal, not the real problem.** To eliminate it, you need to first understand the underlying flaws you're battling.

THE NATURE OF TILT

Anger is not inherently a bad thing. It can be an incredible motivator to act and improve. But it can also lead to the very performance issues that drove you here. Therefore, the first key to solving your tilt problem is to understand the specific causes of your anger. Anger is produced when underlying flaws, biases, or illusions conflict with reality. Anger at a basic level is a signal of this conflict. These moments of explosion become a chance to identify the real cause of your anger.

Conflicts are most obvious when they exist between two people—like debating who is the greatest athlete of all time, the pros and cons of a tax policy, or making monetary decisions with your spouse. When a conflict accelerates, there's a misunderstanding or an inability to see another perspective. If there's an additional component added, like time pressure, frustration can build and cause the conflict to become unproductive, even confrontational.

However, when you reconcile your differences and resolve the conflict, the anger dissipates. Sometimes, that conflict was actually helpful, and whether it got heated or not, it led to greater understanding on both sides.

In trading, the conflicts that most often turn into anger are between you and the market, and you and yourself. The idea of fighting with the market will make sense to you, but an internal conflict within yourself? That may have you scratching your head. If you've ever felt like you were "fighting yourself," that's a pretty accurate way of describing what's happening. Essentially, you're fighting against the performance flaws that I keep talking about in this book, such as believing you're unluckier than other traders, that you should never make a mistake, or that you know what's going to happen.

Logically you know the right way to think or react, and you use that knowledge to fight against your flaws. For example, after losing four trades in a row, there's one part of you that expects not to take another loss, while another part understands how absurd it is to think that way. This is an example of conflict that you have with yourself. You're fighting to prevent the flaw from causing you to overreact to a loss. There are times when you're able to win the fight and keep the beast in its cage. At other times, your conscious mind is overwhelmed by the intensity of your anger and you lose control.

These conflicts, among the countless others, don't have to become heated. Tilt is not an inevitable outcome. However, when the source of the conflict is unknown or unidentified, frustration starts to build and can turn into anger. Anger becomes the signal of a real problem.

Unfortunately, traders typically see anger not as a signal but as the problem in and of itself. That triggers "the tilt of tilt." Essentially, you're angry because you're angry—being pissed off that you can't control your anger, tilting because you took a trade you would never take in the right state of mind, or tilting because you have no idea how to fix your tilt problem.

This secondary anger is like throwing gasoline on a bonfire. This chapter will help you to use your mind to put out the fire, to diffuse the impact it has on your execution, and prevent future fires from starting.

Anger can also go unresolved for weeks, and even years. If you've ever tilted instantly—gone from feeling calm to a bomb going off in your mind—it's because of accumulated tilt. Tilt accumulates most commonly during a prolonged drawdown, where each day it gets easier and easier to tilt because the anger from the day before carries over. It's like a cup that steadily fills with water. Each day you dump water out, but some remains. That means less water is needed before it overflows.

In practicality, you may blow off some steam after another bad trading day, but emotionally you aren't completely reset. You show up the next day thinking positively, but then tilt faster than the day before. That's accumulated tilt, and it can lurk in the background and rapidly compromise your execution.

COMMON SIGNS OF TILT

In a few ways, anger shows up in the opposite way as fear. In the previous chapter I explained that fear takes our ability to assess risk, think, decide, trust intuition, and make predictions, and turns it against us. Conversely, anger makes those abilities inaccessible.

When you're gripped by fear, you're often at risk for overthinking and second-guessing. With anger, the lack of thinking leads you to fire off trades without hesitation. If you're overwhelmed by fear, risk aversion is a big problem. Tilt, and you become blind to risk. When you're angry, there's a righteousness to your decisions and thoughts, and you can't see the possibility of being wrong. This is the opposite of not trusting your gut when you're fearful, where you assume your intuition is wrong and go against it.

For most traders the signs of anger are obvious after they see the external carnage around them: losses, mistakes, overreactions to colleagues, broken coffee mugs, etc. But recognizing tilt afterward is like seeing a trade you could have taken—the opportunity is already gone.

You need a clear map of your tilt so that you can spot the signals in time to avoid the blowup. Let's drill into the details of several common signs of anger to get a more detailed understanding of what happens when you're tilted. While these signs overlap and may seem similar, there are distinctions that can be helpful to more cleanly mapping the way that you tilt.

Fixating

One of the hallmark characteristics of anger is your mind becoming so fixated on something that you're unable to let it go, even if it's to your own detriment. You see this most commonly when you're fixated on a specific outcome or past mistake.

Fixating on an outcome is exactly what it sounds like. You know what you want and won't relent until you get it. On the one hand, this single-mindedness could be considered a strength, and in many other situations, such focus is a driver of your success. But when fueled by anger, it's destructive.

This one-track mind forces such bad decisions that it can actually look like a lack of discipline. You know you shouldn't take another trade, but in that moment, making back your money is the only thing that matters. Another common description is "tunnel vision," where you're like a lion locked onto its prey and the rest of the world is outside of your vision.

Fixating on mistakes is similarly obvious. After making a mistake, you become obsessed by it, so much so that you think about it for the rest of the day. It may even eat at you for days and weeks from the back of your mind. Even an old mistake from years ago can trigger anger—you still can't believe how stupid you were. Your mind snowballs out of control trying to figure out what you did wrong. All of this affects your current ability to perceive what's happening in the market now. You know you shouldn't, but you just keep harping on it. Your mind won't let go. And that torments you more.

Quick Tip: Be clear on the things your mind tends to fixate on. They become signals for you to wake up and realize that anger is putting your mind in a state of paralysis without you realizing it. When you spot that signal, have some physical action that you take, such as a deep breath or standing up, to reinforce your awareness before you start correcting the anger. Something has to change for your mind to start letting go.

Risk Blindness

Another common sign of anger is the inability to see risk or care about proper risk management. These are the two ways this sign can show up. Anger can blind you from seeing the risks that would be obvious in a normal state of mind. It's like you're driving a car and don't see the stop signs. You're in a blind rage and pass by the factors that you would normally consider, or you forget about the risk limits you have in place.

In the second way, you know the risk exists, and you may be aware that what you're doing is potentially wrong, but you're so tilted you simply don't care. There's a righteousness to your decisions, making the extra risk seem justified in the moment. You want what you want, and fire away.

Quick Tip: While I framed the first version of this sign as though you were blind to all risk, there's still a limit. Figure out what risks you're unwilling to take. Then figure out the simplest correction that will allow you to suck less—as you learned from the Inchworm Concept. In the second version, if you get into a spot where you stop caring about risk, write down the common things that justify taking it. Adding that to your map will make it clearer in the moment that you're attempting to convince yourself of something untrue.

No Consideration

Anger can shut down your mind so much that you don't consider the factors that you typically would when making a trade. It's more than being just blind to risk. This is about your decision-making process as a whole, and how it disappears. Anger essentially removes the guardrails that normally guide your decisions and stop your impulse to, for example, get into a trade to make money now, fix a mistake, correct an injustice, or prove other people wrong. It's as if you're driving on a highway where all the lane markings and guardrails are removed, making it easy to drive into oncoming traffic.

Your actions seem random, but instead they simply lack the normal consideration that typically provides a barrier to the entries and exits required for you to execute your strategy. Overthinking and second-guessing are excessive barriers caused by fear. Anger does the opposite and removes them.

____

Quick Tip: Since these barriers exist normally, write down the key
  factors of your decision-making process, and remind yourself of
  them regularly—even if anger isn't present. This will help you to
  strengthen those guardrails in general, so when anger tries to break
  them down, you have a better chance to consider the trade more
  thoroughly.

Toxic Stories

When you can't get your mind to think in a balanced way about a
loss, mistake, or situation, it can create a toxic story. You obsess
about what happened and create a story about, for example, how stupid you are, how the market is rigged, or how the big firms are lined
up against you. And you can't see it another way. Even the efforts of
other people can't get you out of the negative loop your mind has
found itself in.

In some way it's like the toxicity has pulled you underwater and
you don't even realize that you're drowning in blame, regret, assumptions, and excuses. It's a chaotic mess. You can't think outside yourself.
You believe that you're right and convince yourself that your version is
correct.

____

Quick Tip: Typically, these toxic stories will be repetitive either in that
  you'll say the exact same things over and over again or a theme will
  repeat in different ways. Write down the stories or the things you
  say. Recognition is always the first step, and will allow you to come
  up for air when you're drowning in anger and negativity.

MAPPING YOUR TILT

Despite many commonalities, every trader tilts in different ways and for
different reasons. Going through the mapping process is essential for
finding the indicators that anger is affecting execution. This will enable
you to recognize when your anger escalates in real time. Plus, it will

help you uncover the flaws causing your anger and point you to the sections in this chapter that you should focus on most.

Follow the steps below to help you create an actual document that will become the map of your tilt.

Step 1

Over the next few weeks, pay close attention to your **pattern of anger.** Examine and capture the signs that anger has become a problem, including:

- Thoughts
- Emotions
- Things you say out loud
- Behaviors
- Actions
- Changes to your decision-making
- Changes to your perception of the market, opportunities, or current positions
- Trading mistakes

Keep a document open on your computer or a notepad next to you while you trade, and take notes throughout the day. At the end of the trading day, review what you found and add additional details. Be as comprehensive as you can. And remember, one of the best times to better understand your tilt is immediately after tilting.

The beginning of this process is best described as brainstorming. You're not going to identify all the details perfectly the first time you do it. And if this is really hard for you at the beginning, don't worry. Everyone has their own starting point. Use what you find and build on it over time. As long as you keep it on your mind, you'll continually learn more than you knew before. Progress is progress, regardless of the speed. Here are some questions to help get you started:

- What situations typically provoke frustration, anger, or rage?

- How does your body react when you're angry? For example, hands clenched, heat in your head, or smashing your mouse in a fit of rage.
- Can you describe the point where frustration becomes excessive and damages decision-making or execution?
- What specifically is going through your mind? What thoughts do you have?
- How is your decision-making process different?
- What are the earliest signs that anger has become a problem?

Some of the specific signs you may experience include clicking a trade out of frustration, or thinking to yourself *Fuck the market, this is bullshit.* You might find you're constantly bemoaning your luck and how you got screwed yet again. You start chasing the market because you assume it can't go down more.

You might say things like "The market is crazy! How can they buy/sell at this price? It makes no sense." Sometimes it feels like the floodgates open suddenly—you quickly double a losing position and take a trade without much thought, trying to erase earlier losses.

As you identify the signs, be sure to also capture as many triggers as you can. If you need help identifying your triggers, look closely at the thoughts and things you say out loud. Remember, don't criticize what you say or think. Your thoughts are caused by a performance flaw that often directly relates to the trigger.

Here are some common triggers:

- Getting into a position and having it immediately drop
- Going to hit a bid and having the offer disappear
- Losing several trades in a row
- Making a mistake you know you shouldn't
- Seeing that other traders made money while you were away from your desk
- An unforeseen event blowing up a trade

- Making a stupid mistake while you're angry, which then causes rage
- Another trader questioning your trades—it feels like an attack on your intelligence
- Thinking about the amount of money you should have made from a trade

Mapping your tilt is an iterative process. When you spot new details, even just slight adjustments, be sure to add them. Small details matter. They can make all the difference when progress is on the line and you have an opportunity to correct the cause of your anger.

Step 2

Once you've gathered a lot of details, organize what you've found by **putting them in order of severity.** Rank each detail on a scale of 1 to 10, where 1 characterizes a slight frustration, and 10 is what happens from intense rage. At each level, identify details that clearly distinguish it from another level.

As you assign levels of severity, also split them into two categories: the mental and emotional side of tilt, and the technical side. They sit side by side, so level 1 on the mental and emotional side corresponds to level 1 on the technical side, and so on.

Be sure to base this on *your* personal experience of anger, not how other traders deal with it. Everyone has their own range, and if you judge yourself against someone else, you're at risk of over- or underestimating what you're capable of. That, in turn, will make your strategy less accurate.

You also don't need to have details for all 10 levels. Most traders that I work with aren't able to distinguish their pattern of tilt to that degree. Do as many as you can, and do a minimum of three. Here are some questions to distinguish the differences in each level of anger:

- What triggers the initial frustration at level 1? How does it then accumulate or increase to become anger or rage? For example, maybe a standard loss causes you to pound your desk once. Then, you lose again, but this one feels more unjust; you can feel the heat in your head and a strong desire to force a trade. You're able to hold back, but your mind is aggressively seeking a pattern that looks like a home run so that you can double your size. You find one, fire away, get quickly stopped out, and completely lose it.

- What details are present when anger is still small and manageable? What details are present when it's a monster completely disrupting your execution?
- How is your perception of the market different when your tilt is higher? What specific trading mistakes can you avoid at level 1, but can't stop from happening at level 10?

Then take the details you've categorized and put them into a map like this:

TILT LEVEL

Describe the thoughts, emotions, things you say, behaviors, and actions that highlight each level of tilt. Complete at least 3 levels.

1: Gripping the mouse tighter; moving it more like I'm searching for a trade that may not be there. Clicking my chart/DOM, but not doing any analysis. Wondering "Why is nothing presenting itself to me?" Tension in my head.

2:

3: Take a mediocre·trade and get stopped out. If I didn't use a stop, price goes through where I should have gotten out, but I hold. Tension in my head turns into heat.

4:

5:

6: I increase position size, looking to quickly make back the losses. Fighting myself: "You need to stop now!" "No, I can make this back." I fixate on just the price itself, and not what the charts say.

7:

8:

9:

10: Don't care, and trade all the way to a margin call. Cursing at myself. Smash or throw something. Wanting to quit.

TECHNICAL LEVEL

Describe the quality of your decision-making, perception of the market, opportunities, or current positions at each level of tilt.

1: Still able to identify great areas to take a trade, following all my indicators and charts. But considering subpar trades to get on the board for the day.

2:

3: I look for areas that I can possibly scalp but are not in my pre-determined areas that I analyzed pre-market. End up taking the trade. Then take the same exact trade again, or add to another losing trade.

4:

5:

6: Not paying attention to the bigger picture. Adding more contracts and blindly enter a trade with a lot of risk.

7:

8:

9:

10: Gambling and just clicking buttons. There is no decision-making process. I don't know what I'm doing or why I'm doing it.

This step may seem impossible if all of your signs of tilt are extreme. If that's the case, frustration doesn't steadily build and turn into anger—instead, you explode out of nowhere. So you may lack the recognition at this stage to see the signs before you blow up. The smaller signs *are* there; you just can't see them yet. Pay close attention to the buildup, especially after you explode. The clues are there, if you take the time to look.

However, it's also possible that you have so much accumulated tilt, you're instantly exploding, which means you'll need to do a lot more work outside of the trading day to reduce the accumulation.

Step 3

You now have a solid draft that you can use while you're trading to **recognize your pattern and quickly respond with the correction.** Since these patterns can take a lot of experience and training to correct, don't revise your map until you get consistent evidence that it has permanently changed.

Now, use what you identified in this section to focus on the specific types of anger that are most relevant to your trading. I strongly advise that you read through all of them, whether they seem applicable or not, because you may identify issues that you didn't realize you had at first glance. And you may remember additional details to add to your map.

HATING TO LOSE

No one likes to lose money. You sit down every trading day with the intent to make money. Losing it, especially when it's your own money, isn't fun (to say the least). While some traders can easily accept losing as a part of this game, for others, that will never happen and shouldn't be the goal. Your goal is to get to a point where it doesn't cause rage. Your goal is to change how you react to losing—because it's causing you to lose more.

You may have a hard time accepting losses and think to yourself, *The market can't possibly go this way for much longer.* You try to make it work, buy more of a losing position trying to recoup losses, and end the day positive. You know you're in bad positions, but that fact can't get you to close them. You lose more and then force trades to make up for what you've lost.

Anger blinds you, and you become convinced that since they've gone down by so much that you may as well hold out until they recover. Sometimes they do, and the reckless violation of your trading strategy is rewarded—making this mistake one you're likely to repeat. At other times, the losses mount and your anger explodes into the market. You can't give up. You'll do anything to make money, or just to get back to even on the day. You also may:

- Avoid trading for a few days, if the losses are particularly bad
- Quit for the day after getting back to even
- Have a hard time relaxing at night, because you feel like there's more you should be doing

- Get pissed off that mounting losses have put you in a spot that you didn't expect

When the day ends, or when you're able to pull yourself from the onslaught of tilt, your mind can be convinced of all the ways the losses could have been avoided. You obviously know what you should have done. That's clear as day. Sell here. Not buy here. Simple. You instantly feel better about the losses, knowing what you should have done.

Only this is a fool's errand. Knowing what is correct *afterward* is fundamentally different to knowing what to do *before*. You know this, but a part of you can't help but indulge in the fantasy.

While the goal is, of course, to correct tilt, to do that you need to avoid the excuses and rationalizations after losing and, instead, figure out why you can't take the loss. Why, specifically, do you hate losing?

- **Is it the feeling?** Losing often feels terrible, can go on for a while, and even affects other aspects of your life, making you feel less successful in other areas too.
- **Is it that you're overly competitive?** Being fiercely competitive is a trait shared by many successful traders. But problems arise when your drive to win is paired with an inability to take a loss.
- **Is it variance?** Losing is a reality in any competitive environment, and that's especially true in trading, where it can be easy to underestimate how crazy the market can be at times. Variance is built into the fabric of the game, and while you'd like to be friends with it, perhaps, deep down, you hate it.
- **Is it the money?** Making money is ultimately how you're measured in trading. It makes sense why you'd hate losing it. You also may be worried about supporting yourself or your family, which makes losing money harder to take.

Regardless of the reason you hate losing, the goal of this section is to help you to lose less, by correcting the anger that causes more losses.

Trading is a long-term game. It's not about winning or losing each day. It's about executing the strategy that makes you money over the long term. And hating to lose, or more precisely, your reaction to losing, damages your execution and causes more losses.

If you truly hate to lose this much, you certainly don't want to be the cause of it! While no one is ever going to fist pump while celebrating a lost trade or losing on the day, the following sections can you help you to make peace with something that's always going to be a part of trading.

Being Too Competitive

Trading is a fiercely competitive industry, so having an intense desire to win is more a requirement than a problem. But like a lot of things, too much can be problematic. You overreact to losses by overtrading, sizing too big, failing to properly manage risk, and jumping into unfamiliar markets to get a win, or get back to even. You won't allow yourself to lose—your competitive drive to win and achieve your goals won't allow it.

Wanting to make money every day is not a problem. You're no different than the athletes driven to win every time they compete. The problem in trading is that making money is not entirely in your control in the short term. It's unrealistic to expect to profit every day.

There are times when you lose money, but in retrospect you'd make the same decision again because you know it's profitable in the long run. Logically you understand this, but in the moment when you lose, it's hard to see the bigger picture. Since this problem doesn't happen to every trader, why does it happen to you?

To find out why you hate losing so much, it's often easier to first look at what you gain from winning, besides money. Money is the scoreboard. But losing money is not the only reason why you hate losing; it's also what the money represents. Every time you trade, there's more on the line than just money, so it's worth taking time to define what's on the line for you. Here are some examples of what might be critical to you:

- Your goals
- Proving wrong the people who doubted you could make it as a trader
- Ability to sustain a livelihood, pay the bills, and provide for your family
- Your confidence as a trader
- Social status
- Praise from your peers or those you respect
- Tangible results from the time, energy, and work you put into trading
- Better career prospects and an opportunity to manage a larger book
- The possibility of early retirement and getting out of the rat race

When you trade, you're competing to win whatever's on your list. When you lose, it's not just money that's gone—you've also lost confidence, respect from others, progress toward your goals, or anything else on your list. You hate losing because there's so much at stake.

To be clear, being competitive and having an intense desire to win is not a problem. You have goals, there's a lot on the line, and being frustrated when it doesn't go your way means you care a lot about getting what you want. Plus, you now know that low levels of frustration can fuel you to perform and work harder. That's not the problem. The problem stems from flaws that cause your competitive drive to go off the rails, and turn frustration at losing into anger, hatred, or rage.

To start figuring out the roots of your hatred of losing, write down a list of what's on the line for you when you trade, and how you'll know you've won. For example, let's say your goal is to win praise from your peers, and you'll know that you won when it's clear they value your trade ideas and listen to what you have to say. Defining the idea of winning respect this way is particularly important because it's easy to have money be the default metric. But around competent traders, PnL alone doesn't buy respect.

Whether it's respect or another goal, simply becoming aware of what's on the line when you trade can potentially decrease tilt for you. You automatically regain a long-term perspective on things you can't attain in one day. You accept the inherent ups and down, and you don't feel like your social status, confidence, or progress toward your goals rises and falls with every win or loss.

Reread this list at the start of every trading day and use it as a way to frame what winning and losing looks like for the day, beyond money. Set your mind to see the results from this new perspective. It's so easy to get caught up in the old way—it's not like you can just instantly contain your competitiveness.

Next, increase your focus on winning the non-monetary victories, such as improving your execution, focus, and ability to adapt and find new opportunities. Make improvement in these areas tangible and measurable. For example, clearly define the levels of your focus, much like you did in the Mapping Your Tilt section. Rate yourself daily, or multiple times per day. Set goals for duration or average quality. Rate your trading execution, or any other qualitative factor in a similar way.

The key is taking time to define the measuring stick, get a baseline, and track progress. This way, you can see when you have taken steps forward, especially on days you lose money. Without going through these steps, losses can easily overshadow a day of progress and make you feel like you're taking steps backward, when that may not be accurate.

The difficulty with this is that you're at risk of being biased and inaccurate. Don't worry; getting perfect measurements is not the point. The goal is to expand the way you define winning in the short term, and focus your competitiveness on the actions that help you to make money.

Trying to win in a qualitative way like this will never replace the priority of winning money. But you're reading this section because your competitiveness is out of control. It causes you to lose more. You can't control whether you win or lose money day to day, but you can control your execution, focus, and improvement. Be competitive toward all the right things.

Lastly, this section might fundamentally change how you handle losing in general, not just in trading. Have you hated losing for as long as you can remember? Are there stories that family and friends tell of your absurd overreactions as a kid? If so, then you're retraining habits that are decades old and will take a lot of repetition to correct. You may also be fighting against tilt that has accumulated from some significant losses you've taken over the years.

To accelerate the resolution of old accumulated emotion, try using the Mental Hand History on specific memories where you can still feel your reaction to a loss, even though it occurred years ago.

Losing Hurts More than Winning Feels Good

When you enter a trade you not only risk capital, you put your emotional state on the line. Losing hurts, and for many of you it hurts much more than winning feels good. This is a phenomenon first conceptualized by the founding fathers of Behavioral Economics, Daniel Kahneman and Amos Tversky, called Prospect Theory.[3] (You may know Kahneman from his popular book *Thinking Fast and Slow.*)

Prospect Theory identified a pattern of decision-making that showed that the value derived from winning and losing money doesn't come only from the monetary amount. People value avoiding the pain of losing, and they will, for example, make decisions with lower expected value to avoid it. That includes making risky bets when already down money on the day, week, or month, in order to get out of the hole. It also includes choosing guaranteed profit instead of an option that carries a small risk of loss and high probability to make much more than the guarantee.

Losing hurts for all the reasons mentioned in this section. And for many of you, losing also hurts because the feeling of winning doesn't properly counterbalance it. Winning is more of an escape from the torture of losing, rather than something that generates positive emotion on its own. For you, there are more reasons to feel bad about losing than to feel good about winning. Consequently, losing looms larger—you anticipate losses will hit hard—and you make risky or risk-averse decisions to avoid the pain.

The first step in breaking this pattern is to know that Prospect Theory is an observation, not a law of human nature. Yes, this is a pattern that exists, but we're not talking about gravity here. If you believe you can change it, you have that opportunity.

In subsequent articles that build on Prospect Theory, Kahneman and Tversky reinforce the idea that the pattern is based on each person's "reference point," by which each of us classifies the value of winning and losing.[4] The advice in this chapter can change your reference point. Losing doesn't have to be more painful than winning feels good. Resolve the reasons why losing hurts so much, and elevate winning so you actually derive more value from it.

When you *expect* to make money, there isn't much reason to celebrate when you do. It's very matter of fact. You did what you were supposed to do, and you focus on making more of it. But making money the right way, through your edge in the market, deserves acknowledgment.

I'm not suggesting you throw a party every time you make money. Simply recognize that you demonstrated your own competence, and it paid off. Take a moment to feel good about it. You work hard and deserve to end the day with a sense of pride or satisfaction, knowing that you did a good job. Tomorrow you have to do it again, but you'll go into the day with more confidence and motivation to continue to excel and improve as a trader.

Feeling the personal value of winning can seem like a threat, which is part of what takes away the desire to acknowledge it. The assumption is that you stay hungry by starving yourself of satisfaction, but in reality, motivation remains high when you stay committed to your goals.

Expecting to Make Money on Every Trade

You may think it's absurd that any trader would expect to make money on every trade or from every trading session, but it's more common than you think. Do you experience disbelief when you lose? Do you immediately find yourself doing mental gymnastics to convince yourself that it was possible to avoid the loss? Again, logically, you know that variance would never allow anyone to profit from every trade or every day. Yet as you've read many times already in this book, flaws like this overpower logic.

One reason this flaw survives is that traders often cling to the idea that one day they'll become so good they'll never lose. Trading does a great job of feeding this belief. When you run hot, the market seems like a printing press minting money into your account. You're elated. You imagine yourself driving a Ferrari to your beach house. Winning that much brings out dreams of how much money you'll make, and what you'll do with it. It's similar to someone dreaming of what they would do after they win the lottery.

If running hot causes you to have thoughts of making easy money, then you'll hate it when you inevitably lose—it destroys your dream. The resulting anger is your reaction to that fantasy colliding with reality.

Although tilt from losing money is what brought you here, the solution to this problem has to include improving how you handle making money. That begins with being acutely aware of when you start getting caught up by those fantasies. In the short term, you don't have full control over whether you win or lose. There are too many factors. Your focus needs to be on executing every trade as well as you can, because that's where your control lies.

If you're able to keep your emotions from running too high, you're less likely to overreact on the downside when losses inevitably occur. The less high you get when making money, the less low you fall when losing money.

In general, you want to continually work toward attaching more of your emotion to what you can control in the short term and less to what you can't control. You're not becoming robotic or numb to the highs and lows (as people often think they're supposed to). Eventually, it becomes easier and easier to execute your strategy when winning or losing. You have a more balanced perspective and may eventually have some pride for performing well on a day where you lost.

Conversely, when you were profitable but made mistakes, the larger account balance doesn't blind you. You remain focused on how to do better tomorrow, and you don't get swept up in the assumption that you'll make money tomorrow just because you did today.

Here's a sample Mental Hand History tracking this problem:

1. **What's the problem:** If I have a losing trade, I find myself trying to find a way to make the money back quickly. This is almost like a response to a crisis—quick action needed to make the loss go away as soon as possible.

2. **Why does the problem exist:** The quicker I make the money back, the quicker I'll be able to trade well again. My strategy makes money, so I can make the money back quickly by trading something else quickly.

3. **What is flawed:** I'm expecting all of my trades to make money because my overall strategy is profitable. Even if I am a sniper and take only my best setups, I still won't win every trade. Allowing emotion to cloud my judgment means I take more poor trades that are unlikely to be +EV.

4. **What's the correction:** My strategy will incur losses. Thinking all my trades will be profitable is a fantasy, and expecting this sets me up to fail.

5. **What logic confirms that correction:** The damage done by a couple of losses is small, but the damage done by getting angry can be significant.

Attached to Unrealized Gains

Your hatred of losing can be tied up with something that was never yours. You enter a position and get excited as you see the price racing toward your target. As much as you've been bitten in the ass before by getting ahead of yourself, emotionally you can't help but get caught up celebrating. This unrealized profit feels like it's already yours.

When the position starts to go against you, anger builds, because it feels like your money is being taken from you. Some may angrily close out the trade, only to see it reverse and ultimately reach the target. Knowing that if you had done nothing and would have hit your target can make your head explode. Other times, you double the position or force entry into another trade, looking to make up for what was lost.

Not getting ahead of yourself like this is hard for athletes too, especially when there's a lot on the line. In Super Bowl LI, the Atlanta Falcons gave up a 25-point third-quarter lead to the New England Patriots and lost in overtime. Like an athlete in a game like that, you can't allow your mind to go beyond what's right in front of you. It isn't yours until it's yours.

You may be able to correct this problem just by recognizing those instances where you get ahead of yourself, and by training your mind to stay focused on the job at hand. You knew you shouldn't do it, but until now, you didn't realize it was causing you to tilt.

For some, this advice may be too simple—the equivalent of saying, "Just be present." If you can't control your mind from getting ahead of yourself, there's a reason for it, and you've got to figure that out. I've noticed that my clients tend to *need* the win and all it represents. In the section Being Too Competitive, I talk about how winning is about more than just the money. In this case, your mind attaches to unrealized gains because you *need* to win respect, financial security, a career month, etc.

As you address the excessive competitiveness, it becomes easier to avoid getting ahead of yourself. Here's a sample Mental Hand History:

1. **What's the problem:** When I'm up around 3% in the trade, I feel like I deserve the profit in the trade, because I was correct and don't want it to go back down. Once it does start to pull back, I look at the charts a lot more and almost get burned out mentally from staring at them so much. It's like I'm trying to control the price to hit my target.

2. **Why does the problem exist:** I start to think about the utility of the money—I'm up seven months of rent—and feel happy about what I'm up and I don't want to lose it.

3. **What is flawed:** The trade hasn't hit my target yet. It's not my money yet. I'm getting too attached to unrealized profit, and thinking it's already mine.

4. **What's the correction:** Realized profit is the only profit
   that matters.

5. **What logic confirms that correction:** It's true.

MISTAKE TILT

Learning means making mistakes. When you aren't making mistakes, it's because you already know what's correct. Even when you understand their role in learning, however, mistakes can still be frustrating. They're costly. You have goals in trading, and it sucks when your mistakes are the reason you lost money.

Being frustrated by mistakes isn't necessarily a problem. It can even be a good thing when it provides the motivation to fix them, and you actually do. What distinguishes mistake tilt as a problem is frustration so intense that it causes you make more mistakes and have a harder time correcting them. Anger like that shuts down execution in the short term and learning in the long term.

One important distinction between mistake tilt and other types of tilt is the reaction to losing. If you're a trader with mistake tilt, you have no problem losing, so long as you made a good decision. You firmly understand that losing is part of the game and don't hate it. But the combination of being wrong *and* losing money makes your head explode.

You immediately feel stupid for being the reason you lost money and replay past mistakes in your head. Suddenly, an avalanche of past mistakes rips through your mind, along with self-critical thoughts like *How stupid can you be, not to follow your own rules!* You can't get past the mistake. You can't take another loss, because it confirms you were wrong. So you stay in the position, maybe even add to it—doubling down on your desire to not be wrong.

Other times the mistake impacts the next trade, and now one mistake has turned into a second. You swear you'll never make that mistake again. But what happens instead?

You assume the mistake will be easy to fix, so you don't actually work on it. Or you don't really understand why you keep making the wrong move there, and it happens again and again. The problem has snow-balled, leading to short-term damage to your conviction for your next trade idea or hesitation in executing it. You may even abandon ideas that were quite good because your overall confidence has dropped.

Part of the frustration behind mistakes is not being certain of what you're going to learn from them. You automatically assume that you just lit money on fire. But if the trading fairy made another appearance and told you that these mistakes would lead to changes or insight that would make you more money in the future, you would instantly feel different. Remember, mistakes are essential to improving as a trader. Think of it this way: If you hate mistakes, you hate improving.

Mistake tilt is something you may not even realize you experience, as it's often hidden by more obvious reasons to tilt, like losing, injustice, and revenge. To help identify whether this is a problem for you, ask yourself "Why do mistakes make me so angry?" Here are some possible reasons:

- It feels like you missed a great opportunity because of your own incompetence
- You erased a day's worth of work with one stupid move
- There's no excuse to make such obvious mistakes at this point in your career
- It feels like you've taken a step backward in your progression
- You hate what others will likely think of you
- You feel like you're standing in the way of reaching your goals and becoming a great trader

Embedded within each of these statements are the common reasons why mistakes cause traders to tilt. Each reason is connected in some way to fundamental errors in their understanding of the learning process and the nature of performance. The remainder of this section breaks them down, making it easier for you to resolve them.

When these errors are corrected, it not only means that mistake tilt goes away but also that you're going to be better at fixing your trading mistakes and will become a stronger trader. By the way, if you read the Fear of Mistakes section of the last chapter, the themes in the rest of this section will be familiar (but still worth reviewing in the context of tilt).

Expecting Perfection

Perfection is out there. It can be attained. But only temporarily. The roots of mistake tilt take hold when you're at your peak and believe you've found permanent perfection ... a paradise where you never make mistakes and trading is easy. Only you're forgetting it's an illusion.

Perfection is a moving target that, for two reasons, is impossible to sustain over a large sample. Most obvious is that the changing dynamics in the market force you to continually refine your strategy, and thus the definition of perfection changes. Less obvious, Inchworm shows us it's not possible to have perfect execution for very long—as the bell curve illustrates, there's always variation in your execution.

Sure, you can have those days where you're in the zone, spot on with your sense of the market and timing, and making money easily. The problem is that even though, rationally, you know better, part of you believes you can have those days every day, for every trade. Deep down you feel like you've figured it out, have unlocked the mysteries of trading, and found a new standard that will allow you to print money. And now, that's the standard you expect.

Reaching "perfection" means you have minted a new A-game. Your best has just gotten better, and your definition of perfect rises. To continue to expect perfection means continuing to be perfect while your execution improves and continues to hit new high points. In other words, you have to correctly predict and hit a target that's moving to an unknown destination. That alone isn't possible to sustain, but your range has gotten wider and that makes it even more unlikely you'll remain perfect.

Progress at the front end of your Inchworm hasn't yet been matched by improvement from the backend. Traders often expect the opposite. They think perfection eliminates the backend, but that's just not how it works.

For some of you, reaching these new heights, whether in execution or profitability, doesn't even come with much satisfaction. You expected it all along, and it doesn't make sense to appreciate something that you expect to happen. Now any mistake (no matter how slight) causes tilt. You either feel neutral about trading perfectly, or you beat yourself senseless at the slightest possibility of a mistake.

The best opportunity to correct this problem comes from how you handle the instances when you're at your best and doing great. When you've performed at your peak, feel good about it. When you do everything right, you get that pop of adrenaline confirming how spot on you were in, for example, your understanding of the dynamics in the market and your execution.

Take a look at how you got there. Reinforce the steps you've taken to get there so you can identify the next things to improve. Knowing how you achieve results strengthens your ability to achieve future results. Plus, if you eliminate weaknesses in your approach to learning and performance, such as distractions, procrastination, or mistake tilt, then you become more efficient when striving for the next peak and can get there faster.

But also recognize why you can't expect those same dynamics tomorrow. Gain a more realistic view of the learning process, so you can prove why perfection can't be attained all the time. Make sure to mind your Inchworm, remembering that the way to take a step forward and reach your next peak is by correcting weaknesses at the backend of your range. Only when your worst has improved can you take steps toward the next peak in your performance. Rather than expect perfection, keep striving for it by continually correcting your mistakes.

The perspective in this section was particularly helpful for Rodrick, the trader I mentioned in chapter 4, whose greed was really the result of this kind of mistake tilt. Prior to our work together, if Rodrick made even a small mistake, he would feel compelled to fix it, often losing more money to cover that mistake. He once lost $58,000 trying to fix a $4,000 mistake—he just couldn't accept it.

As a trader whose strategy uses global intermarket relationships, he looks at how different markets or assets move together and affect one another, but he often had a feeling like he'd missed an opportunity, even when his plan wasn't to trade that market on that day. He'd chase and take the other side, only to get slaughtered. Rodrick also puts a lot of time into research, and in particular, after days or weekends of intense work, he expected the next day would immediately produce a windfall.

When he and I first spoke, we quickly identified that he was expecting to:

- Make money from every trade or every day
- Never miss an opportunity
- Make more money after putting in a lot of time strengthening his strategy

Taken together, these were signs of a larger expectation of perfection. Interestingly, Rodrick's expectation of perfection also extended to his mental game. He was well aware of the mistakes that were caused by his out-of-control emotions. But deep down, he thought that he could crack the code and achieve trading perfection. It didn't make sense to work on his emotions when he believed that one day he would figure it all out and the emotions would simply disappear.

Ironically, this was how we cracked the code to the faulty logic behind his perfection—Rodrick thought he could become so good that, essentially, he would escape his own humanity and be perfect 100% of the time.

The Inchworm Concept resonated with Rodrick, and it was eye opening to think that he could only truly expect his worst. Of course, that doesn't mean that's what will happen. He just has to earn his best, to aspire toward it, and then work to understand why he fell short and troubleshoot the problem. Also, the idea of improving his back end was something Rodrick had never prioritized. These were key points that got him to accept the cyclical nature of progress.

Accepting this cycle finally got him to do the journaling work that he knew he should do, for his trades as well as his thoughts and emotions. Journaling quickly raised his awareness and made a big difference in fighting against the rise of tilt. The anger is still there, but the severity of it is much lower. The proof of that is seen in the number of trades he takes per day, down from between 70 to 100 to just 10 to 20 now. And even when he takes a suboptimal trade, he quickly recognizes it and cuts it off, rather than allowing it to snowball.

Humbled to accept that he's human, Rodrick now also appreciates more of what he's accomplished in his 10 years of trading, which has taken away some of the intensity around his anger. Although during one session, this recognition also made him momentarily feel bad. He said, "I've accomplished all these things, and yet, if I had learned all these things earlier, I would have been even more successful." I quickly pointed out this was the expectation of perfection once again clouding his judgment—it's a sneaky bastard.

Obvious Mistakes

An obvious mistake is, well, obvious—and that's the problem. This wasn't a close decision that if it happened to work out, you wouldn't be certain the trade was bad. No, this mistake is so blatantly obvious and so incredibly stupid that you can barely comprehend it.

Sometimes you know in real time that you're about to make a mistake but can't stop yourself. For example, you clearly know the setup isn't right, and getting in would be forcing it, but you do it anyway. Taking a trade you know is wrong can be so incomprehensible that you're shocked and ask yourself, "Why would you do something you know is wrong?!?"

It doesn't make sense. You shut it down for the day, but can't get the mistake out of your head. You can't relax. You don't sleep well. You question your ability to stop these mistakes from happening. It's deflating, and all that negativity carries over to the next trading session, making an obvious mistake more likely to happen again.

On the surface, expecting yourself not to make simple errors seems completely reasonable. Why would you do something you obviously know to be wrong? There are two main reasons: One, you're already tilting but don't realize it. For some of you, mistake tilt is the first signal that you're already tilting, or that another emotion, like fear or overconfidence, has compromised your decision-making. Two, autopilot, boredom, fatigue, or another discipline issue has caused your performance level to drop. Either way, your mental and emotional functioning is compromised.

The first step in correcting this problem is to change the expectation that you shouldn't make such obvious mistakes. For the rest of your trading career, the errors that occupy your C-game remain possible. Three years from now, your C-game will (hopefully) be significantly better than it is now, and so your definition of an obvious mistake will change too. But at that point, an obvious mistake is still possible. It always is. By changing your expectation, you automatically place a higher priority on showing up prepared, with good energy, emotionally balanced, and ready to correct the mental game leaks that can lead to an obvious mistake.

Second, change how you view these mistakes. The mistake is not the mistake. The real mistake is failing to see the rise in emotion, or drop in intensity, that made the trading error inevitable. Prioritize improving the leak that's causing your mentality to degrade.

To do this, focus on recognition and mapping your pattern. You need to be able to spot the rising tide of emotion, or the decline downward toward autopilot or boredom. You can't stop what you can't see. The changes to your mental and emotional states must be easily and readily recognizable. Otherwise, making an obvious mistake is your first signal of a problem.

Glorifying Self-Criticism

When trying to reach our goals, we all have moments when we need to coach ourselves. For many of you, this internal dialogue is decidedly self-critical. Perhaps you grew up with parents, coaches, or teachers who motivated you through harshly worded feedback, and that became the voice inside your head. Or perhaps the voice is decidedly yours and has been there for as long as you can remember.

Either way, you berate yourself with questions like, "How could I be so stupid? Why can't I just follow my plan and do what I'm supposed to do?" Or you admonish yourself by thinking, *Why the hell didn't I sell?!? When I follow my rules, I make money; when I don't, I lose money. It couldn't be simpler!* If self-criticism is a problem for you, you know exactly what this voice sounds like and what it says.

To a certain extent, self-criticism is a useful tool for motivation. The problem is that you believe self-criticism is necessary for your performance, growth, or ability to learn from mistakes. It's not. And it can actually slow or shut down your ability to improve. For most people it's not an efficient tool for learning, and tends to backfire. You get stuck in the spiral of negativity, self-loathing, rumination, lost sleep, and wasted time, energy, and opportunity. And strangely enough, you end up dependent on this internal anger to motivate you to do better.

Before long, it becomes a self-perpetuating problem. You have to make mistakes in order to spark that drive. For example, soon after instances of reaching the zone or trading at a high level, you may get a bit cocky, lazy in your focus, or mentally flat. The lack of self-criticism causes a concurrent lack of motivation to keep improving, and you slip backward. Eventually, you make a mistake that triggers self-criticism and the cycle repeats.

Self-criticism can motivate you, but mistakes are the currency you trade for it. Mistakes ought to be used just as feedback to learn, and have nothing to do with your motivation. You don't need self-criticism; you just haven't considered motivating yourself any other way.

To make this transition, use a one–two combo of reducing the intensity of anger or self-criticism and strengthening your commitment to your goals as your primary source of motivation. Identify and correct the *source* of your criticism, which often includes flaws in your approach to learning, such as the expectation of perfection or hatred of an obvious mistake. In addition, write down your short- and long-term goals, and why you're driven to achieve them. Review them regularly, including at the start of every trading session.

Then to keep the progress going, you must also correct those instances when overconfidence and discipline issues derail your motivation. Be sure to rectify them so you continue to improve. Then, as the cycle of self-criticism starts to unwind, it should become easier for you to be naturally motivated toward your goals.

Hindsight Bias

Shoulda, coulda, woulda. You're pissed off, because you think you could have avoided a mistake if only you had . . . Fill in the blank: Worked harder, read about a particular piece of news, not ignored a junior trader's idea—you name it. The excuses are endless.

At its core, these thoughts are driven by a desire to be better. But usually, the consideration of what lesson you learned is done in more of a fantasy or wish type of way. You assume that it was easy to see the error when, in reality, it wasn't.

You don't appreciate that whenever you look back and recognize the mistake, after the trade or at the end of the day, you have more information than you did when you made the decision. After the fact, you have an informational advantage.

From that position you highlight what could have easily altered the outcome, but without really figuring out how you could have made the bet based on that information from the beginning. You shouldn't have listened to other traders and, instead, trusted your gut. You saw the massive opportunity to sell the equity market near the top in 2008, or buy Bitcoin in 2013. You lament the lost money and think about what it would mean to you today.

And of course, you beat yourself up for being an idiot, saying, "If I had just . . ." You can even have hindsight on your emotions, knowing you shouldn't have traded out of anger or impatience.

Nowhere in your analysis afterward do you think practically about what it would have taken for you to do what in hindsight seems easy.

Since you're not proactively figuring out how you could've known better, you're not improving, so the cycle will repeat. At some point in the future you'll say the exact same things as you're saying now about another mistake or missed opportunity. You'll look back with 20/20 vision, wishing that you had made different decisions and thinking what a dumbass you are.

To correct this problem, you must first realize that you harbor an assumption that at some point you'll wake up a genius with an ability to not miss a trade or make a mistake again. You've likely never had that exact, conscious thought, but the nature of your thoughts proves you're thinking along these lines at some level. After the trade you know exactly what happened; before it you don't. Equating the two means you believe there is a genius inside you that will one day emerge and know how to take those trades. Obviously, it doesn't work that way.

New knowledge is built upon a foundation of the old. After these missed opportunities, the questions you need to answer are along these lines:

- How could you have made the "right" trade?
- What steps would it have taken?
- What perspective were you missing?
- What changes to your decision-making process can you make?
- What improvements to your mental game are required?

You need to think proactively about how to be better in the future. Otherwise, you're just wishing that you had the capability to make those trades.

Always Wanting to Be Right

Are you the type of trader who has an excuse for every mistake you make? You have a litany of reasons to explain why you weren't wrong, such as you were distracted, you can afford the loss, or that late entries sometimes work. These knee-jerk reactions spring to mind instantaneously to convince yourself that you were right. You always have to be right. Heck, you may even be defending yourself right now as you read this section, justifying your desire to always be right.

The desire to be right is a worthwhile pursuit, but it must be balanced by an understanding that you have limits, and that being wrong is an eventuality. Ideally you're intensely driven to be right, while accepting when you're wrong, learning from it, and adjusting. Given you're here, my bet is that you know, logically, you should have that balanced perspective, but you're instead driven by a desire that you can't control.

The key to gaining control of those knee-jerk reactions and adopting the correct perspective is understanding what drives you to always be right. Why do you need to be right? What does it provide? Why can't you be wrong? What does being wrong mean to you?

In my experience, the need to be right stems from a confidence problem. Being right is part of your identity. Being wrong is a painful hit to your confidence. You need to be right, like you need food. Without it, you're starving, and it feels like you're losing a part of yourself, so you instantly defend against that happening.

An excessive desire to be right was at the root of Frantz's tilt problems, the trader from chapter 2 who wants to make enough money from trading to travel the world with his wife. Unfortunately, his accumulated emotion prevented him from patiently waiting for the infrequent A+ trades he needed. Instead, he'd force trades and then get back into another trade as soon as possible to make up for his mistake.

Due to the severity of his tilt—his mind could completely shut off—we needed to use several tactics to address Frantz's problem. He started by creating a clear map of his tilt, taking notes in real time, and spending an hour after each session to review what he found, in detail. That post-market routine was particularly helpful to release the accumulated tilt, and it uncovered a lot of details. This gave Frantz greater awareness and prevented some mistakes immediately. But he was still tilting, and didn't have a good sense of what he was experiencing when tilt got particularly intense.

The academic researcher side of Frantz took over, and he decided to video himself talking out loud throughout the session. This practical step gave him invaluable insight into his thought process while tilting. While reviewing the video from a particularly bad trading session, Frantz completed a Mental Hand History, based on what he found. That's when a breakthrough happened, and he understood the root of why he had to be right. Here's an excerpt of that Mental Hand History:

1. **What's the problem:** There are many ways to react to a loss. My way is to get back in another trade as soon as possible, in order to chase a loss. I enter "attack" mode in which respecting my entry criteria and basic trading rules doesn't appear as important anymore. When anger takes over, my judgment is clouded and I become impulsive.

2. **Why does the problem exist:** I fight back to repair the damage I've done. I want to make amends. I'm telling myself I'm urgently going to make back the money right now, because I can't stand the lack of success, the failure, the inability to make my system work. I don't like when things are not working for me, despite my best efforts. I don't accept the loss: *I shouldn't be losing. I can't believe I'm losing. Why is this so? If only I could have a win, just a win, I would feel better about myself again. I would stop feeling like I'm failing. I would stop feeling like a loser. Why is this not working? What can I do to make it work?*

3. **What is flawed:** I don't accept criticism or being challenged because I think I'm always right. Trading directly challenges that, and makes me feel like my sense of worth is at stake. This is huge for me to realize. I've always had unrealistic expectations about what I was capable of doing. It's as if I should have known better at all times. Even in the absence of prior knowledge or any practice.

4. **What's the correction:** I achieved a Ph.D. and two postdoctoral fellowships. I'm capable of achieving whatever goal I fix my mind on, so long as I do it in the right way and with the right mentality. Trying to be right all the time is like thinking I have a

superpower. Embrace the challenge that trading poses and figure out how to be right in a real way.

5. **What logic confirms that correction:** Being accurate about my
capability is the only way I can turn my dream into a reality.

You can see the mixture of anger and confidence at the heart of
this issue. Frantz's desire to always be right also had a personal aspect
beyond trading. That discovery helped him understand why his anger
became so intense, and it gave him an opportunity to address the problem in both places—effectively cross-training like an athlete.

He also uncovered other factors that could influence his focus,
energy, and mood that were subtly undermining his ability to execute,
and leading to the initial mistakes. Essentially, he was making mistakes
and couldn't understand why, until he looked closer. The result of all
this work is that his tilt has reduced by more than 50%, and he continues to work through the process.

Finally, Frantz's problems didn't neatly fit into a single category. He
also needed to use some of the corrections from the Fear of Failure section in the prior chapter, as well as to address overconfidence, using
advice from the upcoming chapter on confidence.

If, like Frantz, the desire to always be right is a problem for you, refer
to the next chapter to get to the core of the problem. Find out how to
expand or redefine your identity, so you can adopt a more balanced perspective on being right.

INJUSTICE TILT

You've been stopped out for the umpteenth time and you're steaming
mad. You can't believe how unlucky you got, stopped out again by a tick,
only to see the market turn around and hit your profit target. You tilt
when you think about what you should have made. The trading gods
have cursed you. The market is against you. You don't deserve this and
wonder when you're going to get your fair share of good luck.

Logic says be patient, and eventually things will turn in your favor. But the scales of justice have gone against you, and you tilt trying to fight against them.

As the name implies, injustice tilt is about fairness, equity, and justice. While you already know there is no fairness in trading, that doesn't stop you from having reactions like these:

- Saying things like, "I can't believe this is happening again—I'm just unlucky"
- Thinking the market is manipulated, or personally out to get you
- Blaming losses on bad luck
- Being convinced you're doing all the right things, but are always unlucky with your timing
- Believing the market owes you after a few losing trades

Trading is complex, highly competitive, and chaotic. You don't operate in a courtroom; neither it is a meritocracy. You know this, and yet you still experience these strong reactions that are out of your control, where you feel like you're getting screwed and owed something. While it may seem as if the only answer is to think in terms of probabilities and not overreact to short-term results, it's clearly not that simple, or this problem would have already been solved.

You may have already tried a number of "cures." You've read the book *Black Swan,* you follow your risk management strategy, you've backtested your system, and you have a sizable sample to prove you have edge. Intellectually and conceptually, you understand variance well. But that knowledge is simply not enough to fundamentally change how you react to bad luck.

Since not every trader suffers from injustice tilt, there's obviously more to it. We have to look beyond the natural desire for fairness, which is observable even in infants,[5] and examine the biases and flaws that skew our perspective on what's fair and what's not.

Let's look at a basic example. You may feel like you're consistently unlucky in the market, and yet the fact that you're reading this book means you're likely living in a first world country, with your basic needs met, and have the capital to trade. Have you factored that luck into your perspective? Likely not. And while I'm not suggesting that appreciating this good luck is the antidote to injustice tilt, failing to account for other forms of good luck in trading or elsewhere in your life means that your perspective is skewed.

With injustice tilt, there's a similarly skewed perspective that needs to be uncovered. To help you find the flaws or biases causing it, answer these questions with your anger in mind, not what you know logically about fairness:

- Does it feel like you never get your share of the luck, or that you're always getting screwed?
- Does it seem as if the money you've lost is being taken from you?
- In what situations does bad luck really get to you?
- Are you jealous or resentful of other traders who you think are luckier than you?
- When variance is really bad, do you wish trading wasn't this way, or that you could somehow control variance?

When your actions cause further losses, it's always harder to swallow. This is especially true when you lose control, despite working hard to increase the size of your edge and understand the randomness in the market and distribution of outcomes. While you have no control over luck or variance, take the time to better understand the reasons *why* bad variance stirs anger, and you can regain command of your execution.

Believing You Are Unlucky

Look beyond how you think you *should* react to bad luck and be honest about why you get angry. Do you feel like you don't get your fair share of good luck, are cursed, or get more bad luck than you deserve? If so, you may have drawn that conclusion from a long-term research project you've been unknowingly conducting since you started trading.

The problem is that your research has been compromised by bad data, and thus your conclusions are wrong. You aren't cursed, you get your share of good luck and not as much bad luck as it seems—you're just not measuring it correctly.

There are two primary errors that cause faulty coding in this way. First, you attribute your mistakes to bad luck, and second, when you have good luck, you attribute those results to skill. These errors bias the scales of trading justice to make variance seem unfair when it's not. The next two figures illustrate this point.

BAD   GOOD

MISTAKES   SKILLS

Figure 1

Figure 1 represents a theoretical ideal, where your view of variance, your understanding of your skills as a trader, and your assessment of the mistakes that you make are accurate. You have a balanced view of fairness. Although theoretical, some are much closer to this view than others. Practically speaking, this means understanding the inevitable outliers, knowing that even the best setups in your system can lose, and focusing more on the big picture, not just the outcome of a few trades. Filtering variance this way allows you to see it more accurately, and focus on what you can control.

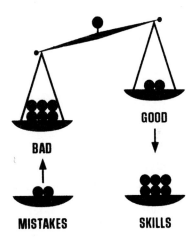

Figure 2

Figure 2 highlights how the two errors I mentioned can alter your perspective on variance and cause injustice tilt. First, if your mistakes were the predominant cause of your losses, but instead you attribute it to bad luck, then some bad luck is added to the scale. Second, if your profits were more likely a result of good luck, but you believe it was solely due to your skill, then some good luck is taken off the scale.

You can imagine what happens when this bias plays out repeatedly, over time. Inevitably you'd believe variance was unfairly against you, or that you were cursed. Consistently attributing good luck to your skill, and your mistakes to bad luck, overweights the scale on one side, making it seem like variance is against you. Bad luck appears to happen more frequently, and you tilt, believing you're getting screwed, when in actuality, you're mentally screwing yourself.

This pattern is further exacerbated by the fact that, typically, traders remember bad luck more than good luck, especially under emotional pressure. Remembering and focusing more on bad luck creates a biased perspective for the simple reason that when you add focus to something, you learn it better. So bad luck gets more attention and thus stands out more easily in your mind. Basically, you're really skilled at spotting bad luck and terrible at spotting good luck.

To make matters worse, not only does this extra focus on bad luck bias your perspective overall, but when under emotional pressure from a drawdown, it's all you remember. A statement such as "I never get lucky," makes total sense when bad luck is all you see. In that moment, you truly believe that you never experience good luck, something that happens primarily because you're so bad at recognizing it.

As chaotic as this problem may seem, you can change your perspective and the way you code results in your mind. Start by improving your ability to spot both positive variance and your mistakes. One idea is to track when you get lucky—in a notebook, word document, spreadsheet, or whatever works for you. Perhaps you got in and out of a trade at the exact right time to maximize profit, happened to be off the desk and missed a losing trade you certainly would have taken, or missed getting stopped out by a tick or two and exiting at your target. Notice these instances and track them.

Conversely, whenever you think you were unlucky, stop and evaluate if you made a mistake. At first, the objective is to simply be open to the idea that you might have made a mistake and consider whether or not that is the case. Sometimes bad luck prevents a win. Other times you made a mistake. In the short term, you'll continue to automatically react to losses by assuming you got unlucky, or whatever characteristics you identified around this issue. But now, by asking a question, you're disrupting that pattern and beginning to alter the coding of your results and balance your perspective about variance.

Lastly, look at your history. Go back through your trading career, perhaps even your personal or professional life outside of trading, and identify instances of good luck that, at the time, you thought happened more because of your skill than variance. Also look for instances when you thought you were getting screwed but were either making mistakes or not looking for distinct points of improvement that you could have made.

Correcting your biased perspective is easier when you also correct your past biases. You obviously can't change what's happened in the past, but changing how you look at the past provides a more accurate and stable view of the present.

Focused More on Results than Quality

In an industry like trading, results are what matter most. And that will never change. This is also true in places like major professional sports, where the old adage is that no one remembers who finishes second. But in sports recently, there has been an increased emphasis on the process of attaining those results. Coaches understand that to build consistency at the top, more than just a ruthless focus on results is required.

Leading coaches across a variety of sports have popularized process-oriented thinking. And within trading, Ray Dalio is an outspoken stalwart of this style. In his popular book *Principles*, Dalio says, "Choose your habits well. Habit is probably the most powerful tool in your brain's toolbox."

While this isn't a new concept, what may be underappreciated is the extent to which the results-are-all-that-matter perspective has to be upgraded to value the process more. Right now, your default reaction when results don't go your way is to feel like you got screwed. When you're in a stronger process- or quality-oriented state of mind, you view results from a balanced perspective that can automatically handle bad luck, losses, and even your mistakes with greater ease and less anger.

If you're like most traders, however, putting greater emphasis on the process is a general idea that sounds good, but you're not actively training to be more process-oriented. Which means that you see this as a perspective that should just be there without any effort, not as one that follows a learning process like any other skill.

Recognizing progress is easier when you track your progress for your process-oriented goals. Daily PnL is easy to see and your mind is already well trained to think about it. When you focus on how you're doing in these *non-monetary* pursuits, you train a process-oriented mentality.

In your daily journaling at the end of the trading day, review your progress with process goals, such as reducing tilt, improving execution, or decreasing distractions. With the goal of reduction of tilt, you could pay attention to, for example, a general ability to review lost trades more easily without immediately tilting, reduced frequency checking your PnL during the trading day, and a sense of accomplishment on a day where you lost money but executed your strategy well. These outcomes signal progress, both in reducing tilt and becoming more process oriented. You get two benefits from one action.

Ultimately, you must get to the point where focusing on signs of progress becomes second nature. Until then, you're still learning this new perspective, and at times you'll tilt because you're focusing too much on results. It's easy to fall back into old habits. Stay focused on training your process orientation until it's automatic.

Thinking You Know What Will Happen

Your immediate reaction when you see a position going against you is to believe losing is a foregone conclusion and the only question is how it will happen this time. You start having thoughts like *Here we go again*, or *Really? Again?!?* You sense what's coming and are already pissed off about it before it happens.

This pattern typically happens when you're already on a losing streak and have some built-up accumulated tilt. Then these predictions start popping up and create a cycle like this: You predict a loss, and when it comes true, you tell yourself, "I knew that was going to happen." This subconsciously fosters a belief that you actually can make accurate predictions, exaggerating your sense of control.

Part of the resulting anger from a loss is being pissed off at yourself because you *knew* it was going to lose and you didn't close it immediately. Now, tilt starts to snowball. You become so angry that you'll do whatever you can to avoid the loss. Over time, the cycle perpetuates and reinforces the idea that you're cursed. Which, hypothetically, could be true—thus far in your trading career you could have had more than your fair share of bad luck.

Regardless, that reality doesn't say anything about what kind of luck you'll have going forward. You can't know what's to come. But you think you do, and that's the root of the problem: the belief that you know what's going to happen.

The mind has the ability to anticipate the future, just as the body does. When your body is moving, it's constantly making predictions so it's prepared. One example of where this prediction goes wrong is when you walk up a flight of stairs without paying attention to how many steps remain. If you anticipate a step that isn't there, you'll practically trip because your body's prediction was wrong.

Whether in reference to the body or the mind, a prediction is based solely on the information available at that time. During a drawdown your mind draws from a pool of data that's skewed toward losing, because that's what's happened recently. Naturally, your mind predicts more losses to come, and tilts in anticipation.

But the flip side can also occur. When you're on a great run, you assume profits will continue to come your way. For example, when you're in a trade that quickly moves toward your target, you assume it will hit your target. The idea that it would reverse doesn't cross your mind.

Either way, when your predictions come to fruition, the belief that you know what's going to happen gets stronger. Then, in subsequent drawdowns, tilt becomes more intense, because you're even more certain that losses are coming.

At the root of this problem is a belief that you can predict the future. Unless you have real psychic power (and, then, why are you reading this book, if you do?), believing that you actually know what's going to happen is an illusion that needs to be corrected—in connection to both predicted losses and profits.

Make sure to closely map your positive and negative predictions for a trade, and the thoughts that confirm your predictions afterward. Seeing them in real time is the only way to correct a flaw that on the surface seems crazy to believe.

Hating Variance

Underlying the sense of injustice for some of you is a hatred for variance. Deep down, you know that variance is an unextractable reality in trading. You know that there are factors beyond your control. And yet . . . Deep down there is a part of you that wishes trading were more predictable, or wishes you had more control over your results. You hate how things can seem so unfair. You hate how profits can be eviscerated in seconds. The lack of control makes you crazy.

Let's assume you have actually had worse luck for far longer than the math says is likely. It's completely reasonable to be pissed off, but the question is whether that frustration or anger affects the quality of your performance. Traders with a hatred of variance often end up losing control of their decision-making and execution.

Since you can't control variance, and can only control how you respond to it, the goal is to build up more mental muscle so that you can respond effectively and focus on your execution. Of course it's hard. Variance is a major reason why trading is so challenging.

Assuming that's all true—and many of you already know that it is— what's the wish for more predictability really about? Wishing variance didn't exist in trading is another way of saying, "I can't handle the emotion variance causes me," or "I can't handle my results being out of my control," or "I can't continue to execute properly when I lose in unfair ways."

You can't control variance, but you can understand it better—admittedly, you may have a real deficit in this regard. But you can understand and correct the flaws that variance exposes. Most likely, if variance didn't cause you to tilt, you'd love that it causes other traders to tilt.

Jealousy

Jealousy specifically relates to luck when you believe you aren't getting your fair share of it and are envious of those who you think are. If you think, or say to another trader, "I wish I had your luck," do you actually have proof they've had more luck? Or does it just feel that way?

Think about the scales of justice from earlier in this section. When you look at other traders, you might falsely assume they're having good luck when it's actually the result of them being more skilled than you think. You perceive their scale is overweighted to the right (lucky). Plus, you may be discounting the errors that you're making, so in your mind, your scale is overweighted to the left (unlucky). Which means that you may feel jealous about something that isn't real.

Alternatively, maybe this trader really is luckier than you. But even if that's true, what does it mean for you? Not much. You can't control variance, and wishing you had their luck won't make it come true.

In its most basic sense, focusing on the fortune of others is a distraction. Unless you're learning something from them that makes you better, you're simply wasting time. But the source of jealousy can also run deeper. Is your comparison isolated to just luck? If not, what other things do you compare yourself to others about? Your career as a whole? The amount of money they make? The position they may be in, in terms of title or opportunity?

Injustice tilt can be a signal of larger problems, like a sense that your abilities are lacking, your career isn't stacking up to expectations, or a general confidence issue. To start making improvements on the issue of jealousy, answer the following questions:

- What do others have that you resent or wish you had?
- What would having it mean for you?
- What more can you be doing that you aren't already?
  (There's always something, even if it's just being patient.)
- What have you achieved that you haven't celebrated enough?

Your answers will give you some direction, so you can focus less on the fortune of others. It's easy to say, "Don't focus on them; focus on yourself," but if you don't correct the reason why you're compelled to focus on someone else's good fortune, following that edict is difficult at best.

REVENGE TRADING

Revenge is common in everyday life, so it's no surprise it also exists in trading. And in the market, just as in life, the long-term consequences of seeking revenge often outweigh the short-term satisfaction of achieving it.

Of course, when revenge gets triggered, the likelihood that your actions will lead to losses is the last thing on your mind. You're glued to your screen and focused on every tick, driven by a relentless urge to take back what you believe is yours. It's as if you're saying to the market, "Oh no, you're not going to just screw with me and get away with it!" There's no thinking, just a pure impulse to make money.

Revenge is not irrational. It has a history of contributing to creating laws, unwritten codes of the street,[6] and the unwritten rules that you define as acceptable and unacceptable in trading. So long as the outcomes of your trades follow what you expect to happen, it's all good. You're making money and there's no reason to want revenge.

As soon as you lose money, make a mistake, or get unlucky, the desire for revenge starts to rise. You try to control yourself and not make a big mistake, like in the past. But you can only hold on for so long. Eventually you crack and fly off the rails. Then you wake up, wondering what the hell just happened and how you could lose control like that.

Reacting in a vengeful way is especially surprising when you're not like that in everyday life. But consider how you've reacted in previous competitive arenas in your life. Was a desire for revenge triggered by a particular opponent who always seemed to get the better of you? Were you fighting for self-respect after a loss, or trying to prove to others how good you are? Sure, you couldn't really control what they thought, but it doesn't mean you didn't try.

While revenge in life is usually directed at a person, in trading, it's not like there's someone specific you can get back at—you're often fighting the whole market. Logic and reason have been overrun by the strength of your anger. As inexplicable as your actions may be, the post-blowup self-criticism rarely solves the problem. You instead need to understand the reason you seek revenge.

Revenge trading is unlike any of the three types of tilt covered earlier in this chapter, because the source is not just anger. Instead, the secret ingredient mixed into revenge trading is a confidence problem. The two seemingly explode when they come together, and that's how the intensity that characterizes revenge is created.

On the anger side, look out for a hatred of losing, mistake tilt, or injustice tilt. But if you have any of those tilt issues independent of a problem with confidence, you won't seek revenge. Even if you don't think you have an issue with confidence, try not to make any judgments until after you read the next chapter.

While you'll learn significantly more about confidence in the next chapter, it's important to point out that confidence is not an all-or-nothing proposition. You don't have it or not have it. Confidence has a number of dimensions, like pieces to a puzzle. Weakness in one small area—such as an excessive desire for respect, being overly focused on results, or maintaining the illusion of control—when mixed with anger, is enough to spark revenge.

You may see this as you complete your map of tilt. For example, you may recognize that levels 1, 2, and 3 are actually related to confidence, where you become overconfident after seeing a number of your positions in the green, but then anger is triggered after they appear to unjustly turn into losses.

Or perhaps it's the opposite, where the lower levels are marked by anger, and a mixture of revenge and desperation (a confidence issue) come in at levels 6 through 10. Either way, to solve revenge trading, you need to understand and correct the roots of both the anger and the confidence issues.

Revenge trading can be a problem even for 20-year Wall Street veterans. Joe is currently an independent trader from New York City, with years of experience trading and working at a bulge-bracket investment bank before going out on his own five years ago. His background is heavily weighted toward options and higher periodicity trading that he managed as a rolling 20- to 60-day portfolio. On his own, however, Joe became increasingly focused on adding an intraday-futures trading vertical to his existing strategies, and this change led to a lot of anger that impacted his subsequent performance.

With options trading, Joe could have, for example, 30 positions open over a rolling 30-day period and if one position blew up, it wasn't a big deal, because he was managing the risk over a larger portfolio of complementary positions that tended to offset one another to differing degrees.

Managing a strategic book like that had been his bread and butter for years. But now, trading futures intraday on a directional basis, he was overly hung up on the outcome of individual trades, where any single trade might be the only active position. He would mess around with trades, cutting them short of his target, and became hyper-focused on the outcome of each individual trade at the expense of the overarching process.

When the market would stall out in an area in which he expected it to move swiftly through, Joe would often immediately get out before the loss got larger. Then, if it ultimately went in his direction, he would think about how unlucky he was, feeling like the market (including algorithmic market makers) was out to get him or toying with him.

In his mind he would get everything right, to the exact tick he wanted, and then suddenly, for example, the trade wouldn't fill, despite hitting his bid or lifting into his offer, because the market would turn right on that price. It was incredibly frustrating.

Then with residual feelings of FOMO, he'd be inclined to enter at a slightly less favorable price only to get stopped out, and then possibly forced back into the trade again when that stop appeared to be too tight. Although he was always managing risk, he still might do that two to four times more, before recognizing he was on tilt and walking away.

Having reactions like that made his head explode. Joe couldn't comprehend how he could think like that when, intellectually, he knew that the market was never out to get a single trader and is largely indifferent to the intentions of the participants. But those types of situations still sparked a deep desire to get the next trade right.

Joe also wanted to be right, not for the sake of money but because he prided himself on his skill and abilities. And when he was wrong, like when he read too much into the price action and believed he could predict what was going to happen next, his confidence would take a hit.

Bad predictions were a primary reason he curtailed winners, rationalizing to himself, "Oh, you're wrong again—look at the flow going against you. You'd better get out of this trade before you take another full loss." Then at other times, he would book small wins, just so he could feel good.

Joe couldn't understand why he was screwing up. He got pissed off at himself, and at the market. This mixture of injustice tilt, mistake tilt, and the need to be right (a flaw in his confidence) sparked revenge. He became impulsive and vengeful toward the market. He would overtrade, taking the same trade over and over again after getting stopped out prematurely. As he doesn't use hard stops, this gray area was the perfect rationale his revenge needed to get back in, thinking, *I'm not letting the market stop me at the very high/low of this retracement. I'm going to get this trade right.*

Joe was very aware of the revenge problem, and even kept detailed stats, tracking what he did and what each trade would have done if he'd left it alone. Over the most recent three-year period, he was generating an R-factor of around 1.5, but it could have been 2 to 2.25, had he managed to remain more objective in his management—he was easily losing a full third of his available profit potential.

Through our discussion, which is summarized in the following Mental Hand History, you can see how the underlying flaws caused so much chaos:

1. **What's the problem:** I have a lot of experience in this business, and even though I know losing is an integral part of the game, I get myopic when trading the intraday timeframe. I'm just not seeing the winners and losers as a collective process, and I'm only seeing this one trade, this single outcome as a standalone occurrence. When it goes against me, or something unexpected happens, I can lose my composure and interfere with the trade.

2. **Why does the problem exist:** I'm convinced I know exactly how the trade is going to play out. That it's going to immediately break out, or reverse. But when long and I see sellers come in, for example, and it stalls, I second-guess my premise and lose trust in my judgment. I feel like I should get out of the trade, even though I know it doesn't unfold the same way every time, that it's inherently unpredictable, and that I have the hard proof of that in my data.

3. **What is flawed:** I'm holding onto this unreasonable expectation, and I have a hard time seeing that this trade could be one of the 50% or so that unfolds in a different way. The expectation that it should work out exactly how I anticipate it is overriding my ability to see the process objectively. I can become so drawn up in my reading of the orderflow that I'm almost fooling myself that I can predict what's going to happen next. Plus, there's a part of me that wants to win all the time. I want to be that good. Maybe I can't get 10 out of 10, but I believe I have the knowledge and experience to get 8 out of 10. I simply want to be that good. It's driving me to hold onto something that is unrealistic, and yet I'm reluctant to give up on that belief. Any threat to that fact—like a narrow loss—causes me to immediately attempt to prove it in the next moment. Once I'm in a trade, I'm seeking validation of that proficiency, and if I see the flow going against me, I'm doing everything in my power to predict what's going to happen next, despite knowing it's a futile task. But the very reasoning that got me into the trade, when apparently invalidated, is the same reasoning I feel should get me out.

4. **What's the correction:** I can only be assured that the trade fits within my system and that it has edge over time. My goal is to have a win rate close to 60% and a 1.75 to 2.50 R-factor, not an 80% win rate, which I believe is unrealistic for my style. I can be incredibly successful, but not like that, so I need to let the trades play out.

5. **What logic confirms that correction:** There is a thorough data set that grounds my strategy. The process has edge over time, but I'm only going to make money on roughly half of my trades.

Essentially, Joe was comingling daily PnL with long-term profitability, and he was equating PnL with being right. In our work together, I pushed him to become more process-oriented and that led him to revisit a tracking idea that he had kicked around but not fully explored.

Joe created a sheet with 100 boxes on it where each box related to an individual trade. Every time he would execute his strategy correctly, he would check off one box and wouldn't even think about the outcome until he had at least 25 in a row. Looking at these 25 completed trades at one time allowed him to more easily see them as a whole portfolio, replicating the process he had with options trading, as opposed to standalone occurrences. This made it a lot easier for him to avoid hyperfocusing on each trade, individually, in the moment, and to reframe his objectives in a more familiar light.

Joe knew he had an edge, and implementing such a strategy allowed him to let it work itself out over time. Laying out the trades in this way gave him the validation of success that he desired—the feeling of being a winner.

And the results showed. His R-factor rose to 3—although, to be fair, he noted that the market environment was different during the bulk of our coaching than previously. Yet, he estimated that if the environment had remained the same, it would likely still have risen to at least his goal of 1.75R.

Joe's work isn't done. While this process-focused strategy has significantly improved his execution and removed some of his emotions, there's more emotion pinging around than is ideal. As this approach becomes more standard, he'll free up mental space to focus on correcting those incremental emotions as aggressively as he corrected his execution around revenge trading.

If revenge trading is a problem for you, look closely at the types of trades that typically trigger the revenge. It's unlikely that every losing trade sets off this reaction. Is it the ones that are more discretionary, where you have less conviction about your strategy, or have more uncertainty about the outcome? Could it be a sign of a weakness in your strategy or technical proficiency? These questions will help you get to the heart of the anger, as well as the weakness in your confidence.

ENTITLEMENT TILT

Entitlement tilt happens when something you believe to be rightfully yours has been taken away. The act of winning is akin to possessing something. You now own it, and when losses mount, it's as if the market has robbed you.

After losing the first trade you expected to win on the day, you might experience some shock or disbelief. You might even laugh, because you can hardly believe what just happened. But it's not that big of a deal; you know trading is like that. As losses pile up, however, tilt settles in and you start to lose your mind.

At the root of entitlement tilt is an underlying belief that you have the right to win, or deserve to win, for such reasons as working harder than others, being smarter, or having a longer career. You may say to yourself, "I have a great track record and do all the right things," "I should be the one getting paid for my effort," or "I've suffered more than anyone—I deserve to make a killing now."

You're incredulous over the idea that you could make less in the same situation as traders with less skill, knowledge, and experience. How did you not score a massive winner when they did? It annoys the heck out of you. In your mind, the implication is that you have earned the right to have whatever it is you believe you deserve.

Entitlement is a problem that you may not realize affects you. Not only can it be subtle—who wants to admit to being entitled? Just the sound of that can be hard to swallow—but once you look more closely at why you're getting so pissed off, you may notice a sense that you deserve to win, or that losing takes away what's rightfully yours.

The reality is that everyone has some weakness to work on, and it's better to be honest about yours, so you can get past it. You may actually feel relieved by acknowledging this problem and no longer protecting these lies.

While anger is the most common signal of entitlement, the problem is really caused by overconfidence. Overconfidence simply means that you have exaggerated or inflated beliefs about your skills or results. In other words, you believe things that aren't true. The idea that your past results, efforts, or suffering have earned you the right to make money is absurd. You know that, of course, but trading can do a good job of feeding these false beliefs.

Periods where you make a lot of money not only pad your account but your confidence as well. You dream of how much money you could make, and a small part of you feels like that money is already yours. This inflated confidence sets you up to tilt when the market takes the profits you thought were already yours.

The anger that shows up is often an attempt to preserve the false confidence. You want to believe you're that good. The question is why do you need to believe it? To help you answer that question, and get to the heart of what's causing your overconfidence, keep going to the next chapter.

CHAPTER 7

CONFIDENCE

"Confidence is a feeling, which reflects the coherence
of the information and the cognitive ease of processing it."

—Daniel Kahneman,
Thinking Fast and Slow

Right now, there are new traders out there who feel more confident than 20-year veterans. How can this be? The gap in skill between them is immense, and if we were to bet on who was going to make more money in a year, you'd only take the new trader if you were looking to gamble. Their levels of confidence and skill are not aligned.

For many of you, the confidence you have in your trading is not an accurate measure of your competence as a trader. If it were, you wouldn't get caught up in a rush of euphoria after closing out a huge trade and then make questionable bets, thinking you can't lose. You also wouldn't lose conviction for trades that you're normally certain about during a drawdown.

But confidence is an emotion, and—just like the other emotions described in this book—it's vulnerable to the influence of flaws and biases. You make decisions based on how confident you feel. When feeling strong, you size up, take on more risk, and trade more. Of course, if you're overconfident, those actions are problematic. Low on confidence, and you're likely to hesitate, cut down on size, lean toward consensus, and look for a new system.

For those of you skeptical of the role of confidence in performance, I agree that it has been oversold as something that you need to have to be successful. That's not the case. There is no causal connection between confidence and how much money you'll make. You don't need to feel confident to be a profitable trader.

Being confident that you can make money doesn't mean you will, just as lacking confidence doesn't mean you won't. You need to be *competent* as a trader more than you need to be confident. Regardless of how you *feel* about your ability, after a large enough sample, your results tell the real story.

But confidence does help you navigate the short term, when you don't exactly know what your skills are capable of producing. And having confidence helps you to perform at a higher level compared to when you lack it. Confidence is like the oil in an engine that allows the parts to move with less friction—it allows you to make the most of your skills and knowledge as a trader. Just like the oil in a car, however, too much or too little causes problems. You need the right amount to operate at peak efficiency.

Many of you will come to this chapter as you'd come to me for coaching, when your engine is seizing and your confidence has stalled. There's a natural tendency to focus on correcting a lack of confidence, when having too much of it could be a bigger problem. Let's look at both more closely.

In today's day and age, it might sound strange to suggest **too much confidence is a problem**, particularly in Western society, where confidence has been anointed as the be-all and end-all. The idea that you could have too much of it doesn't jibe with that perspective. Remember, however, that confidence is an emotion, and when emotions rise too high, because you're excited, greedy, or euphoric, higher brain functions decrease and mistakes are made.

Being overconfident doesn't mean being outwardly arrogant, cocky, or a greedy blowhard. Many traders are plagued by overconfidence, but exhibit only subtle signs of it. When there's a feeling of certainty about market direction, especially without having done a complete analysis, that's overconfidence. When you get amped up about how you've figured out the market and are going to make a killing, that's overconfidence.

It can also manifest as a refusal to admit mistakes or an insistence on being right. On a winning streak you take trades just for the sake of it, or you don't think leveraging a position means you're adding risk. You cut corners and avoid pre- and post-market routines. Or you may be discounting the role of variance, assuming that if you timed a trade perfectly to make the maximum, that was all you and not luck.

From a performance standpoint, being overconfident means that you're overestimating your real competence. Basically you're operating more in a bubble, relative to what's real. On some level, every trader needs a little bit of that.

In the short term, you can't know precisely what your edge is, and there's arguably more upside than downside to having a small amount of overconfidence. For example, having an extra bit of confidence helps you execute your strategy in the face of uncertainty, learn from mistakes, and adjust to changes in the market faster.

On the other side of the coin, **when you lack confidence**, it can be easy to say, "I'm not feeling it," and avoid trades you'd normally take easily. Maybe you start out feeling less confident than usual, and slowly it becomes a bigger trend. You're more consistently down, unsure, depressed, or whatever the traits are that you associate with someone who isn't confident.

At a certain point, these traits begin to feel bigger and all encompassing. You might wonder if there's something wrong with you, or that maybe you're just not cut out for trading. Suddenly it's all doom and gloom. You're stuck and can't get out of it. Or you might end up denying it's a problem, and do whatever you can to minimize the idea that you could have a confidence problem.

But there's a far more practical way of thinking about it, which is that confidence, as it relates to trading performance, has many dimensions. Think of it more like pieces to a puzzle rather than a singular thing that you either have or don't. In my experience, it's far more common that a couple of flawed, incomplete, or missing pieces create a weakness in confidence than for the entire puzzle to be missing. You simply need to isolate each weakness and correct it, much like we've addressed every other issue in the book. In surgical fashion, find the flaw, fix the flaw, and confidence is restored.

While some traders tend to struggle with either overconfidence or low confidence, others go through big up and downs with both. This especially happens when your confidence is based primarily on results. You end up riding the highs and lows of winning and losing like a roller coaster. You become more obsessed about the intraday up-and-down ticks of your PnL, and your confidence goes along for the ride. The more you make, the more your confidence rises, and the more likely you are to become overconfident.

Execution begins to degrade without you realizing it. Variance continues to be on your side, so small mistakes, or subtle drops in execution, don't get punished. Part of you feels like you're just going to keep making money, and you get so caught up in riding the high that you don't see the losses coming. When results suddenly take a nosedive, it's like getting the carpet yanked out from under you, and you're face first on the ground, with your confidence flattened. You try to talk yourself through it and stay positive. You show up the next day, optimistic and ready to execute. But losing again is deflating, causing you to question what you're doing.

The way you can stop these emotional swings from being so dramatic is to develop what I call "stable confidence," which means your confidence is based upon something more solid and independent than just results.

Stable confidence happens when your perspective is untainted by the flaws that cause instability. You become automatically better able to withstand the chaos of the markets, variance, and things out of your control, so you can adjust your strategy more quickly and accurately. It's like you're anchored to something solid enough to withstand a tornado.

Stable confidence enables you to focus much more on your execution than on PnL in the short term. Of course, profitability matters a lot, but emphasizing execution in the short term is how you can make more money (or lose less) and learn faster.

THE NATURE OF CONFIDENCE

Confidence is the foundation of your mental game because it's the emotion that directly reflects your skill as a trader. Viewing confidence as an emotion may be a novel idea when it seems like something solid, that you either have or don't, but think about how you or other traders talk about it. You'll often use the word "feel," like "I'm feeling confident," or "I'm not feeling it." Skill is solid and much harder to change. Confidence is fluid and can change in a flash—just as other emotions can.

Confidence problems develop as a result of beliefs, flaws, biases, wishes, and illusions that alter your perspective on your skill. That's what the bulk of this chapter will focus on. But first, it's important to highlight that a drop in confidence can be a signal that something is off in any of your individual trading skills.

Other, more ancillary skills can also be off. These might include studying or researching, networking and collaborating, and the mental side of being a trader, which includes skills like focus, discipline, work ethic, and emotional control.

More experienced traders should first analyze a drop in confidence as a signal of a drop in skill. Maybe you're in a slump and out of synch with the market. The game has changed but you haven't caught up yet. Or maybe your confidence is down because your ability to execute your strategy is inconsistent. Despite your best efforts, you continue to take marginal trades because you lack the necessary discipline or nuanced skill to navigate discretionary trades. Either way, the drop in confidence is not the problem—it's signaling the real problem to be addressed.

When you lose confidence like this, it can easily be misinterpreted as something mental, when the solution will actually come from the technical side of the equation. The drop in confidence is deserved because something is off skill-wise; you just haven't identified it yet. It's better to lose a little confidence, however, than to be overconfident and blindly continue as though nothing was wrong. That's how problems become magnified.

The key is not overreacting to the signal by becoming pessimistic or negative, and losing more confidence. Traders with stable confidence can remain more objective in this spot, knowing they'll eventually figure it out.

On the flip side, a surge of confidence can reflect an expansion of your skill set and reaching higher levels of competency. Something has clicked. It almost feels like you're cheating. Your hard work has allowed you to see these trades so clearly that you can't believe it was so hard to see before. From a practical standpoint, this increase in confidence is confirmation that the front side of your Inchworm is expanding.

But watch out, as this can easily turn into overconfidence when you assume that you've figured "it" out, and you believe you'll continue to make more money now, or that your future goals are assured. Take the rise in confidence as confirmation that your work is paying off and continue your efforts. Don't use it as evidence that you can passively ride the wave, or you'll eventually get into trouble.

COMMON SIGNS OF OVERCONFIDENCE

Being overconfident is like having your head in the clouds while thinking you're on solid ground. I imagine it like a cartoon character who unknowingly runs off a cliff and is suspended in mid-air until realizing what's wrong.

When you become overconfident, you don't realize that your perception, analysis, and execution have begun to degrade. And as they degrade, you become looser with your risk management parameters. Your focus and energy on finding the next idea or adapting your system decreases, and you start to justify getting into a marginal trade. You become more complacent in your decision-making process and put on weaker trade ideas that lack the usual rigor.

Overconfidence is often fueled by a big swing in profitability—perhaps you've had some outsized returns, like your biggest win or your biggest month ever. It also can show up when you start to feel like your understanding of the market or your development as a trader is really clicking. You can overestimate the extent of what you know and start to feel certain about market direction. You become more stubborn and can't admit a mistake, take a small loss, or accept advice from more seasoned traders.

You assume losses are temporary and that you'll continue to print money. You get overly excited about a trade and, at the height of this euphoria, think *This is going to make me rich*, or *I've figured out the market!* For some of you, your head will inflate so much that your sense of superiority will make you criticize other traders or the market as a whole, saying things like, "People don't know what the hell they are doing."

When you're expecting to make money, it doesn't make much sense to bring the usual focus and energy. You might spend less time in front of the charts, or even if you're there, you lack vigilance compared to your optimal state. Overconfidence can pump you full of adrenaline and make you feel on top of the world, and on the flip side, lead to complacency and taking it easy.

As I said in the intro of this chapter, traders experience overconfidence in a wide variety of ways. If you're not showing this emotion outwardly, in a big, dramatic way, then you may assume you're not overconfident. But overconfidence can show up in understated ways too, such as when you:

- Are overly convicted on a particular trade
- Refuse to take profit at your target because you assume you'll make more
- Are eager to trade, but less rigorous in your preparation and execution
- Quickly make decisions because it feels like you can't lose
- Justify more risk by saying, "This has to go up"
- Want to always have action, regardless of the risk
- Neglect valuable signals and focus on only a few pieces to make a buy/sell decision
- Impulsively enter or exit trades

Subtle signs of overconfidence were the reason Brendan, a commodities and futures trader from Canada, hadn't solved his problems executing a morning strategy, which resulted in a lower win rate than his afternoon strategy. He would become certain a trade was going in his favor and think, *100%, I can't possibly be wrong here.* Then the trade would blow out. But his excessive conviction wouldn't allow him to exit—he couldn't admit that he was wrong.

This led to big losses, sometimes up to 30% of his account, as well as to revenge trade. Intent on ending every day green, Brendan would force trades and, instead, too often hit his daily stop/loss. This was particularly painful because easier trades would pop up 20 minutes later, and he couldn't take them.

Brendan also struggled to take profit at his target. Logically he knew a fight for the absolute top wasn't worth the risk, but a desire for perfection compelled him to fight for every cent. Then after a pullback, swirling thoughts about how much he lost would cause him to start looking for trades, rather than letting the trades come to him.

The last sign of overconfidence, and, to Brendan, the most surprising, was in his goal-setting. If he made $10,000 in a month, his goal for the following month wasn't to make 10% or 20% more. No, Brendan would look to make $100,000. He didn't realize how much pressure he was putting on himself with this big of an increase. It made him do things like break the rules he set for how many trades he could take in the morning. His big goals were setting him up for failure, and he was spinning in circles due to the large drawdowns.

When I lay the examples out, one after the other, like this, it may make these signs of overconfidence seem obvious, but in the midst of the daily grind, they weren't obvious to Brendan. Not until he and I started digging into these problems did his outsized conviction, desire for perfection, and unrealistic goals become clear.

At the heart of all of them, we found two main flaws: believing he could be right on every trade, and expecting perfection. Brendan was able to resolve these problems by using the advice in this chapter and the real-time strategy I discuss in chapter 9.

He discovered that he never gave himself credit for any of his successes. The advice I've included in the Perfectionism section was particularly helpful to Brendan, helping him steadily build the muscle, so to speak, of recognizing that he knew what he was doing and was profitable. While it took some time for the new perspective to become second nature, he had the data to see that, over a large sample, he's winning at 60%. Now, when Brendan takes a loss, he just thinks, *This trade is one of the 40%, I'm still playing my game, and in the long run, I make money because I'm following my strategy.*

At this point Brendan is much more consistent, both emotionally and in how he trades. He can take losses easily, doesn't force trades, and is able to "stay out of harm's way," as he explained it. He's able to immediately get back to watching the market for the great opportunities he couldn't capitalize on before.

Similarly, the corrections to his desire for perfection allowed him to take profit at his target, and accept just catching the meat of the move, not the entire thing. His new perspective allowed him to use the logic that perfectionism had hijacked—that one cent is insignificant and not worth the risk to chase it.

Taken together, these improvements have made a substantial impact on Brendan's bottom line. His winrate has stayed the same, but the big losses that caused carnage to his PnL and emotions are gone, and as a result, his PnL is steadily climbing.

COMMON SIGNS OF LACK OF CONFIDENCE

Lacking confidence is like getting a car stuck in the mud. Sometimes, with a little effort and luck, you can get out quickly. Other times, the more you struggle, the deeper you sink, and the more desperate you become. That's when you floor it, looking for a quick escape, and end up digging yourself into a deeper hole.

Confidence can get stuck like this as a result of some big losses, a sustained drawdown, seeing others making a lot of money while you're not, or continually missing opportunities. Suddenly it seems like nothing you try works. You get creative. Lose more. You try to figure out why it's not going well, but you can't come up with an answer. That leads to more doubt and more instability. You force. Lose more. You become negative, thinking things like: *I suck at this! I can't come up with a single winner. I just keep losing.*

You take the rest of the day off, but when you see the juicy trades you missed, you lose even more confidence, now related to weakness in your emotional control or mental game. You don't know why you struggle so much with it, and you assume that no one else does. You question whether you're as good a trader as you thought, and wonder, *If I missed a big move like that, how could I be any good?*

If you're not any good, then what? You can't quit—you've invested too much time. But this is as far as you've gotten. Was it for nothing? Will you fail?

For some, this description will hit home. For others, it's too severe. Obviously, there's a lot of variation in what traders are like when they lose confidence. Here are some additional descriptions of what you might be going through:

- Overly focused on PnL, account balance, or the size of a drawdown in an unproductive way
- Uninterested and making excuses not to trade or find opportunities
- Wondering if your strategy has stopped working
- Difficulty finding new ideas, and unable to trust that what you do come up with will work
- Embarrassed and comparing yourself to other traders who are doing better
- Beating yourself up for not having what it takes
- Thinking you've lost it and can no longer perform up to your prior standard
- Discouraged that you're not making progress
- Depressed or down about your performance
- Feeling like previous success means nothing

- Desperately jumping from system to system looking for something that will work and make money—as if you're looking for *the answer to your poor results*

While some of these signs you will recognize easily, others are less obvious. The following scenarios are examples that you may not immediately associate with having a lack of confidence.

Trying to Hit Home Runs

A hidden signal of a lack of confidence is taking an extreme setup that can have a big return, aka trying to hit a home run. Taking a trade like this can arise from a lack of trust, belief, or confidence in your strategy and your ability to consistently create profit. You're looking for a windfall to give you confidence that what you're doing is right. But a trade like this is outside your system. It's akin to gambling.

Even if it pays off, you're not getting the right confirmation about your skill set and you're actually in a weaker position going forward. Sure, at that moment you have more money in your account, but you got lucky. And you know it. That weakens confidence, and when you inevitably lose confidence again, you're more likely to look for a similar type trade. Next time you might not get so lucky.

The attempt to force a home run type trade is a subconscious attempt to make up for prior losses and escape negative thoughts about your trading—a big win means you must be good and would eviscerate any doubts to the contrary. That's not something you're thinking about consciously when you attempt a trade like this, but often, traders have a hard time understanding why they take them. On the outside it looks greedy, and others around you may accuse you of that.

But it's important to analyze the problem cleanly. If you have a cluster of other signs that show you're actually struggling with a lack of confidence, look closely at what the real intent of taking a trade like this is. It's likely that you're looking to win a lot of confidence quickly.

Quick Tip: When you're feeling low in confidence is not the time to overhaul your strategy, because you're unlikely to do so correctly. Put extra emphasis on executing your existing strategy. You know it can make money, and you'll be able to start rebuilding your confidence in a more sustainable, long-term way. As you start to get back on solid ground again, that's when you can take what you've learned recently and adjust your strategy.

Lack of Confidence Can Pull You Out of the Zone

When you become aware of how incredibly well you're doing, that awareness is a signal that your confidence has not grown large enough to support the idea that you could be this good. Your skills and confidence do not match.

You're surprised by how much money you made, the year you had, feedback you're getting from other traders, or your own uncanny sense of the market. Your perspective on your own competence is artificially low. This often shows up in traders who struggle after going on a heater or who have the best month of their career. If your confidence was in line with your skills, you wouldn't be surprised by what you accomplished, or what you were able to sense about the market. You don't get surprised by things that fall in line with what you expect of yourself. You're only surprised by the truly unexpected.

If someone rings your doorbell and it's your neighbor, you're not surprised. You may wonder what they want, but it's not out of the realm of possibility for your neighbor to ring your doorbell. If, on the other hand, you answered the door and it was the president of the United States, that would be surprising. If you're truly surprised at your performance, you don't yet believe that you could actually be that good.

Quick Tip: If you want to build a bigger pyramid, you need to build a bigger base. When you become surprised by how good you're performing, or how good you've become, don't try to force your intuition or do anything crazy. Return to your B-game and make your base wider by removing technical and mental errors from your C-game.

STABLE CONFIDENCE

In a sense, you can consider stable confidence as the middle ground between overconfidence and lack of confidence. That doesn't mean you feel neutral, robotic, or numb. In fact, it's quite the opposite. You're full of emotion, but that emotion more accurately reflects your real skill, not misperceptions caused by flaws, biases, or short-term results.

Having stable confidence means that your confidence never swings to extremes because of variance, or any other reason. Of course minor fluctuations occur, since growth and variation in your performance is constant, but there is a degree of solidness that remains. The major flaws, habits, or biases have been corrected. As a result, you're more easily able to:

- Perform at a high level
- Evaluate your strengths and weaknesses
- Maintain a clear mind, even during periods of market chaos
- Access and trust your intuition
- Avoid big mistakes
- Adapt to changes in the market
- Focus on finding opportunities and executing
- Focus only on what's most relevant, without getting distracted

Since your level of confidence influences execution, development of trade ideas, adjustments in your strategy, sense of the market, and other decisions around trading, it's important to have your confidence be as stable as possible. For obvious reasons, the goal of this chapter is to help you build stable confidence. As you resolve the flaws and biases you have about your trading skill, you'll get there automatically.

Take David, a retired actor who has been trading bonds, futures, and options part-time for the past six years with the intent of making it a full-time gig. When he and I started our sessions, he was not yet profitable, and confidence issues were part of the problem. Flashes of entitlement and overconfidence would strike when he was doing well. Market movement seemed so easy to understand that he would size up too large and overtrade.

On the flip side, when he was losing, confidence would go way down, and thoughts like *I have no reason to believe that my strategy will ever work again* would lead him to jump to another methodology he thought was better suited for that market. There was a distrust, both in himself and those he was trying to learn from.

For the past few years, David had a "grass is always greener" state of mind, and he leap-frogged from one strategy or instrument to another, based on small samples of data or erratic market conditions. Driven by a life lesson that there was always a better way, he would quickly lose faith in a methodology, even before getting a big enough sample to properly evaluate it.

Through our work, he realized that he had to commit to a strategy and focus more on implementation and understanding his rules under changing market conditions. By sticking with it and gathering a larger data sample, he found the limits of his knowledge and owned up to his shortcomings, instead of jumping ship, all of which led to greater stability in his confidence.

Reducing the loss of confidence was the first step. After that, we needed to tackle the overconfidence. The flaw driving this surge in confidence was essentially the polar opposite to the flaw lowering his confidence—he felt like he had found "the strategy" that would dump money in his backyard, forever. Saying this out loud helped, but he needed a little something more.

After getting to know David, I suggested he create a poster that detailed all aspects of his overconfidence. David took that idea to the next level, actually hiring an artist to draw a cartoon caricature of him with the details listed from his confidence profile to reference during the trading session. Then whenever he would start to become that cartoon version of entitlement, looking at that picture immediately helped him gain some perspective and stabilize his confidence.

For him, this strategy really made a difference, because for the first time in his quest for emotional discipline, David got to use comedy instead of negativity. This fit with his general worldview that life is funny and often absurd. Recognizing his emotional state as cartoonishly overconfident made the faulty logic behind his emotions easy to challenge.

This lighthearted perspective has allowed him to manage the peaks and valleys of trading with stability in his confidence and consistency in routines. He now trusts his methodology—no more jumping ship—and that has led to consistent growth in his account.

MAPPING YOUR CONFIDENCE

Recognizing the signals that confidence is rising too high or falling too low allows you to quickly contain and minimize the damage to your execution. Going through the process of mapping those signals is essential to being able to recognize, in real time, when your confidence has become unstable, so that you can quickly regain stability. Plus, it also provides insight into the flaws causing your confidence to fluctuate and the sections of this chapter you need to emphasize. Follow the steps below to help you create an actual document that maps your confidence.

Step 1

Unlike the prior three chapters, you're not just going to focus on recognizing the signals of a problem. You're going to start out by mapping what **stable or optimal confidence** looks like for you. This gives you a target to aim for, and makes it easier to identify when confidence has risen too high or fallen too low.

Even if you don't experience it very often, every one of you has a version of stable confidence that's unique to you. Write down a short description of what it looks like. Here are some questions to get you started:

- What does it feel like when your confidence is balanced, neither too high nor too low?
- What is your decision-making process like?
- Describe the quality of your focus.
- Describe your energy level. Do you feel calm, fired up, or somewhere in between?
- Are you in the zone?
- Does your mind seem clearer?
- Does your sense of time speed up or slow down?

Take notes after each instance when you have stable confidence. Build your understanding of what it looks like, until your notes become repetitive and it's clear there's nothing more for you to add. If you're currently in a period where you're struggling, and your confidence is low or too high, you may find this step hard. Do the best you can now, and then add more details the next time your confidence is stable.

Step 2

In addition to describing stable confidence, pay close attention to the **fluctuations in your confidence.** Do you tend to predominantly become overconfident or lose confidence? Or do you cycle back and forth from one to the other?

Examine and capture what causes your confidence to go up and down. Be specific about signs of overconfidence and/or a lack of confidence, including:

- Thoughts
- Emotions
- Things you say out loud
- Behaviors

- Actions
- Changes to your decision-making
- Changes to your perception of the market, opportunities, or current positions
- Trading mistakes

Even when your confidence is low, I encourage you to look for the subtle signs of overconfidence too, such as having excessive conviction, being too certain about the future, or being overly complacent.

Keep a document open on your computer or a notepad next to you while you trade, and take notes. At the end of the trading day, review what you found and add additional details. Be as comprehensive as you can. Mapping is an iterative process. You're not going to identify all of the details perfectly at first. Keep an eye out for new details and be sure to add them. Small details matter, and can make the difference when you have an opportunity to improve execution.

If this is hard at the beginning, don't worry about it. Everyone has their own starting point. Use what you find and build on it over time. As long as you keep it in your mind, you'll continually learn more than you knew before. Progress is progress, regardless of the speed. Here are some questions to get you started:

Low Confidence

- What situations typically cause you to lose confidence? For example: losing faith in your strategy, seeing other traders make money, or finding it hard to come up with new ideas.
- How does your body react when you're low in confidence? Do you move more slowly, or slouch in your chair?
- Can you describe the point where confidence drops too low and becomes a problem?
- What, specifically, is going through your mind? What thoughts do you have?
- How is your decision-making process different?

Overconfident

- What situations typically cause you to feel overconfident? For example: big winning trade, getting a lot of praise, or being ahead of your goal for the month.
- How does your body react when are feeling overconfident? Are you restless and can't sit still, amped up, or aware of adrenaline pulsing through your veins?
- Can you describe the point where confidence becomes excessive and turns into a problem?
- What specifically is going through your mind? What thoughts do you have?
- How is your decision-making process different?
- If you also go through periods of lower confidence, is that drop preceded by overconfidence?

Frequently, traders have a tendency toward one or the other, overconfidence or a lack of confidence. But you may have to go through a few cycles of results being up and down to get a clean map. Some of the triggers for the swings in confidence may not happen that often, so you may not get a "perfect" map for a lot longer than would be ideal. That places a greater emphasis on spotting the smaller fluctuations or triggers, because they're typically still related to the larger ones.

Step 3

Once you've gathered a lot of details, organize what you've found by scaling them. Due to the unique nature of confidence, there are a few ways that you can do this. If you tend to only lack confidence, you could set ideal confidence at 10, with 1 as your lowest level. If you tend toward overconfidence, you might do the opposite, where 1 is your ideal level, and 10 describes you at your most overconfident.

Finally, if you tend to cycle between the two, you can do one for each, or combine them, by making 5 your ideal level of confidence, levels 1 to 4 reflecting a lack of confidence, and 6 to 10 highlighting overconfidence.

However you organize your levels, at each one be sure to identify details that clearly distinguish it from another level.

As you assign levels of severity, also split them into two categories: the mental and emotional side of confidence, and the technical side. They sit side by side, so level 1 on the mental and emotional side corresponds to level 1 on the technical side, and so on.

The example below illustrates a scale that puts 5 in the middle as the ideal level of confidence, with 1 to 4 reflecting lack of confidence, and 6 to 10 reflecting overconfidence.

CONFIDENCE LEVEL

Describe the thoughts, emotions, things you say, behaviors, and actions that highlight each level of confidence. Complete at least 3 levels.

10: Feel invincible. Euphoric. Thinking about what I'll do with the all the money I'm going to make.

9:

8: Everything I do is right. Not thinking about potential for losses. Amped up and feel blood coursing through me.

7:

6: Expect the next trade to hit. Excited.

5: Confident and calm. No extra thoughts. Certain on what I'm looking for. Able to trust my intuition. Losses barely register.

4: Pessimistic, assuming open positions will lose.

3:

2: Self-critical and discouraged. Question the viability of my strategy. Feel like I want to give up, but am still fighting.

1: Knot in my stomach. Can't see how I can make money.

TECHNICAL LEVEL

Describe the quality of your decision-making, perception of the market, opportunities, or current positions at each level of confidence.

10: Get even more aggressive with targets, certain they'll hit.

9:

8: Take bigger position sizes. Harder time letting go of trades, and adhering to stops. Take more trades than normal.

7:

6: Making faster decisions and taking on more risk than ideal.

5: Easily stick to my game plan, while sensing what the market is giving me and adapting to it.

4: A bit hesitant, but still executing well.

3:

2: Looking for perfect trades, so don't take many.Overly worried about a reversal when I do.

1: Stop trading.

With that, you have a solid draft that you can use while you're trading to recognize your pattern and quickly respond with the correction. Since these patterns can take a lot of work to correct, don't revise your map until you get consistent evidence that it has permanently changed.

Now, use what you identified in this section to focus on the specific causes of instability in your confidence most relevant to your trading. I strongly advise that you read through all of them, because you may identify issues that you didn't realize you had at first glance. And you may think of additional details to add to your map.

CORRECTING COGNITIVE ILLUSIONS AND BIASES

As I've mentioned before, there are some people who believe cognitive biases can't be changed and that your only defense is to learn about them so you can avoid them. However, biases *can* be changed when you correct the faulty reasoning behind them. The first step is to identify the ones that affect you, and then to dig in to see what's feeding the illusion or bias.

There are many biases and illusions that affect traders. You can do an online search and find hundreds of them, such as the Gambler's Fallacy (where your sense of probability is altered) and the Recency Effect (where you overweight the relevance of information that you've heard recently). This section focuses on the biases that most commonly cause instability and impact the confidence of traders. You might find others that affect you personally, and by all means, use my system to break down and address them.

Illusion of Control

Having control is fundamental to our existence as people, not just as traders. We constantly strive to increase our ability to control our lives, and the same is true as traders. But problems arise when there are elements of trading, the market, or your mental game that you believe are within your control when they are not; for example, price action, opportunities to make money, and tilt, before having worked on it.

Too often traders assume they're in more control of these elements than they are, and that further impacts confidence. In the short term it's hard to know for certain the limits of our control. It's in this uncertainty where illusions thrive.

Believing you're in more control of your trading or mental game than you really are is the primary reason for instability in your confidence.

Here are seven common causes:

1. Belief That You Can Make Money in Every Trade

There is a distinct difference between wanting to make money from every trade, and believing or expecting that every trade should be profitable. This belief gets reinforced when you're running hot, fueling overconfidence. Then as your results turn negative, you force trades in an attempt to make even more money.

In the beginning of the drawdown, some traders will remain defiant and overconfident, generating more mistakes and losses. Others crack, and the belief that used to provide confidence is shattered. The downward mental slide turns into a freefall. After moments like this, when confidence is shattered, traders look to put the pieces back together and rebuild the confidence they had before. But when your confidence was based (in part) on an illusion, your aim needs to be to rebuild your confidence in a new way.

On the surface, it's the idea that you can make money from every trade. No trader can possess that kind of control of the market or their results, and you know that.

So why then does the idea hang around in the recesses of your mind? There must be a deeper reason why part of you believes that it's possible, or wishes that it could be. Perhaps you have a desire to prove yourself, or a belief that you're special.

Or, perhaps, as you'll see in this example of a Mental Hand History, it comes from a desire to be perfect:

1. **What's the problem:** It's so hard to accept when I have down days, and I force trades, average down, and move my profit targets to be profitable every day.

2. **Why does the problem exist:** I want to make money every day. I have the skills to make 5 to 10 times more than what I'm making now. To me, that's perfection, and that's what I'm capable of.

3. **What is flawed:** I can make 5 to 10 times what I'm making now and have days where I lose money. That's not my problem right now. My problem is that I lose my mind and disregard a strategy that I know works, trying to be perfect.

4. **What's the correction:** Perfection doesn't mean profiting every day. If I'm going to try to be perfect, I should focus on perfect decisions . . . knowing full well that I'm unlikely to reach it, but driven to try.

5. **What logic confirms that correction:** I can't control the market or my results in the short term, so even if I were perfect in my execution, I would lose, often. But I'll lose a lot less by focusing on making the decisions within my system.

Make sure the correction to this illusion is at the forefront of your mind. Start the day by reinforcing the limits of your control and where your control lies—your preparation, execution, focus, etc. This trains your mind to focus more on what you can control and less on what you can't.

2. Illusion of Emotional Control

Traders who haven't yet worked extensively on their mental game often have an inflated sense of the degree to which they can control their emotions. Simply put, you expect to always be in control, regardless of how intense your emotions are. You don't consider the brain's ability to shut down higher brain function when emotions become overactive.

When this happens, you can't control your emotions as well, because the part of the brain responsible for emotional control has stopped working. Consequently, you lose confidence when failing to prevent yourself from making greedy, risk-averse, or tilted trades. The assumption is that you should know better, and that they should be easy to avoid. It's inexplicable why you couldn't stop yourself. There must be something wrong with you, but you can't determine what it is, so confidence drops.

This illusion of control is such a problem that I often warn clients that once they've gained knowledge and recognition, they'll mistakenly believe they can control their emotions. Despite the warnings, the problem still crops up because of the hidden belief that they should always be able to control their emotions. Burn this into your brain: *Recognition does not equal control.*

The good news is that the answer to this is quite simple, but for some, it may require a lot of repetition. Deep down you believe that controlling your emotions should happen as easily as breathing. That means you're trying to correct a larger myth: that you can magically control your emotions. It's not magic. Instead, you build that competency when you firmly understand how the brain functions and how to truly correct your emotional reactions—something I'll discuss more in chapter 9. Be really honest about how weak that skill is, and understand and accept that it will take some work, time, and effort to get right.

3. Predicting Outcomes

The mind is always trying to predict the future. However, problems arise when you start to believe your predictions will definitely happen. For example, when you're in a drawdown and assume it will never end, or when you're running hot and feel like it's only a matter of time before you're driving the Lamborghini you've always wanted.

You may also find yourself making more subtle predictions at times, such as thinking *Today is my day!* You start the day excited and eager to battle the market, and this excessive certainty helps you manage small losses or wins. But if your results become outsized in either direction, your ability to maintain discipline and manage your reactions may be compromised by the overconfidence that started your day.

Conversely, when you're thinking negatively about the future, it wears on you. You assume that today isn't your day and you won't make money. You check out mentally, lose focus, put in less effort, miss trades, and undersize the good ones. You say things like, "I'm not feeling it," and stop trading to avoid losing. You lack confidence simply because you believe your negative prediction is accurate.

Both scenarios are caused by the illusion that what's happening now will continue indefinitely. In your mind, it's as if you've pressed the repeat button and today's reality will just continue to play out the same way in the future. A great run or a drawdown is assumed to continue, and that causes an excessive rise or fall in your confidence.

This, in turn, affects your preparation, execution, and ability to respond when problems hit. I've talked in the prior two chapters about this problem contributing to anger and fear. If you haven't made as much progress in correcting those issues as you would like, it may be because the issue is more rooted in confidence than pure fear or anger.

The correction to this problem comes by firmly understanding that your predictions are not certainties; they're estimates. You're not considering a range of possible outcomes and assigning probabilities to their likelihood. Instead, you're convinced that you're going to make money on a trade, lose money for the day, get stopped out, or hit your profit target on the trade, even when you're only 75% there.

You feel justified in these predictions because they feel like they're going to happen, and *that's* how you know there's an illusion at play. Your job isn't to know what's going to happen. You manage the inherent unpredictability in the market by making probabilistic bets within a system.

Recognizing the feeling of excessive certainty (whether positive or negative) is a big part of how you correct this illusion and develop stable confidence. Write down a list of things you think or say when your conviction is excessive and when it's optimal. This will help you to distinguish the difference in real time, so you can dial down your degree of certainty in spots where you actually don't have it.

You may also need to dig deeper and use the Mental Hand History to understand why you need that excessive certainty. What's the weakness in your confidence that forces you to make assumptions about the future? For example, excessive certainty could come from:

- A desire to mask weaknesses in your decision-making , process. Perhaps it's not as robust as it should be because you're half-assing the process.
- Attempts to emulate the confidence that you see in traders you respect and aspire to be like.
- A wish that you could know what's going to happen. Obviously, you'd make quite a lot of money that way.

Getting to the root of what drives your need for excessive certainty is key to being able to consistently treat your predictions as predictions, not as fact. You know that's how it should be, but you have to do the work to get there.

4. Ignoring the Influence of Variance

Some traders think, in the short term, that they're in full control of their results. They revel in profits that aren't entirely their doing, and they berate themselves over losses they didn't cause. Variance is tricky, making it difficult to distinguish the degree to which your PnL is a result of your edge. But traders who struggle with this illusion of control neglect to actively develop a skill that can stabilize their confidence and emotional reactions to their results: the skill to recognize variance.

Your first reaction after reading this may be to assume that your ability to recognize variance can't improve. But think about your ability to spot variance now, compared to your first year. Even though it may still be weak, relative to what would be optimal, you've improved. Now imagine if you worked on it directly. At a minimum, it will help you to reduce overreactions due to variance in either direction.

Here's how: Before looking at your PnL for the session, make note of the trades where you suspect variance was a larger factor, and estimate the degree to which it impacted your results. Then gauge your performance or level of execution and estimate your PnL for the day. Finally, compare it to your actual results.

Following these steps will give you a different feeling. If you were unhappy with your execution, but had higher profit than normal, you should feel less positive and more concerned with how to execute better.

On the flip side, if you lost money, but were very happy with the trades that you took, you should feel less negative than normal. The value here is not to attain perfect accuracy. It's getting you to account for variance in a more deliberate way, so you can view your results more objectively.

What if you already know this, account for it, but still can't help but get caught up in the wave of blaming yourself for losses and/or getting too high for the wins? Then you know it's really not about variance, and is connected to one of the other confidence issues discussed in this chapter.

5. Unrealized Potential

This problem is more commonly found among aspiring traders than veterans. You deeply believe in your potential and envision yourself being successful, maybe hugely so. You're highly motivated to prove yourself and realize that potential. Your belief is so deep that you can actually feel the success you envision as if you've already achieved it.

Confidence artificially rises because imagined results produce positive emotions, even though they could take a long time to attain. It's as if your confidence has already priced those results in. Not surprisingly, like an inflated market, it doesn't take much for your confidence to crash. It's fragile, and even a standard losing day is enough to expose the illusion.

It's easy to get caught up in enjoying the confidence and inspiration that comes from being excited about your potential, which makes this flaw easy to miss. You don't see the harm because the consequences aren't immediate. You enjoy the feeling of success, unaware that it creates instability in your confidence. For instance, normal risk calculations are based on the size of your book today. When you suffer from this illusion, however, you get ahead of yourself and take on more risk, because you just assume growth in your account is inevitable.

When you revel in your own future success, you also make losses more painful. Why? Because now a loss feels like something is being taken away from you, even though, in reality, you haven't earned it yet.

You must understand the importance of balancing a strong belief in your potential with appreciation for all the steps required to realize it. The more you embrace those steps, the easier it is to keep yourself from enjoying future success prematurely. Be both aspirational and realistic. Dial back your level of certainty about the future, and keep working until you have the results, knowledge, and experience to realize the success you envisioned.

6. Handling Feedback

You can't control what people think of you, just as they can't control what you think of them. But it's easy to overreact when being praised or criticized. Pay close attention to the way you're overly influenced by those comments, as it highlights the weaknesses in your confidence.

For example, some of my professional golf clients were standout juniors who received heaps of praise from those around them. "You're going to be on tour, competing with Tiger," people would say. After a bad tournament, however, those same people would pepper them with questions, inquiring what went wrong. The players felt like they needed to defend themselves and prove that they played pretty well, even though that wasn't reflected in their scores.

You may similarly feel the need to defend yourself against questions that come after some losses. The key is to assess the legitimacy and competence of the person making the comment.

As junior golfers, my clients didn't yet possess the sophistication to understand they needed to be skeptical of even the praise they receive—it often came from uneducated sources. A part of their confidence needed that praise, and loved the idea that other people thought so highly of their game. But the reality is that no one could say for sure whether they were going to make it on the PGA Tour, just like no one can know for sure that you'll be a successful trader, long term.

If there's a part of you that needs assurance and praise from others, you risk those comments artificially raising your expectations and causing overconfidence. On the flip side, negative comments can prey on that need for approval and cause you to be defensive, more doubtful of your prospects, or defiant and motivated to prove them wrong.

External feedback, both positive and negative, should ideally represent only a small portion of your overall confidence. Otherwise, your mentality, emotional state, and execution is overly dependent on others. You give up control. Recognize the times where you defend yourself, or revel in praise, as signals of a weakness in your confidence.

7. Expecting to Always Be at Your Best

Being at your best mentally requires that you have full command of the variables that cause your energy, emotions, and mental state to fluctuate. The traders who frequently perform at their best operate from a base of stable confidence. They don't expect to be at that level; they do the work necessary to reach it. In contrast, you just blindly expect to be at your best, and that's a cause of instability in your confidence.

Remember back to chapter 3, where you learned from the Inchworm Concept that your C-game, or your worst, is the only part of your skill set you can truly expect? Everything else is in the process of being learned and requires effort and attention to attain.

You can't control your A-game. When you expect to be at your best, you signal to your brain not to focus on the skills currently being learned. You believe your A-game is automatic, so you presume to have full command of the variables that produce it. Ironically, by expecting to consistently be at your best, it's practically guaranteed that you won't be. Expect your worst and drive hard to be at your best.

An extreme version of the illusion of control that many newer traders have, and that's important to correct, is highlighted by Goro, a client from Japan who started trading cryptocurrencies early in 2017. At that time, he was still working full-time as an engineer, but by the end of that year he would quit his day job to trade full-time.

Soon after he started trading, however, Goro began to feel tremendous pressure. The crypto market was bullish at that time. He made money in his first trade, and soon after, he was making a lot more than he was from his full-time engineering job. He started thinking he could quit and easily make six figures just by working an hour a day. But the market was volatile and had several major corrections that this novice couldn't handle, tactically or mentally.

The tension was exacerbated by the fact that his wife was pregnant with their first child and they were, at the time, living in the U.S., with no friends or family for support. He became obsessively focused on the crypto markets, and he wasn't sleeping well, because he'd get alerts throughout the night. This strained his marriage, because not only was he not there for his wife during her pregnancy and in the months that followed his son's arrival, but he started losing money on top of it. Goro felt like he was failing his family, and it was at that low point when he and I began working together.

In the first several sessions, we found that at the root of Goro's issues were the illusions that he could make easy money, make money from every trade, and always be at his best. One day, we discussed whether he would rather be the luckiest trader in the world or the most skilled, and he immediately replied that he would rather be lucky. That was the turning point, and this Mental Hand History helped him to clearly see the problem:

1. **What's the problem:** I want to have superhuman power that will allow me to maximize profit and eliminate loss from every trade in an extremely unrealistic way.

2. **Why does the problem exist:** I have had this illusion for a long time that it was possible to have superhuman abilities, and deep down I must think it's possible.

3. **What is flawed:** I have 25 years of life experience to prove that it's not possible to have such power, and if I continue to think this

way, I'm basically a seven-year-old. Look at the chaos this one belief is causing in my life—I'm essentially thinking that I can win the lottery. What if I win it? Will I have anything left, other than money? If I don't win, then I'll have neither.

4. **What's the correction:** Since I don't have superhuman power, the only thing I can do is to do the work necessary to become a skilled trader, and accept that no matter how good I become, I can't always be at my best and that not all trades will be profitable.

5. **What logic confirms that correction:** This is the only way to achieve financial freedom through trading. Unless I want to be a lucky fish who wins the lottery, I need to correct this illusion or risk ruining my life.

From that point, Goro started to treat trading with the seriousness required. Three years later, as I write this, he continues to trade crypto, as well as other markets. Emotionally he's graduated from the deeper illusions to more practical problems that I typically see with veteran traders. FOMO and anger pop up from time to time, with some flashes of overconfidence.

Goro estimates that his emotional volatility has decreased by probably 75% since we first began working together. Of the 25% that remains, he's very aware of when it happens and knows how to correct it. For example, as soon as he thinks *I'm a genius*, he makes certain to stick to the plan and looks for a good opportunity to take a profit or close the trade.

Illusion of Learning

If you previously were unfamiliar with the Inchworm Concept, you may have developed errors in your beliefs about learning. These flaws cause emotional volatility, including confidence problems. You falsely assume things about your development as a trader, creating confusion and pessimism.

Or, conversely, you get ahead of yourself too easily and think aspects of your skill set have already been mastered, when they haven't yet. Correcting these errors is necessary to develop stable confidence.

Additionally, here are some of the more common illusions of learning that impact confidence:

1. Premature Mastery

When on a good run, it's easy to be fooled into thinking that aspects of your skill set that are currently being learned have actually already been mastered. This mistake essentially means you think you have crossed the finish line when you haven't yet, like being at mile 21 of a marathon—close, but you're not there yet.

Perhaps you've been in a good emotional state for several weeks, making some money, and you've relaxed a bit, assuming your tilt is handled. Then tilt pops back up unexpectedly, because you stopped actively thinking about the corrections to your tilt. A couple of losses triggered tilt, your mind malfunctioned, and you made a bunch of mistakes.

In the aftermath it's easy to lose confidence, both in your ability to control tilt and the strategy to correct it, even though the actual problem was getting ahead of yourself. The same thing happens when you make trading mistakes you thought were no longer an issue, and you start to question your competency as a trader.

When you reach this stage of the learning process, you feel in such command that it *seems* like you've mastered it. However, reverting back to incompetence, at any time, and for any reason, is proof that skill is still in the process of being learned, and requires more work before being fully mastered. Prior to this book, you didn't have the theory or structure to understand why these mistakes were happening. You got ahead of yourself, because you didn't know any better.

One thing that can help you avoid this problem is understanding the signals that indicate when you've achieved mastery. A critical marker is consistent preservation of your competence under intense situations where you might previously have hesitated, tilted, been fearful, greedy, or emotionally volatile. Another signal is the complete absence of those mistakes within your B-game, whereas before, you still had the thought or impulse to tilt or force a trade.

Until you've gotten those indications, keep running the race—those mistakes are still possible. And if you do make one, be a detective, curious as to why you made them and get aggressive at fixing them.

However, if you can't stop yourself from assuming you've achieved mastery prematurely, there may be a part of you that's desperate for success. As a result, you latch on to any indicator that you're going to be great, will be able to quit your job and trade full-time, or make a ton of money. You're compelled to get ahead of yourself because you're desperate to attain your goals. (Desperation is a topic I talk about later in this chapter, so be sure to read it.)

2. Assume That You're Smarter Than Others

Like athletes who assume their athletic talent is greater than others, traders with this bias assume they're smarter than others to bolster their confidence. It's a subtle issue, and a bigger problem for traders who are more competitive with other traders than with themselves.

If you're the type to constantly look over your shoulder to see where you rank within the firm, or even within a trading group, you're likely jockeying not just for profits and dominance monetarily but for proof that you're smarter. You may say things about other traders like, "This guy is an idiot. I can't believe he made that much last year."

When you miss opportunities others capitalized on, or losses pile up, you're quick to make excuses. Taking the blame would be an admission that you aren't the smartest in the room, and you can't allow your confidence to take a hit.

The main cause of this is a fixed view of intelligence, which comes from an old-school mentality that you're either smart or not. When profit is how you prove intelligence, your confidence ends up rising and falling based on the movement of your PnL. You feel like you're only as good as your last trade. There's no lasting permanence to it. Some traders feel this movement more dramatically, while others deny there's a problem, become defiant, or become arrogant to prevent their fragile confidence from dropping.

Changing your view of intelligence is important, because it's harming your ability to compete with other traders. You end up underutilizing your capacity—you're not learning from losses and mistakes, or at least not efficiently. You're more focused on preserving your position as the smartest, rather than understanding that intelligence is a tool that helps you execute and learn.

The key to evaluating yourself in the short term and still preserve confidence is to embrace the Inchworm Concept. For argument's sake, let's assume you really are the smartest one in the room. Like athletes who rely too heavily on talent alone, you'll still get beaten by traders who work harder, who learn from mistakes faster, and who are more open-minded.

To broaden your view of intelligence, you must remove the association that PnL equals intelligence. Embrace the reality of your own weakness, and more firmly reinforce the idea that everyone has weaknesses. The faster you embrace yours, the faster you'll be able to improve upon them and move your entire range forward.

If you haven't already done so, I recommend you complete the A- to C-game Analysis that I describe in chapter 3. It gives you a way to see intraday performance in a non-monetary way. You'll also better understand the causes of fluctuations in your performance and correct them faster. If you can shift the use of your intelligence in a much more practical way, it will give you greater stability in your confidence, improving your overall performance.

I also suggest you read Carol Dweck's book *Mindset: The New Psychology of Success*. It's a fantastic resource for understanding a fixed view of intelligence.

3. Hindsight Bias

You believe a mistake or a loss could have been avoided if you thought longer, had read an obscure piece of news that others saw, hadn't hesitated, or . . . Fill in the blank with another excuse. As discussed in the section Mistake Tilt, hindsight bias includes a fantasy-like way of analyzing what you could have done differently. You believe your mistake should be easy to fix because you now see what you could have done differently. That's fiction. If it were that simple, you would have made a different decision. This fantasy comes from an inflated sense of your own competence.

This problem is called hindsight bias, but really it comes from an expectation that you know the future. As if you should have the ability to know what factors to consider, what to read, when to pull the trigger, or whatever else could have avoided the mistake. As you look back and identify your mistakes, it feels like you should have known better. But to do that, you have to know a mistake or loss will happen before it happens. Of course, that's impossible, so what's this really about?

What would happen if you were honest about why you failed? What would happen if you didn't make excuses and, instead, acknowledged that you could have done better? Does it feel bad? Would it cause you to lose confidence? Do you become pessimistic about your prospects as a trader? Do you expect yourself to be perfect, or believe that you could be?

The answers to your questions reveal what hindsight bias is protecting. Once you know what you're protecting, that's the problem to work out. Make that problem Step 1 of the Mental Hand History, and use the corresponding section in this chapter to help you fill out the remaining four steps.

Confirmation Bias·

One of the fundamental skills of successful traders is the ability to quickly recognize when you're wrong. When you suffer from confirmation bias, you lose that skill because your confidence is based on the need to be right. Instead, you automatically seek out information to confirm your existing belief and ignore opposing viewpoints.

You lack a thorough analysis of what information is filtered in or out and can have a hard time reevaluating your opinion. You're more likely to ignore contradictory suggestions from other traders. You rigidly hold on to a position in the face of mounting evidence that it's a dog. Or you might quickly jump on the first bit of information that confirms your opinion about a potential trade.

In reality, you can have confirmation bias for almost anything. It could be views of another trader, assumptions about the opportunity in the market this quarter, or thoughts about the type of job a CEO is doing. Perhaps you believe that you're unlucky and destined to lose, or that you're going to make millions. You could be certain a stock will rise because you personally love their products. You can believe a tech stock is poised to pop, pointing to the positive media coverage, and you're so certain of this that you don't evaluate the trajectory of advertising spend, or whether the customer base is shrinking.

Confirmation bias is less about the specific belief and more about a rigid attachment that you have to it. This attachment blocks out opposing viewpoints and shuts down rigorous analysis. Or worse, a more severe version of confirmation bias: you just have to be right.

As a trader, your livelihood depends on a clear perception of what's happening, so you can evaluate opportunities as they are, not as you want them to be. Only when you're realistic do you put yourself in the best position to succeed long term.

To begin cracking through confirmation bias, you need to understand what's driving it. Why do you want to confirm what you already believe is true vs. finding out what's actually true? Why would you want to stop learning? At a basic level, you might lack the skill to properly evaluate opposing viewpoints without losing your perspective. Perhaps you're too easily influenced by other people.

Or you could be afraid that you're going to look stupid. Maybe you're unconsciously protecting yourself from finding out that you're not as good as you think, and that your results to date have had more to do with luck than skill. Perhaps you want to be top dog in your firm or group and want the respect of your peers, but you don't have the results to prove it yet. So you think less of them to boost your own confidence.

Confirmation bias blocks you from identifying gaps in your skill set, knowledge, and perspective. And it stops you from learning. The most basic way to begin correcting this is to identify the beliefs that you're most rigidly attached to. Look for beliefs, ideas, or statements that have been looping in your mind—day after day, month after month, and even year after year—without changing.

If you were truly evaluating information objectively, the story would at least evolve. Instead, the story hasn't changed. Your bias is fixed and you're not open to counterarguments.

Get better at being rigorous in your analysis. Learn how to understand arguments on the other side and prove your point in the face of that argument. Blindly making assumptions is weak. Try to understand, and have your perspective grow or evolve. In the end, your belief might not change, but the rationale that surrounds it becomes strengthened by having to defend it in a more rigorous way.

If that doesn't sufficiently correct your bias, then it suggests that you have a deeper need to "just be right." Proceed to Step 2 of the Mental Hand History to uncover why you're so rigidly attached to being right. It could be caused by some of the examples I gave previously, or you may be defending against the idea of being wrong—indicating a deeper insecurity or weakness in confidence.

In that case, you need to understand what's so threatening about being wrong. It's possible the answer extends beyond trading and is personal. Here's a sample Mental Hand History:

1. **What's the problem:** I have a strong urge to prove to myself that I can do this. I try to force a high R-multiple so that I can step it up.
2. **Why does the problem exist:** If I'm getting high R-multiples, then it's proof that I'm doing this right, and validation that I should step it up.
3. **What is flawed:** Actually no, it's not proof. I could be getting lucky, and if I were getting false confirmation, I would unwittingly set myself up for a crash that would be far more painful than the short-term "missed opportunities" that I could have had trading outside my system. I'm also developing bad habits that I'll have to fix later on.

4. **What's the correction:** I want and need validation through the system. I need to focus solely on execution for the next several months. Nail it, so that I can build the competence and set the foundation to level up.

5. **What logic confirms that correction:** Getting this far is valida-tion in itself that I'm doing something right. I don't need valida-tion day to day, from results.

The Dunning-Kruger Effect

This concept refers to the tendency of poorly skilled performers to over-estimate their abilities, and, conversely, for highly skilled performers to underestimate their abilities.[7] In trading, that means on one side, trad-ers with very little skill become overconfident because they're unable to recognize their own incompetence. They're unaware of how bad they are, and they falsely assume they know more than other traders.

On the other side are highly skilled traders who falsely assume that others share their level of knowledge, and who undervalue their own competence, resulting in artificially low confidence. This concept epitomizes why confidence isn't an accurate measure of competence or future success. If anything, reality would suggest that traders on either side of this issue should feel the opposite of how they do!

The commonality on both sides is a false assumption about your knowledge relative to other traders. Let's look at why your analysis might be flawed from the underconfident side. Perhaps you were raised to be humble, never gloating about yourself, your accomplishments, or what you know. Or it may come from anxiety, nervousness, or fear of standing out, and not wanting the attention or perceived expectations that come with it.

You may also be aware of how many massively successful traders and investors are out there. Not having reached that level, you auto-matically undervalue what you know. This false perspective can be rein-forced, because it's so much easier to look at traders more successful than you, especially those covered in the media, than it is to look behind to see how many traders are less successful than you.

On the flip side, if you're overconfident relative to your actual competence, why are you so unskilled in recognizing your own weaknesses? One reason can be a belief that dominates in Western societies that you can accomplish whatever you put your mind to. This often comes with a general tendency toward denying weaknesses and emphasizing strength.

Or your overconfidence might come from insecurities where you demean other traders in order to elevate your own confidence—the classic "step on somebody else to make yourself feel bigger." So, you assume other traders who don't think like you are dumb, even if they're far more accomplished.

Whether you're an overconfident weak trader or an underconfident strong trader, to correct this problem I suggest completing the A- to C-game Analysis in chapter 3. While you may never achieve a flawless analysis, gaining a clearer perspective on your strengths and weaknesses can help you avoid adopting a misleading level of confidence.

You may also need to establish if there's insecurity or a deeper weakness in your confidence that caused you to become overconfident or underconfident. The Mental Hand History is the tool to help. In my experience, this is often connected to a personal issue that extends beyond trading.

When completing the Mental Hand History, I encourage you to think in more personal terms, even if the problem isn't showing up anywhere else in your life. Often trading can challenge you in ways that other parts of your life don't. So unresolved personal issues emerge when trading, and need to be fixed to stabilize your trading confidence.

Black-and-White Thinking

Evaluating mistakes, losses, the market, or others in a black-and-white, all-or-nothing way is a hidden flaw that can underlie many of the illusions and biases I've already described. When you have a knee-jerk reaction that's truly polarized, your language contains words like "always" and "never." Or you assess your performance as either perfect or terrible, and you often oscillate between one and the other, based on your results. Results in trading are black or white, but you can't evaluate yourself as a trader like that; otherwise you're going to have strong over-reactions.

To see if this is a problem for you, pay attention to whether you often make extreme statements about yourself, other traders, the market, or trading opportunities. The common denominator is whether you have a polarized way of categorizing things—classifying them without any gradation or range.

For traders who tend to cycle between being overconfident and underconfident, this flaw may be part of the reason. You flip from one side of the coin to the other. Feeling confident, you see yourself as a genius; not feeling it, you consider yourself a fraud who has merely gotten lucky.

This flaw was a main cause of Max's problems with greed and, ultimately, confidence—remember he's the forex swing trader who had a 10-level map of his pattern of greed. If he had a losing trade, Max would begin to worry about his competence and his monetary return. He wanted to be more profitable than other traders to prove that he could be successful. There was a distinct need for his competence to be recognized by others, as well as himself.

Losses would make him hesitate to take another trade. He would overly focus on what he was doing wrong and, at times, start to doubt his competence and think he just wasn't a good trader. He'd have to shut it down for a few days to reset.

Before we began our sessions, Max assumed all traders had emotions that interfered with their performance, and he didn't know he had the potential to eliminate these problems. (Another example of black-and-white thinking.) In our first session, we were able to unearth what lay behind his greed and confidence problems. This Mental Hand History shows what we found:

1. **What's the problem:** When greed is at its worst, I am driven by an uncontrollable urge to make the absolute best return, right

now. I'm only focused on making money right now. There's no longer-term thinking.

2. **Why does the problem exist:** When I'm in a drawdown, my confidence weakens; I have more doubt about my ability and my goals. There is less certainty that I can hit my targets. I need to make money now to get back to breakeven or profit, eliminate any doubt, and feel confident enough to say that I'm a consistently profitable trader who could eventually take on investors.

3. **What is flawed:** I have a deep desire to prove that I can do this. The more that I can support myself, the more I prove that I can do this. This desire is healthy, but is taken to an extreme because I need to prove it right now. I don't want to prove it in one or two years; I want to prove it now.

4. **What's the correction:** I can't skip steps. If I want to build a big house, I can't build the third floor before I build the second. I know what I'm capable of, and I know what I've proven to myself already.

5. **What logic confirms that correction:** My confidence is weakened because my perception of my skill is too black and white. Clearly understanding the base of my skill allows me to know that there are always some aspects of my skill set that don't disappear. That allows me to progress in a more linear way, and have the patience to avoid impulsively jumping into marginal trades and, instead, only take the best ones.

To help break out of the black-and-white way of viewing his competence, I had Max identify all of the skills and knowledge that he's mastered in trading so far—all of the things he's good at automatically, and doesn't need to think about anymore. For example, being able to identify the market structure, where the key trendlines are, and support and resistance levels.

I suggested he read and think about the list daily for three to five minutes. What Max quickly realized was that he is a competent trader with a solid foundation that had been built up through thousands of hours of testing, by being involved in the market.

Shortly after completing this exercise, his first signs of progress emerged. Max began seeing short-term decisions from a long-term perspective, allowing him to take trades he otherwise would have avoided, and to accept losses without the urge to immediately make the money back.

He also found he could avoid the urge to close a trade below his target and stay away from trades that didn't meet all his criteria. The latter bit of progress was quite remarkable, and in two instances, he noted, "It was way easier to be on the sidelines, even though they were both in profit. I'm happy that I didn't take them. Why would I break my plan that I spent thousands of hours to create?"

Max still experiences the signals of greed and a weakness in confidence, but his awareness is so strong now, it rarely affects his execution. Plus, with such a strong ability to handle losses, he's now taking more trades and even doing some day trading—something he could have never successfully done before because of his emotional volatility.

For you to correct a polarized way of evaluating, you must, as Max did, identify the situations where you tend to be the most polarized, and integrate a perspective with gradation to it. If your polarized reactions are related to your own competence, completing the A- to C-game Analysis is a great way to start. You'll likely only have an A- or C-game to start, and the task of identifying your B-game will significantly help to correct this flaw:

If your categorization is related to other traders, build an understanding of where their performance contradicts how you label them. For example, if you have written them off as idiots, consciously look for indications where they have performed well and have had good ideas. Conversely, if you lionize them as infallible, bring them down to earth a bit for yourself by identifying weaknesses and the places where they make mistakes.

If your polarized language is related to the market because you're "always getting screwed, and never getting a fair share," begin tracking variance. Look for examples that disprove those statements. Then begin to build in more nuance.

This may be enough to get you to change the specific places where your reactions are too extreme. If not, you need to further investigate why your evaluation is so polarized.

PERFECTIONISM

Perfectionism is complex, with different degrees of severity. Entire books are written on just this one topic. I have also discussed it several times in this book already. In Fear, you learned that the standard of perfection can loom over you and add so much pressure that it can paralyze your decision-making. In Tilt, you saw how expecting perfection caused anger that further degraded your execution. Now, let's go a bit deeper, exploring how perfectionism or high expectations damages confidence, and some different ideas on how to solve it.

The crux of perfectionism is having outsized beliefs about your own capabilities. This is why the advice that "Nobody is perfect" or "Failure is an opportunity to learn" are niceties that don't strike at the root of the problem. Traders are analytical and need more information. You don't make trading decisions based on general advice. You dig. The same is needed here. That doesn't mean we have to delve into the personal. There are some common performance-based causes of perfectionism that you may not yet be aware of.

While some traders have a healthy striving for perfection, often a driver of high performance, it can also be a double-edged sword. The downside occurs when the drive for perfection becomes excessive and creates emotional volatility. That volatility can cause every type of trading error you can imagine. It can also slow progress and create dissatisfaction, which can then lead to burnout, and to finding your motivation and dedication slipping backward.

I want all of you to be driven to be your absolute best, and to find your own version of perfection. But in order for your attempts to strengthen confidence, they need to be balanced with some understanding about the nature of perfection. Perfectionism is not bad. That's too crude of an analysis, which also doesn't account for the upside it provides.

Instead, let's put a spotlight on what's excessive to transform perfectionism into something more productive. In doing so, you can blunt one edge of the sword and minimize the self-inflicted damage, while sharpening the other side that allows you to excel.

First off, Inchworm is the antidote to the "Nobody is perfect" line. Here's why that statement is, in fact, functionally incorrect: It's not about being perfect. That idea of being perfect is too large. No one is perfect. We all have a C-game. We always have relative weaknesses. But that doesn't mean we can't, at times, reach our own version of perfection when we're in the zone and maximizing our capabilities at that moment in time. That's a version of perfection. You can attain it at times, just not over a large sample.

Being perfect in that sense doesn't mean that you squeeze the most profit out of every day. After all, given variance, that's not even entirely in your control. It's more about your own version of perfect decision-making and execution, given your current range. Also, once you reach perfection, the standard rises; performing at that level means the front end of your Inchworm moves forward.

Your capacity grows and a new definition of perfection emerges. You have a new A-game, and the easiest way to reach perfection again comes not by pressing forward from the front but by correcting aspects of your B- or C-game and moving forward from the back.

Whether or not you're aware of perfectionism being an issue for you, it may be helpful to read through the following list. There may be signs here that you would not have recognized that fit under the perfectionism umbrella:

- You put a lot of pressure on yourself to be great
- Constant internal pressure doesn't allow you to relax or take a break, which leads to burnout
- You feel like nothing is ever good enough, even after big profitable days

- You never applaud good results and assume that anyone in your shoes could achieve them
- Self-criticism bubbles up over the slightest missteps, and you treat all mistakes as equal
- You continually feel you're not doing enough compared to others; there's always somebody doing better
- You have a hard time moving on, letting go, or getting over a mistake, because you obsess over them and have regrets
- You perform at your peak infrequently
- You feel like you're falling behind

With those in mind, let's look more closely at two causes of perfectionism: a faulty self-evaluation caused by an accumulated deficit in confidence, and mistaking expectations for goals.

Faulty Self-Evaluation

All of us have an internal measuring stick, in a sense, to evaluate our level of skill, get feedback on how we're performing, and identify what to improve on. At the beginning of the chapter, I stated that confidence problems arise from flaws in your perspective of your skill. In this case, perfectionistic traders have flawed methods of evaluating themselves. It's common for traders to achieve milestones, such as their first five-figure month, and shortly afterward think nothing of it. They fail to give themselves any credit, and miss an opportunity to strengthen their confidence.

Think of evaluating your skill as a game: You gain or lose points based on the quality of every trade you take or pass on. Total it up and you get a score for the day. Daily tallies feed into monthly, monthly into yearly, and so on. The game doesn't stop until you stop trading. Perfectionists consistently fail at this game, **essentially accumulating a massive debt**.

Your internal measuring stick is used to determine how many points you gain or lose. Perfection, or high expectations, represents the standard that you expect and forms your baseline. That means that when you reach that level of expectation, you get zero points—you don't give yourself credit for doing what you're supposed to do. Only when you exceed expectations do you get points. But . . . they can also get taken away after you move the goal posts, or increase your expectations.

The majority of the time you fall below your expectations and lose points. For some of you, this scale is proportional, so when you underperform slightly, you only lose a few points, and when you massively underperform, you lose more. For others, it doesn't matter whether you've fallen slightly below or far below, failing is failing and you lose the same amount.

In this game, points equal confidence. So where does that leave you? In debt. While there have been times you've earned some points, they are strikingly low compared to the massive number you've lost. That produces a hole, or a weakness, in your confidence that can underlie both a consistent lack of confidence and overconfidence.

High expectations initially get you into debt, but as this problem evolves, you begin to believe that reaching perfection will get you out of it. There's a subconscious sense that if you can perform perfectly, your debt will be wiped clean and you'll now feel consistently and justifiably confident.

However, once you've reached a new height in performance, you now expect this standard to show up every time. The goal posts move again. You've just jumped higher, and now expect to jump even higher. The moment of satisfaction is fleeting, as your mind immediately moves on to what's next. Or you don't even experience that fleeting moment, dismissing the value of what you've attained, having already moved on to the next expectation.

Either way, rather than being debt free, you're deeper in the hole. The process repeats, and you think that bigger accomplishments—more money, status, responsibility, etc.—will finally do the trick. This is why you have incredibly successful traders who are miserable; they're so driven by money, they think more of it will finally allow them to be satisfied. Money can't get them out of this debt. External sources—even heaps of praise from others they hold in high regard—can't reconcile the debt.

What you need to do is recalibrate your internal measuring stick and make it more accurate. To do that, you need to recognize that you've been mistaking expectations for goals.

Expectations vs. Goals

The difference between an expectation and a goal is significant. Basically, an expectation implies a guarantee. In this case, it's a guarantee to attain the results you want, which means that you believe that you either have the requisite skill or you're certain to attain it along the way. On the other hand, a goal implies uncertainty. The exact road to that end is unknown, and while the skills needed may be known, whether you can attain them and how you'll acquire them is not.

Expectations just want the outcome and don't care how you get there. Goals come baked in with a recognition of the potential for chaos along the way. While you can be driven with the same level of intensity by a goal or expectation, there's a distinct difference in how you feel when, for example, you pursue a target to make $500,000 in a year.

If it's an expectation, when you face mistakes, setbacks, or failures along the way, you're unprepared and overreact. There's a lot more self-criticism, as well as the potential for overconfidence or a loss of confidence. If you're actually able to attain your expectations, you get zero points and feel nothing, or perhaps you even feel worse.

Whereas with goals, you're prepared to handle the setbacks, and you understand the lessons and value they provide. Goals imply learning and a lot of ups and downs. There is an implicit understanding that you'll discover new things on the road to getting there. You also gain a sense of pride and satisfaction for each step along the way.

The result of an accurate internal measuring stick is that you have a chance to collect points as you make progress at each step along the way. You build up a reserve of confidence with each milestone you hit, so the finish line is not the first time you feel proud or satisfied. The net result is a stronger foundation of confidence that you leverage to pursue your next goal.

Perhaps the most obvious difference between an expectation and a goal is how you evaluate the outcome when you fall short. As a goal, you might get upset, but rather than dwelling on it, you look proactively at the results:

- How or why did I fail?
- What did I not prepare for?
- Could this have been avoided?
- In what areas have I succeeded and made progress?
- What have I learned?
- How will I do better on my next goal?

The answers to those questions immediately make you better, not only at achieving your goals but at setting future goals.

Many of you will look at this problem and assume my advice is to lower your expectations. No. I want your aspirations to be as high as you want them to be. The problem is not that you want to be perfect; it's that you expect it. The correction is not to lower your expectations. Instead, convert them into a goal.

Conceptually, the only thing you can truly expect is you at your absolute worst, or your C-game. That's the only thing that's guaranteed. The rest of your range—B-game and A-game—have to be earned every day. You get credit, or earn points, when you do. Proportionally, of course. You also get points when you learn more about the cause of variation in your performance, and when you make corrections. Spotting progress is easier when you create an A- to C-game Analysis as outlined in chapter 3, and use it as your measuring stick to get real-time and daily feedback.

Changing how you evaluate your daily performance is **the first step** toward correcting perfectionism. But for it to truly stick, you must go back into your history as a trader and correct the damage caused by your old measuring stick. You need to get yourself out of debt. Obviously, you can't change what has happened in the past. But changing your perspective on it can reconcile the lost confidence that you earned but didn't accumulate.

Very often there are past accomplishments or benchmarks that, at the time, weren't given the proper respect, praise, or acknowledgment. It doesn't matter if your spouse, friends, co-workers, or boss lauded you with praise and even threw you a party. Your perspective is what matters.

Go back and look at all the accomplishments you've had since the start of your trading career—successfully getting off the sim, your first profitable month, the first time you made more than $10,000 from a single trade, etc. Big or small, write down as many of your accomplishments as you can, especially the ones where you felt ho-hum, and didn't feel particularly proud of, or satisfied by, them.

As you start going through your accomplishments, keep an eye out for "Yeah, but . . ." entering your mind. This common phrase is used to downplay what you've accomplished. "Yeah, but . . . I could have made more/done more/worked harder." "Yeah, but . . . compared to so and so, it's nothing." More is always out there; that's the way of the world. And the accomplishments of others have no relevance to what you've attained.

The second step is to list all of your past accomplishments and write precisely how you achieved each one. What were the steps you took? What did you learn? What difficulties did you encounter, and how did you get through them? Now, looking back on it, how was it a building block or stepping stone to where you are today?

You also don't have to have a completed list before you start delving deeper into each accomplishment; you can go back and forth. More important is how you go about listing your accomplishments and writing about them. This can't be a task you do for two hours on one day and that's it. You're trying to reshape your perspective. It's far more effective to do it regularly for, say, 5 to 10 minutes a day.

An accumulated deficit makes you feel like you're starving for confidence and the next accomplishment on the horizon seems like the feast that will finally satisfy you. Only it's a mirage, and you're just eating a pile of sand. The process of doing 5 to 10 minutes per day, perhaps even several times a day, is like eating. You're feeding yourself the confidence you have been starving for. Once you've gone through this process for all of your accomplishments, review them. You might learn more as you go through a second round, further instill the correction, and strengthen the new way of evaluating yourself.

Step three is to extract and confirm the skills or assets you've learned as a trader, especially those you take for granted. You can do this along-side your review of past accomplishments, but keep them listed separately. The point here is that your perfectionism doesn't care about the details of your skill set; it just demands perfection. This is your way of easing back that intensity. For example, your skills might include:

- Making quick and accurate decisions
  when the market goes crazy
- Estimating future price
- Preparing a clear strategy for the day
  and applying it at the right time

Your skills and your past give you stability; review them at the start of the trading day. Then use your A- to C-game Analysis as a new measuring stick at the end of the trading day, and evaluate performance and progress. The combination of these serve to steadily reshape your perspective, fill the hole in your confidence, and allow you to climb higher. You'll be able to capitalize on what comes next by standing on the foundation of what you've already built.

This won't happen overnight, so be aware of perfectionism related to the process of correcting your perfectionism. It can undermine your progress.

The advice in this section was particularly important to Chris, the trader from chapter 4, whose greed was connected to the pain of missing out on life-changing money. Even though it happened years ago, the regret remained constantly on his mind. If, for example, he sold a position for profit, he would immediately think about how he could have made more. As a result, Chris would often get aggressive once a trade turned profitable, and he'd try to turn it into a home run.

In addition to greed, Chris experienced waves of other emotions. At times he felt invincible, as if he had cracked the market, and in this state, would go after losers harder, assuming he'd get the next one. (He'd figured the market out, right? So the next one had to win.) Not surprisingly, his biggest drawdowns came after these periods of over-confidence. The boom-and-bust cycle crashed his confidence, and Chris would question whether his strategy was still viable. That would spark a strong urge to make money in order to feel good again.

Chris also had twinges of FOMO and doubts about the viability of his strategy. After a string of losers, he would try to recoup them to end the day positive by forcing more trades. In addition, anger would arise after he'd get stopped out several times in row—he'd become more aggressive and impatient, and stray from his strategy by entering too soon. However different they may seem on the surface, for Chris, the signals of greed, fear, anger, overconfidence, and a lack of confidence were all related to an expectation of perfection.

Chris knew he had an edge with the system he traded, but he was struggling to comprehend why he wasn't allowing that edge to play out in the long term. Over the years he had read a ton of trading books, but hadn't gotten to the root of his problem. He was trapped in a cycle of managing emotions and couldn't sustain progress. Chris would have high moments and weak moments. There was no middle ground—he'd swing from one end to the other, and there was a direct impact on his execution.

In our first session, we discussed the concepts and strategies from this section. It immediately hit home and provided a new perspective on the trade that continued to haunt him. Between our first and second session, Chris spent some time writing in detail about the trade and realized it was the catalyst for taking trading seriously.

At the time, he had been in an unfulfilling job, with long hours, and was looking for a way out. Despite having no proven system or trading education, he got lucky and found a company that had good fundamentals. It was on the brink of bankruptcy, but there was talk that a big-named bank was coming in with funding. Chris sold his entire portfolio and dumped it all into this one stock, thinking this could be his ticket to a better life.

While he made a small profit, and it was painful to leave a lot on the table, this experience was a turning point in his life for the better. It made him realize that if he really wanted to trade, he needed more expertise. He invested his profits in training and was eventually able to leave the other job and trade full-time. Looking back on it, he realized, "I would have paid $200,000 to be where I am today." Even though the regret is still there, it's significantly less, and no longer triggers greed.

In addition, Chris really benefited from the A- to C-game Analysis, and by journaling during trading sessions. He once swung from A-game to C-game, but now, even if taking losses, he's able to maintain a solid B-game and doesn't trade outside his system.

Also, his awareness of his emotions is high enough that he can quickly recognize and correct emotional reactions before they get too big. His baseline level of emotion is lower, and it no longer feels like a problem he has to manage. For Chris, knowing that he has a system for the mental game has freed him up to make progress, knowing perfection is no longer the standard.

DESPERATION

In a flash, a mixture of anger and greed takes over. *Fuck it.* You don't care anymore, you switch to a one-minute chart, triple a position as it falls, and fire off several more trades without even thinking. For some traders, their desperation is so intense, it's as if they black out, and wake up unaware of how they lost all that money.

Maybe you're one of those who struggle more with fear and are overcome by a desperate need for certainty. Nothing you do works, losses pile up, and panic rises. You hop from one system to another, convinced these new ideas are creative, but really, you're just frantic for something to work.

As losses mount, greed, anger, or fear builds, making it impossible to avoid the urge to do something—anything. It gets increasingly stronger, like an itch you *have* to scratch. For some, winning is the only thing that can make the itch go away. Squeeze out a few winning trades or a profitable day and you get some breathing room. But that's only temporary. Once losses pile up again, desperation returns, as though it had never left.

Some traders actually need to lose more in order to scratch the itch. Losing feels good, because it gets the pain over with quickly, and provides relief from the pressure and uncertainty.

Desperation is distinguished by an intense urge to do almost anything to make money or avoid taking a loss on the day. It's often hard to recognize desperation because you're paralyzed by fear, or blinded by rage or greed. Those emotions are so big and obvious, they're what get noticed. But regardless of whether desperation includes greed, fear, or anger, the underlying cause is connected to weaknesses in confidence. Those emotions would not reach extreme levels if your confidence were stable.

Confidence is your emotional foundation, and weaknesses are the cracks in it. Up until this point in the chapter, the weaknesses in confidence that I've covered, while problematic, have been on a smaller scale. Desperation, on the other hand, is a big, gaping hole.

The question becomes: Why does this gaping hole in confidence exist, and what are the flaws that have made it so large? It's not just one issue. To have your mentality fall to this level means the problem is complex. You'll have multiple flaws or biases revealed in this chapter, as well as likely from the Fear or Tilt chapters. Self-criticism, too, is a common and large part of the problem that makes desperation exponentially harder to correct.

Desperation is also marked by a significant amount of accumulated emotion. The intensity of the greed, fear, and anger that show up is so strong that it instantly takes over your mind, drowning you in so much emotion that your reactions are beyond reason. Intense emotions at this level create a sense of disconnection, where you do things that don't make sense.

Even though you may be aware in the moment of how irrational your reactions are—in some extreme cases forcibly trying to control your hand on your mouse, or yelling at yourself to do something different—you still can't stop from making absurdly bad decisions. Being in this state is like sitting in a movie theater watching a horror movie and screaming "Don't open that door!" And then watching as they (you) open the door.

If this problem has been going on for a while, the emotions have been building up for years. Even if it only recently became severe in trading, working on this problem away from the trading desk is mandatory to both decrease the old emotion and build up the discipline needed to have any chance of remaining in control in these situations.

Accumulated emotion is the real wild card, and if you try to take on desperation without serious preparation, you have little to no chance of correcting it. Rather than showing up unprepared, work with a sense of urgency, as if your trading life depends on it.

It does.

Having your mental game devolve to this point is not something that happens to all traders. This is as extreme as it gets from a performance standpoint. When it happens to skilled traders, it's hard to comprehend afterward just how badly they performed. The gap between normal execution and when desperation strikes can make it seem as if the trader's possessed by a demon.

Much like a person addicted to drugs will do anything to score their next fix, a desperate trader will do almost anything to make money. But *almost* is the key word. The distinction between what you will and will not do determines whether you have a performance issue that could be addressed by using this book, or whether you have a clinical, non-trading problem that requires the direct assistance of a therapist or psychologist.

Think about when this problem is at its worst, and consider whether you can remain in enough control to function as a trader, afford the financial losses that may happen while working on this problem, or tolerate the implications in your personal life. If you're going to work on this issue by using this book alone, you're accepting those and other potential risks, and you must be ready to work hard. You're in for a battle.

In a few other sections I alluded to the possibility that the flaws or biases affecting your confidence may have personal roots. In this case, there is a near certainty that it does. As you dig through the performance issues, ask yourself questions about why your emotions are so intense, how they're connected to your past, and if they show up in your life outside of trading. Resolving the personal side of this problem is necessary to have any success, and, of course, this book alone won't do that.

Although sometimes hard to accept, an idea that has helped clients with this issue is thinking of themselves like an injured athlete. Some of you may have such a severe injury that you need to step away from trading to heal and work on the problem for days, or weeks, or longer. This amount of time is what it will take to build an understanding of what's causing it, and to personalize the strategy that I outline below to prevent desperation from destroying your trading.

1. Maintain a Sense of Urgency

It's a major mistake to take desperation, or the steps to correct it, too casually. If you think that you'll wake up one day and the problem will be gone, you're delusional. Problems of this severity aren't fixed overnight. To have a chance of fixing this problem, it has to be your top priority.

2. Map Your Desperation

Map the greed, fear, and tilt that are the day-to-day issues that eventually lead to desperation. These details become an early warning system. Desperation is possible every single day you trade, until you have proven that it's not. You have to take aggressive steps at these early signs, even though they might not turn into that big of a problem yet, to have any chance of preventing desperation.

3. Set Strict Daily Stop-Loss

Sure, you've probably set these before and blown through them, but that doesn't make it a bad strategy. Especially since it's unlikely that you've combined a daily stop-loss with these other steps, meaning you had little chance to control the emotion that forced you to disregard it. A daily stop-loss is not just important to preserve capital; it also protects confidence and prevents it from taking too big of a hit.

4. Book Wins

In normal situations, you want to keep your foot on the gas pedal. But in the early stages of correcting desperation, the losses that come after some big profits can be more painful and damaging than losses at the start of a day. Since overconfidence and fear can negatively impact execution after earning outsized profits, booking a win and shutting it down is a temporary crutch that you should use. You have significantly less to gain than what you have to lose, from a mental and emotional standpoint.

Greed might compel you to push too hard—driven by a desire to instantly correct your confidence problems. Or the slightest drop in profit might induce tilt and cause you to force entry into a marginal trade. These setbacks reinjure your confidence. Book a win to preserve confidence so that you can go into tomorrow with something to build on. Do it with tomorrow in mind.

5. Take Regular Breaks or Use a Timer

Maintaining emotional control throughout the session is critical. If greed, fear, or anger take over your ability to think, you're far more likely to succumb to the intense accumulated emotion that follows close behind. A timer increases the likelihood that you can disrupt and correct these problems. While this strategy is disruptive, and may even keep you from trading your best, it's far better than the alternative.

6. Take Aggressive Action Toward the Early Signs

To take action early, go through the steps in chapter 9 to devise a real-time strategy to disrupt the problem and gain control of it.

7. Recognize Small Steps Forward

Recognizing sessions where you make progress gives you a boost in confidence to keep you working hard. Remember, increased recognition or awareness, not emotional control, is often the first signal of progress. Desperation is a major problem, and eliminating it takes sustained effort over a long period of time. When small improvements go unnoticed, you might abandon a strategy that's actually working.

8. Release Day-to-Day Accumulated Emotion

In the early stages of containing and correcting your greed, tilt, fear, or confidence issues, you'll create a pressure-cooker-like effect. You'll get better at containing the emotion during the trading session, but if you don't release it, several days can go by where you feel like you're making improvements mentally and emotionally, which you are, but then one day you'll snap, and it will feel like the emotion just came out of nowhere.

Use the Mental Hand History at the end of *every* trading session to digest and release the emotion. This is especially important after days that sparked a lot of emotion, where you were still able to prevent desperation from setting in. Celebrate that win, but digest and release the emotion. Otherwise, your odds of blowing up tomorrow are greater.

9. Correct Self-Criticism

I have yet to work with someone grappling with desperation where self-criticism wasn't a massive problem. When your reactions are so out of line, it makes sense why they deserve criticism. But it doesn't help. You need to think practically about why you failed, and why desperation occurred. Learn from it and improve your strategy. Keep working the problem in a practical way. The faster you can do that, the more likely the next iteration of the problem will allow you to take another step forward.

10. Correct the Fuck-Its

When you're so deep in a hole, a common tendency is to say, "Fuck it," and try to hit a home run. What's the harm? If it pays off, you get the benefit of escaping hell today. But that might also reinforce the idea that you can pull off an escape like this again. That makes you less vigilant about the work needed to keep yourself out of such spots to begin with.

Trying to hit a home run in such a compromised mental state is weak. You don't reinforce quality decision-making. Instead you reinforce the option to gamble as part of your range. Sure it's really hard to walk away with a loss, especially a big one, when you have capital you could use for your escape. But you have to think about tomorrow.

What's the value of the capital and confidence you preserve for tomorrow? When you're strong enough to be able to take a loss and show up stronger the next day, you've got something to build on. The fuck-its may be fun and make for a good story when they pay off, but that's not why you're here, right?

Before every trading session, review your strategy to prevent desperation, as if rehearsing for an emergency that has a high chance of occurring. This keeps all the details of your plan fresh in your mind, so that you're ready to act. Be especially firm on this after several days or weeks of success. Complacency in your preparation is dangerous. Realistically, you'll need to go through several market cycles, or a minimum of three to six months, before you'll have firm evidence that desperation is improving or no longer a problem.

This is a major issue, and, like a severe physical injury such as tearing your ACL, the rehab is long, so buckle up. But if you're serious about trading, you must tackle this problem, and your best shot may be by working with a psychologist, therapist, or coach. You could even bring them this section of the book to further bolster your regimen.

Gurdeep, a part-time trader from the U.K., can attest to the time and effort required to correct desperation. Using the 10 steps that I outlined above, it took him around three months to see any progress, and another six months to prove he could trade without blowing up. That was with my help. So, on your own, it will be a challenge to say the least.

Let's look more closely at how Gurdeep managed to get on the other side of desperation. When he and I started working together, he had been day and swing trading for three years without having made money. He had a mentor, who described him as a good trader with a lot of potential, who had to gain control of his emotions.

Every month, even every few weeks, Gurdeep would go through a series of boom-and-bust cycles—making $10,000 and then losing it all back and then some. At any moment, a normal loss or the threat of a losing day could trigger a cascade of revenge trading, doubling down on losing trades, and raising his stake on subsequent trades, all in an effort to make money back and end the day green.

Out of the gate we worked on mapping his revenge, which was the big problem that could eventually lead to desperation. It took about a month, and a few big blowouts, to get a clear map, and another month before it was precise. Gurdeep really embraced the detective role, and mapping the details of his tilt immediately afterward proved to be a big eye opener—seeing every step on paper was a boost to his confidence that he could eventually beat this. Even though he knew the problem was going to take a lot of work, he had previously felt consumed and overrun by his emotions. Now, he could see the emotions coming, and that was powerful.

At this point we established a zero-tolerance policy, deciding that if his tilt rose to level 3 on his scale, he had to shut it down for the day. That was the last point where he could possibly retain control without needing luck from the market to avoid a massive losing day. Over the next two months, the boom-and-bust cycles continued, but Gurdeep showed small signs of progress after each cycle.

Sometimes the progress was a clearer understanding of the performance flaws or personal issues causing the intense emotions. At other times, he was able to recognize the urge to get his money back and seek revenge, and instead, quit the session.

At the heart of Gurdeep's desperation lay personal issues of low self-confidence. Losing money was devastating, and made him feel worthless. That was further reinforced by the self-inflicted losses that came from his lack of emotional control, and a growing sense that he was running out of time to make trading work out. For him, every trade felt like his identity and future were on the line. Add in a mixture of high expectations, intense self-criticism, and common performance flaws, and Gurdeep had a prototypical recipe for desperation.

As we worked through these issues, the intensity of his emotions began to stabilize. We doubled down on this progress by tightening his routine. He would spend one to two hours on the simulator before a trading session to practice executing his strategy.

During the session, an alarm would go off every 15 to 30 minutes to remind him to check on his emotional state and review corrections to his flaws. Then after every session, Gurdeep evaluated his process, looking for mistakes to improve and improvements to praise. When he tilted, instead of getting angry at himself for tilting, he tried to understand why it happened and what was driving the anger.

Seven months in, the cycles became less frequent and less severe, but Gurdeep continued to work the process. He'd take weeks off when personal issues added emotional volatility to his trading that he couldn't control. He set realistic goals to ease back the time pressure. He continued to work on his confidence issues and understand more about what made him a competent trader. He maintained a strong commitment to his routine.

All of that hard work paid off. Now, Gurdeep's tilt is caused by flaws that are more normal among traders—like being too PnL-focused, or getting stopped out by just a few ticks. More important, he believes he can make it as a trader and is motivated to realize his full potential.

HOPE AND WISHING

After an intense section like desperation, you might read the title of this one and assume that I'm going to talk about hope and wishing in a positive, uplifting way. Well, the opposite is true. My goal for this section is to kill your hope and wishes. *Welp.*

To be blunt, there's no place for hope or wishes when it comes to trading, or any area of performance, for that matter. Sure there's a place for hope and wishes in other parts of your life, but in this environment, they're dangerous, undermine your confidence, and stunt your improvement.

For those of you who routinely succumb to hope and wishes, it may be so common, or such an ingrained part of how you operate, that you may not even realize they're there. They come out only at particular moments, showing up in isolated ways and giving you the impression that they don't affect you.

Hope

Hope is an emotion connected to things we can't control. Hope can be a useful emotion in society, with so much of our lives affected by things outside of our control. We can hope for good weather when we host a BBQ or go to an outdoor wedding. We can hope our airplane lands safely, and on time. But hope has no place in performance.

Time and energy spent focusing on things that you can't control are wasted, and they need to be redirected to places where you have the opportunity to improve your control—like on your execution, or how you handle your emotions. Here are some of the ways that hope seeps into trading:

- Hoping that you don't get stopped out, that you'll reach your target, or that your loser will get back to breakeven
- Babysitting a trade, hoping your presence will yield more profit
- Hoping you have a great month, or that your results turn around
- Losing hope that you can get over the hump and realize your goals
- Becoming so hopeful about your own potential that you feel like your future has already been realized

At your lowest points you may have felt hopeless. Essentially you believed there was nothing you could do to achieve your goals, and you had thoughts like *I can't see how things are going to turn around; I should just quit,* or *No matter what I do, it's not going to make a difference, so why bother?* You believe that you don't have control and that you never will. Your hopes have been dashed.

To begin correcting this problem, think about the reasons why you turned to hope in the first place. For one, since it's common in society, you may have assumed it was ok here. Or you might have deep doubts about your ability to succeed. Rather than deal with those fears about your incompetence, you automatically turn to hope as a way to manage that. Start by identifying where hope exists and ask yourself: What's it protecting? Basically, what do you not feel in control of, and why not?

Then—as I sometimes joke with my clients—fuck hope. It's that simple. Putting energy into something you can't control or, worse, giving up control in spots where you need it, is dangerous. Even though it's small, and seemingly innocuous, what happens when what you hoped for doesn't happen? Whatever it was that hope was protecting gets exposed. Like ripping off a Band-Aid.

Immediately, your lack of control becomes obvious—higher emotional volatility as you overreact to losses, mistakes, and setbacks. Or, if what you hoped for materializes, you assume control of more of those big wins.

In a larger sense, when you rely on hope, you're not controlling all that you actually could control. Like a lot of things, the first step is awareness. If you have confidence issues and, by this point, haven't figured out what's causing them, or if you're missing something in your analysis, hope may be affecting you in a subtle way.

Wishing

Identifying the wishes that are hidden in your mind is critical. Wishing not only causes instability in your confidence but also negatively affects your ability to correct the flaws, biases, and illusions already impacting it. Wishes, such as to always perform at your best, know the direction of the market, or learn easily, are usually harbored deep in the recesses of traders' minds. Surprisingly so.

Many traders are stunned to realize their confidence is affected by wishes like these. They're illogical; that much is obvious. And yet, as impractical as they may be, many traders have them.

It's one thing to want to always perform at your best, know the direction of the market, or learn easily, but it's quite another to wish those outcomes could be real. When you have wishes such as these, it means that you actually believe they're possible, and hold out hope that, one day, they could come true.

Why would you work as hard as you could to improve as a trader when, deep down, you believe you could predict the direction of the market? Why would you be openminded or try to learn about the mental game if you believed your emotional problems could be corrected easily? If you believe your wishes will be granted, it would be illogical to work hard.

Since spotting these wishes is tough, try this process that I go through when I'm working with a client. First, take a few deep breaths to relax your mind and suspend logical thinking. Logic believes these wishes are absurd and will deny their existence. Put that part of your mind aside for a moment and allow your gut to react to the following questions. Answer them as honestly as you can:

- Do you wish that variance wasn't part of trading and that you could make what you deserve?
- Do you wish that you could have perfect discipline and always execute your strategy correctly?
- Do you wish you had the perfect method, system, or indicator that would allow you to print money?
- Do you wish you could have masterful control of the markets and make millions?
- Do you wish you could make money every month, every day, or from every trade?
- Do you wish you could watch a video or read a book and be able to instantly apply all that you have learned?
- When in a big hole, do you wish for one trade to get you right back to even?
- Even if you don't wish for any of these directly, as you read them, does a part of you think any of them would be cool outcomes?

Your answers will range from a firm no to a resounding yes, or to somewhere in between. Wishing isn't a black and white thing. Wishes show up in matters of degree. Regardless of how small they may appear, correcting them is vital to developing stable confidence.

Wishes are hard to eliminate. They're like a stubborn mule that won't budge; the more you try to force them to go away, the more intractable they become. Force won't cut it. This should make sense, as you're essentially trying to wish them away. Instead, you need to get to the heart of the wish and resolve it.

To make working through this process easier to conceptualize, here's a story of a trader whom I worked with who found that a wish was surprisingly at the heart of an issue he had with FOMO. Nick is an aspiring full-time trader from the U.K. When he and I worked together, he was an office worker in local government, but due to the coronavirus pandemic, he was able to trade for an hour when the U.S. market opened.

Here's what Nick described in Steps 1 and 2 of his Mental Hand History:

1. **What's the problem:** I don't want to miss out on the opportunity of the day. So when I do, I want to make it back somewhere, and begin searching for a trade that will make the money I should have made. That FOMO can even carry over to the next day. I get hyped up and go into the day thinking *This is going to be a big day*, but I instead end up with massive losses.

2. **Why does the problem exist:** On days where the opportunities are there, and clear, I should be good enough to take them. I also look back and see that my plans are working, even if I haven't traded them well. I realize that hindsight trading doesn't make sense, but I expect the market will provide the same opportunities again, the following day, and that those next trades will be winners.

When he said, "I expect the market will provide the same opportunities," I sensed there might be a wish behind such a statement. I asked him to do a gut check: to take a deep breath, shut off the logical side of his brain, and allow his gut to answer if he wished the market provided the same opportunities each day. He immediately said yes, and added that he also wished that he could trade perfectly and go on a big win streak that would never end.

We continued with those wishes as the new first step in the Mental Hand History:

1. **What's the problem:** Part of me wishes the market could provide enough good opportunities each day that I could trade perfectly and go on a big win streak that never ends.

2. **Why does the problem exist:** If the market gave me perfect opportunities and I traded them perfectly, then I would catch all the big moves and that would prove I'm successful. Leaving money on the table when the market leaves it there for me says that I'm behind everyone else who was able to take advantage of the day, and that I need to make up for that.

3. **What is flawed:** Opportunities are easy to see in hindsight. I often look back on a chart and think, *That was the most obvious thing.* But it's only obvious when you already know what's going to happen. That doesn't mean that I will be able to see and take them in the future. What I'm really looking for is to eliminate the doubt or uncertainty that I am profitable enough to make it as a full-time trader.

Working through the layers of this problem, you can see that Nick's FOMO on the surface was actually caused by deeper concerns about his ability to make it as a trader. When nailing down a correction in Steps 4 and 5, it was important that it corrected both the FOMO and the wishes. Here's what we came up with:

4. **What's the correction:** It's ok to have uncertainty. That's an inherent part of this game. Continue to learn and develop your competency, and that will allow you to capture more of the opportunities, but never all of them.

5. **What logic confirms that correction:** I can't be perfect, and trying to be puts my dreams at risk.

For Nick, the biggest benefit of the process came from realizing how silly these wishes sounded. He prides himself on being a logical thinker, and having to admit that he was invested in these wishes made him quickly realize how unrealistic they were. This immediately removed some of the pressure to be perfect, and his work around trading became more efficient, such as focusing on screenshots and journaling.

Additionally, his view of the market, and how he needed to oper-ate, became much more realistic. Perfect patterns rarely present them-selves the way Nick wished them to, and letting go of this wish allowed him to recognize the edge he was previously missing by trying to be perfect.

He also became better at spotting those moments where a wish would pop up; for example, a reaction like, "Ahh, I should have been able to take this." As a result, he could focus more on what was actually real-istic. The more he did that, the more comfortable he became with what was realistic and unrealistic, and that further decreased the power of those wishes. Plus, he stopped daydreaming about unrealistic situa-tions, freeing him up to see opportunities in the market without a false narrative that had plagued him before.

Such wishes can never come true. Believing in them is no different than believing Santa Claus delivers presents to millions of kids in one night. Instead, change your wish into a realistic goal and come up with a strategy and plan. Then look for the subtle, or not so subtle, ways in which wishes hijack your efforts, and correct them in real time. As you work that process steadily, over time, your confidence will become more stable, and you'll notice how much easier it is to be at your best.

No matter where your confidence problems stem from, you now have a good understanding of how to create stable confidence in your trading. As this aspect of your mental game improves, so will your abil-ity to be consistent in your decision-making.

Now that you've learned how confidence, as well as the other primary emotional problems, can interfere with your trading, it's time to dive into discipline. We couldn't take a close look at this problem until you had experience teasing out the effects of greed, fear, tilt, and confidence on your execution. But at this juncture, you're ready to see if any discipline problems are holding you back. That's coming up in chapter 8.

DISCIPLINE

"Talent without discipline is like an octopus
on roller skates. There's plenty of
movement, but you never know if it's going to
be forward, backwards, or sideways."

—H. Jackson Brown, Jr.

So far, I've covered the emotions that cause problems you previously thought were due to a lack of discipline. You now understand that emotions compelled you to trade against your strategy; for instance, by forcing a mediocre entry, jumping into a sideways market, or impatiently closing out a trade before you hit your target.

You've learned that your attempts to remain disciplined weren't going to work. A lack of discipline wasn't the problem. Powerful emotions were the problem. If you've taken steps to correct the flaws that lie beneath those emotional issues, you're ready to take on any actual discipline problems that remain.

If you've come to this chapter directly, or you're unsure if you've made enough progress correcting your emotional issues, don't worry. You'll get feedback pretty quickly on whether the issue is related to emotion or discipline. If you make a good effort to use the advice in this chapter for two weeks of full-time trading and you don't make progress, the odds are high that you need to address underlying emotions first.

Or, if you only make temporary progress but quickly slip back into old habits, you need to prioritize correcting your emotions *alongside* the advice in this chapter. If you're unsure whether or not you're ready to take discipline head-on, make your best estimate and the feedback will tell you whether or not you're ready.

For some of you, achieving emotional resolution has already led to automatic improvements in discipline. Essentially, you had the capacity or skill to be disciplined, but it was hidden or impaired by those emotional issues. Once they were removed, your capacity for discipline sprang to life.

But for others, resolution is like building a house in a forest. Resolution comes in and clears the land, creating the space to erect new habits. But you still have to get in there and build the house. It's not like, all of a sudden, when the ground is cleared, you have a beautiful house to live in. You need to build your discipline from the ground up in the newly created space.

For help in building discipline, there are a ton of general resources out there, such as *The Power of Habit* by Charles Duhigg, *Atomic Habits* by James Clear, or the Stephen Covey books. This subject is widely covered by experts who specialize in developing structure and discipline, and the advice applies well to traders.

In addition, the general framework for what makes a disciplined trader has already been pretty well defined. I'm not going to talk about that structure, or tell you to do a daily trade journal, track your trades, or analyze charts, for instance.

But if despite knowing what you ought to be doing, or having read resources like the aforementioned, you continue to lack discipline, something is missing for you. What I provide in this chapter is some advice on how to tackle the problems preventing you from establishing the consistent habits you know will enhance your trading. And maybe even to think about discipline a little bit differently.

Discipline is not a one-and-done deal. You don't just become disciplined. It's not a static achievement that's accomplished once—"I'm disciplined!"—and then never thought about again. Neither are you someone who is either disciplined or not. That's too basic an analysis. All of you, right now, are disciplined. Everybody has their own degree of discipline. It's impossible to be at this stage of your life without having some of it.

You have areas of strength, regardless of how weak they may be compared to other traders. Maybe their discipline C-game ranks above your discipline A-game. But you have to look at it through your own range. You must establish where you're currently weak to make progress.

Discipline follows the Inchworm principle—you have both a range and an opportunity for continual growth. The definition of an optimal level of discipline changes as your goals change. But for a lot of traders, there's a large gap between where they aspire to be and where they are now. This chapter is designed to help you eliminate your current discipline C-game and narrow your range.

Your ability to be at your best is linked to how strong you are when you're weak. Being stronger, or sucking less, at those times when it's easy to slip back into your discipline C-game is essential to becoming more disciplined. That perspective should motivate you.

You don't have to focus on becoming disciplined, like it's a personality trait, but instead you can pinpoint specific habits at specific times to improve. As you build those habits, becoming more disciplined in executing your trades and the actions around your trading, you create an internal process that's built for growth.

Discipline, however, comes with a cost. There's a freedom that comes with trading, especially for traders who work independently. You get to participate in this worldwide marketplace with massive opportunities. Obviously, there are rules as to how the industry operates, but there's open runway to make it what you want for yourself. Discipline runs counter to that idea, and it can take away some of that excitement. It can make discipline feel more like a chore rather than the thing that unlocks your potential.

In some respects, traders are like artists. Artists usually don't like constraints either. They want to be free to unleash their creativity in whatever way their instincts or intuition guides them. But artists need tools to create—paintbrushes, chisels, etc.—and their creativity is bound by their ability to use those tools. Developing their technique in the use of those tools unlocks their creative potential.

In the same way, discipline is a tool that you use in trading, and if you're not continually upgrading your abilities with that tool, your potential is capped.

THE NATURE OF DISCIPLINE

Discipline comes from a combination of mental strength and willpower. Your mental strength comprises the muscles, and your willpower the energy that fuels them. While mental strength is a concept that gets thrown around a lot, it often lacks a strong operational definition. **Mental strength is the strength of your connection to an idea, concept, or belief.**

Mental strength isn't some esoteric, intangible idea. We can evaluate it much like an athlete would assess their muscular strength: How well does their body hold up under the conditions of competition? Where is it strong? Where is it weak? Where does it break down and fail, and why? At some point your muscles will eventually weaken or fail, in competition or doing hypertrophy training in the gym, and that gives you an indication of your current capacity.

In the same way, when you look closely at breakdowns in discipline, examine the ideas, concepts, or beliefs that fail to hold up in your mind. Then try to determine what makes them weak, what flaws might exist, and what ideas might be acting against them.

Think about the people that you believe are mentally strong, and consider the ideas that most deeply personify that strength. Perhaps someone is devoutly religious—they have an intense connection to the religious doctrine they follow. How about a U.S. Navy Seal who lives by the creed that "If knocked down, I will get back up, every time. I will draw on every remaining ounce of strength to protect my teammates and to accomplish our mission. I am never out of the fight."[8]

Or the athlete who always believes they can win, no matter what, even against insurmountable odds. These ideas are so deeply embedded in their mind that they hold up under the most intense circumstances, and make that person mentally strong.

In trading, consider the idea of preparing for the trading day and properly reviewing it afterward. This is part of a daily routine that you intellectually know is important, but how strong is the connection you have to it? Does it hold up on days when you've slept poorly, or tilted? How about after big winning or losing days, or in an extended drawdown, or after months of consistent profits?

Those situations challenge the degree to which the importance of a daily routine is strong in your mind. When you have a rich understanding of the value it provides, the consequences for half-assing it, the steps to completing it, the methods of adapting it—*and* you have practiced enough to master it—there's such strength behind the routine that it happens automatically in those situations. You can't help but do it. That's just how you operate.

COMMON SIGNS OF DISCIPLINE PROBLEMS

Many of you already know the instances where you lack discipline. Think about the times when you fail to follow your daily stop-loss, to take a break to reset when you're bored, or log your trades at the end the trading day. Worse, you're aware you should be doing these things but can't will yourself to do so. You force trades even when you know there are no opportunities, you get in sooner than your strategy tells you to, and you get sucked into looking at other markets outside your strategy. You trade just to trade.

Lacking the will to do what you know you should do is the most notable sign of a problem with discipline. Willpower is the name for the energy you use to be disciplined. Unfortunately, like physical energy, willpower is a finite resource. When you're running low on willpower, you lack the energy to power your mind and maintain discipline.

Your willpower isn't just affected by trading activities; your lifestyle can drain you as well. Much like athletes organize their lives around training and competition, you may need to do the same thing in trading. Make trading the center point of your life, so your energy and willpower are at peak levels when the market is open.

You don't need willpower to be at your worst. You do that easily. Willpower is the energy you deploy to build the habits, routines, and processes that build strength and improve discipline. This should be freeing. Sometimes willpower is talked about in an all-encompassing way, like you're someone who just "lacks willpower." But in truth, we all have it. The question is, are we able to use it in a precise way?

When it comes to trading, decisions themselves cause fatigue. Every decision burns energy and eventually you can run out. Think about the periods of time in the day when you lack the energy to properly think. It becomes easy for your mind to wander, you spend too much time on Twitter, start looking for opportunities outside your strategy, or think about plans for the weekend.

Steve Job's famous turtleneck and jeans wardrobe wasn't just about branding; it was an energy saver—he made one less decision each day. Energy is finite, and while there are ways of replenishing it during the trading day, preservation can sustain disciplined execution.

Ultimately, you only want to use the amount of discipline that's necessary to achieve your goals. The traders who overwork themselves and repeatedly burn out could, arguably, be excessively disciplined. That workload is not only counterproductive for trading; it can suck the life out of your life. Resentment builds and decreases your longevity in the profession.

You don't want to be more disciplined than you need to be. Many of you are here because you don't have enough. But it's not black and white. Where do you need it, and in what way? Get precise, because, like any other problem, the details matter—a lot.

Lastly, it's important that you distinguish whether discipline is breaking down because of emotions or a lack of willpower. If you're unsure, here's a simple question to ask yourself in moments when discipline breaks down: Are your emotions too high, or is your energy too low?

If emotions are too high, it's not a discipline problem. Emotions do put pressure on your work habits, but they do so in ways that I talked about in chapters 4 through 7. If, on the other hand, your energy is too low, you're in the right place.

GENERAL STRATEGIES TO IMPROVE DISCIPLINE

Traders often wish they had more discipline, but are unprepared to build it in a sustainable way. The biggest opportunity to improve your discipline actually happens at the times when you're weak and more likely to fail. Maybe you're weak in a certain type of market, entering a particular type of trade, or at a specific time of day.

Regardless, you need to be ready to take advantage when the opportunity arises. In addition to the advice unique to each of the six discipline problems addressed later in this chapter, here are some general ways you can improve discipline.

Take Full Responsibility

The first step to becoming more disciplined is to acknowledge that your success in trading is entirely on you. You're the only one responsible for your goals, decisions, time, and work ethic. If you rely on external things, make excuses, or hope someone else or some event will drive your success, you'll never reach the level of discipline you aspire to.

Even if you work in a firm or a proprietary shop, success is still ultimately in your hands. Regardless of your reporting structure at work, you're effectively your own boss and need to behave that way. Sure, you could argue that that's not actually true in an office setting, where you report to someone who limits your risk and the types of trades you can make.

Except you chose to take a seat there, you make important decisions, and you're to blame if anything goes wrong, so it is true. You're still your own boss, even if you don't get to make all the decisions—think of it as having decided to set up your shop in their office.

The reason you may shy away from this idea is because you feel less pressure when someone else is running the show. The ultimate responsibility is on them, not on you. Knowing you, alone, control your fate can feel like a heavy burden on your shoulders. Sometimes it just becomes too much to bear, and discipline problems are an attempt to relieve some of this weight.

Taking responsibility isn't just about making that declaration; you need to understand clearly why you give up responsibility in the first place. Not surprisingly, there are often unknown factors and influences that undercut your efforts. You need to tease them out, so they can be corrected.

Quick Tip: Review the ways in which your discipline breaks down, and write down the benefits of breaking your rules. The idea that a breakdown in discipline could be beneficial can sound strange, but our actions always serve some benefit. Going through this exercise can make you more aware of why you're willing to let go of your responsibility for your own discipline.

Increase Mental Strength and Willpower

Break out of the idea that you either have discipline or you don't. You have it; you just want more. A big part of how you develop more discipline comes from increasing *both* mental strength and willpower. As I mentioned earlier, mental strength is the muscle behind the rationale for your habits, while willpower is the energy that drives the repetition needed to form those habits.

By pushing yourself to be more disciplined at times when it doesn't come easily, you can increase your mental strength and willpower. The process is simple: In the moments when you have the option to succumb to the weaknesses in your discipline, push yourself to do better. At the same time, reinforce the rationale around the habit.

If, for example, you consistently fail to log trades, go through your pre-market routine, or analyze charts, start with the minimal amount you can possibly do. It doesn't matter if it's as pathetically small as one minute. Choose the minimum you can do *consistently*, under any circumstances, no matter what—except during random emergencies.

Even when you're tempted to give up, think about your goals and push yourself to take steps toward them. Sometimes making just a little progress can be transformational.

Obviously, you can do more than the minimum if you get on a roll. Over time, as the habit gets stronger, you can scale up and work on making your small actions automatic, and then use your discipline on the next habits. This is not something you can do in a day. It requires consistency. If you fail to maintain that consistency, you're instead ingraining bad habits, making good ones harder to establish.

Quick Tip: Traders often make the mistake of aiming for levels of discipline that are beyond the front edge of their Inchworm. That's like going into the gym and trying to bench press 200 lbs. when you can only lift 150 lbs. While not beyond the realm of your potential, it's not realistic yet. Start with what you can do and improve upon it. And be sure to reinforce the progress that you're building, not what you're still lacking. Otherwise, self-criticism will slow down the process of building greater discipline.

Use (Don't Abuse) Inspiration

Inspiration is a tool. When used in the right way, it can assist in developing discipline. Use it incorrectly, or abuse it, and you'll perpetuate the same problems that brought you to this chapter. In order to avoid making that mistake, let me explain some background theory first.

Although you may consider them to be one and the same, there's a significant difference between motivation and inspiration. While each play an essential part in developing discipline, motivation is like a marathon runner and inspiration is like a sprinter. Motivation is a more stable energy that keeps you consistently working over the long term. Inspiration is high energy, and it provides short, intense bursts of energy needed to get you fired up or to stay on track.

Inspiration isn't what's going to allow you to consistently train yourself to adopt all of the habits you need as a trader. For that, you need consistent and stable energy to keep you motivated over the long term.

We all have habits that have become automated, some of which we call bad habits and attribute to a lack of discipline. Training to that degree, however, doesn't differentiate between good or bad. It just knows what it has learned to the point of automation. Overtrading, constantly checking PnL, and getting distracted by social media are habits you're really competent at, even if you consider them "bad." You abuse inspiration if you rely on it to change these old habits.

If you need a daily intake of things to fire you up, such as challenges or bets with other traders, watching clips of *The Wolf of Wall Street*, or new trading courses, you're compensating for an underlying problem. Inspiration makes you feel like your bad habits are gone, but eventually they return, because you didn't upgrade or correct them.

Inspiration is best used sparingly, and just as an extra boost when you're most likely to fail. It's like the personal trainer egging you on to get in those last reps. If you need a trainer to even get you to the gym, you have a deeper problem with discipline that inspiration can't fix. That could be your way of trying to manage any of the discipline problems described in this chapter, or it could be your way of dealing with fear or a confidence problem.

Quick Tip: If you're going to use inspiration, plan out the specifics in advance. You don't want to search for something to inspire you when discipline is falling apart. Be prepared with the music, movie clips, quotes, videos, catchphrases, etc.—whatever can quickly and reliably inspire you when you need it most.

MAPPING WHERE DISCIPLINE IS NEEDED

The ability to increase your discipline must come from a realistic assessment of your current strengths and limitations. Remember, it's not black and white. Regardless of whether or not you think of yourself as someone who is mentally tough, strong, gritty, or has good willpower, you're missing the point. Inchworm teaches us that we still have room to improve.

Completing the discipline mapping will give you a good picture of the work you need to do. From there, you get to define the workout—the places where you're weak and can get stronger. The following steps will help you create a document that will become the map of your current level of discipline.

Step 1

Start out by writing a short description of what **ideal or optimal discipline** looks like for you. Think about instances where you've demonstrated it. Be specific about what that means in terms of your routine, motivation, focus, energy, executing your trading strategy, and the actions you take around trading.

A written description not only provides clarity on what you're striving for; creating one makes it easier to recognize the subtle signs that discipline is breaking down. This is critical. Regaining discipline is always easier when the problem is small. Here are some questions to help you think about what it means for you to be optimally disciplined:

- What's unique about your decision-making process and execution?
- How do you manage the ups and downs in PnL?
- Describe your focus, motivation, and energy.
- Describe what you do at the start and end of both the trading session and the day.
- Under what conditions do you have it?
- If you've never attained that level of discipline, what, realistically, is your current peak?

Step 2

Over the next few weeks pay close attention to **breakdowns in discipline**. Examine and capture the signals of a breakdown, including:

- Thoughts
- Emotions
- Things you say out loud
- Behaviors
- Actions
- Changes to your decision-making
- Changes to your perception of the market, opportunities, or current positions
- Trading mistakes

Keep a document open on your computer, or a notepad next to you, while you trade and take notes throughout the day.

At the end of the trading day, review what you found and add additional details. Be as comprehensive as you can. And remember, times when you lose discipline are great for identifying what's happening and understanding why. Here are some questions to help get you started:

- In what ways do you typically lose discipline? (Impatient, bored, distracted, lazy, etc.)
- What are the things you do instead of what you're supposed to be doing?
- How frequently does it happen?
- In what situations do you most likely lack discipline? Do problems occur more when you're winning, or losing? In certain types of markets? At the beginning, middle, or end of a session? After or before trading sessions?
- How impactful are fluctuations in sleep, diet, and exercise?
- What excuses do you make for instances when you lose discipline?
- What's the first sign that discipline is breaking down?

For example, you can't sit on your hands. You know you need to just walk away, but you remain glued to your screen, watching PnL fluctuate, and looking for more trades to take. Or, when volatility dries up, you get bored and start looking at social media, but you miss opportunities that still present themselves.

Perhaps after a rough losing session, you don't sleep well and the next morning you look over your pre-market data too quickly. The combo of less sleep and poor preparation lead you to enter impulsively, chase price, and take random trades outside your strategy.

Keep an eye out for signals and patterns like these. And remember, mapping discipline is an iterative process. When you spot new details, even just slight adjustments, be sure to note them. Small details matter, and can make all the difference when the opportunity to make progress is on the line.

Step 3

Once you've gathered a lot of details, organize what you've found by listing them in order of severity in a document, where 10 is optimal discipline and 1 is your worst level of discipline. At each level, identify details that clearly distinguish it from the other levels.

As you assign levels of severity, split them into two categories: the mental and emotional side of discipline, and the technical side. They sit side by side, so level 10 on the discipline side corresponds to level 10 on the technical side, and so on.

You don't need to have details for all 10 levels, however. Most traders whom I work with aren't able to distinguish their levels of discipline to that degree. Do as many as you can, but do a minimum of three. Then take the details you've categorized and put them into a map like this:

DISCIPLINE LEVEL

Describe the thoughts, emotions, things you say, behaviors, and actions that highlight each level of discipline. Complete at least 3 levels.

10: Energized, totally consumed by the process, waiting for the market
    to come to me, not concerned about money.
9:
8: Wondering why it's not working and trying to convince myself that
    it still can. A bit on edge, leg bouncing.
7:

6:

5: Heartrate accelerating. Moving the mouse faster. Care what other traders are thinking, and looking for something newsworthy. Thinking about how to end the day green.

4:

3:

2: Can't step away, even though I know I should. Checking PnL every 10 minutes. Body feels itchy.

1:

TECHNICAL LEVEL

Describe the quality of your decision-making, perception of the market, opportunities, or current positions at each level of discipline.

10: Taking action only at my predetermined spots, and able to let the trades play out.

9:

8: Have trouble letting go of losing positions, and looking to enter new spots sooner than my strategy tells me to.

7:

6:

5: Forcing trades for valid reasons, but not my ideal.

4:

3:

2: Overtrading. Getting in and out of positions more randomly. Moving my stops.

1:

In this example, impatience is the primary problem. However, if you have multiple discipline problems, you can include them on a single map.

Now, you have a starting point to dig into your discipline problems, so you can identify the cause and devise a strategy to move your C-game forward.

IMPATIENCE

Impatience comes in different sizes and exists on both a micro and macro level. Think about how you feel in a drawdown, and when lacking opportunity in the market. Maybe you get tired of waiting and can't sit on your hands anymore. The itch to fire off a trade is so strong that you find an excuse to justify a mediocre one. Or you have trouble watching a position as it closes in on your target; the up-and-down ticks drive you crazy—you want it to hit your target now! You're like a sports fan sweating the back and forth of a tight game, and you close it prematurely, just to kill the tension.

Perhaps you make decisions too quickly—you see a flurry of activity and want to jump in. You don't take enough time to properly manage risk, and then you overreact to a move in the market and end up chasing it. All of these are signals of how impatience presents itself on the **micro level** in your day-to-day trading life.

You may be well aware of impatience on these micro levels, but not recognize it on a macro level. You can be impatient with lulls in your career, or are itching to make a lot of money really fast. You can be impatient with the learning process, effectively wishing that you could learn things instantly or far more rapidly than is realistic. Or maybe you can't tolerate a new strategy or system's inevitable drawdowns, and so you're constantly searching for new one.

Other signs of **impatience on a macro level** include believing you can make opportunities appear (a version of the illusion of control), an inherent distrust or uncertainty around your overall strategy, and losing sight of how you make money.

All of the emotional issues we have covered in the book are large contributors to impatience, most notably greed, FOMO, and tilt. You simply can't sit on your hands, allow the trade to play out, or properly consider all the key factors when making a decision, because the emotions build up like a pressure cooker and you feel compelled to act.

When addressing impatience as a discipline problem, you're not going to become patient by forcing yourself to be patient. Patience is a byproduct of working the process. When you have a firm grasp of process—whether it be building a career, executing a trade, or correcting a mental game issue—you're automatically patient. Provided there are no underlying flaws that alter your perspective on that process, impatience ceases to be a problem.

The reason why this is so important is because when someone has told you to "just be patient," they're advising you to slow down and take your time. That's not what you should be doing. What you should be doing is moving as fast as possible while maintaining the process necessary to be successful. Imagine an assembly line moving too fast and the final product ends up with missing or broken parts. On the other hand, you don't want the process to move too slowly either. That assembly line needs to meet its quota.

When impatience causes a breakdown in your decision-making process, the solution isn't simply to "slow down," but to train yourself to automatically consider the pieces of your process that typically go missing when you're impatient. For some of you, that's impractical. You have too much discretion in your decisions. But the places where impatience shows up could still be an indicator of a hole or weakness in your strategy. For instance, you may not know all of the reasons why what you're doing is right or wrong—and this leads to impatience.

Ask yourself: Why do you feel this need to move faster? What's pushing or compelling you? If it's a purely competitive drive, maybe you're not actually impatient. Maybe that's just a criticism you hear from people who aren't as motivated as you are.

Another reason could be that you wish skill or competency could be acquired instantly. Outwardly, you may be committed to the learning process, but deep down you wish you didn't have to go through all the ups and downs that come with it.

Sometimes traders are so driven to succeed and make a lot of money that they aren't thinking about longevity and building a solid base of skill. But think about it. Do you want to be the flash that comes out of nowhere, makes a ton and then has a high risk of losing it back? Or would you prefer the lower risk route, where you consistently build an edge in the market over the long term? Sometimes traders race for financial security without realizing that security also comes from developing a process that creates and maintains an edge in the market.

BOREDOM

Boredom is a signal of the absence of opportunity—either the opportunity to execute trades or the opportunity to learn and develop. Or you're burned out and lack the energy to focus as you would normally.

From the execution side, being bored could indicate that current market conditions are unfavorable for your strategy or system. In that spot, your mind will turn off, or go flat. You'll feel unenthusiastic about anything you see and should scale your expectations appropriately.

The problem is, instead of a scale, your mind only has an on/off switch. In that situation it's easy to overreact to the size of the drop in opportunity. A 50% drop in the number of opportunities suddenly feels like nothing is happening, and you shouldn't even be trading. As a result, you miss trades because your mind lacks interest in finding them.

It's hard to calculate the cost of these lost opportunities, but they exist. You need to keep your mind sharp enough to capitalize on them. Yes, you may not make as much as you would have in a normal market, but isn't something better than nothing? Isn't what you could make now ammunition for when conditions turn and you can capitalize on it more?

From an execution standpoint it's easy to overreact and think there's nothing you can do. You're physically there, but mentally on autopilot. The key is to shift your mentality from that of a starting quarterback to that of the backup quarterback. Assume there's opportunity and you just need to be ready. Remember, assuming there's nothing you can do is a form of thinking you know what's going to happen—and you don't. For some, this requires developing a new level of focus or mental activity. You need to look at it as a skill and train it.

First, write up a clear description of what readiness looks and feels like for you. For example, having a strong, engaged level of energy that's not overly intense, and being present without being detached. Then, when a moment of boredom strikes, challenge yourself to figure out how you can achieve a greater edge in this type of market. What are the little things you can do?

Focus on what keeps your mind active. Market cycles like this will continue to happen. If you find ways to improve, cycle over cycle, you'll find the antidote to boredom. You can't change the market, but you can change how you operate in it.

This advice proved helpful for Michael, an energy trader from the U.S. who started his own fund in 2004. He ran into periods of significant boredom every few years. Before he and I talked, he mistook these for periods of burnout, and he'd take two to six weeks off to decompress. He'd come back refreshed and go on to crush it.

After years of tremendous success, however, Michael noticed that something was different. Instead of taking a vacation, what he wanted to do was quit. Days that had once been busy, dynamic, and packed with action now felt boring. Part of it was due to the market. Around 2014, the volatility and liquidity in the natural gas market dried up and it truly was less busy. He went from 100-plus trades per day to 20. There was less opportunity for risk or reward, and Michael started to wonder if he should get out.

It turns out, however, that what was silently killing his passion for trading wasn't the reduced opportunity; it was an assumption that nothing was going to happen. Michael was showing up physically, but mentally he would give up if there weren't plenty of opportunities right out of the gate. Talking through it, Michael recalibrated his expectations.

Sure, an 80% reduction in the number of trades per day was significant, but 20 wasn't zero. He committed to making a serious and conscious effort to participate in the first few hours of the morning, and then, if there was nothing going on, he could call it a day and work on other things, such as charitable pursuits or other investments.

With that effort to participate came a renewed sense of pride and satisfaction that can only come from working hard. And he soon remembered that he still loved trading. But what sustained this progress long term was recognizing his effort. Michael rated himself daily on the following dimensions:

- How hard he worked
- Quality of energy
- Level of interest in the market
- The effect of outside emotions

The daily repetition built up a strong sense of accountability and responsibility. Even if the results didn't pay off that day, Michael felt better about himself and his performance when he knew he was putting in the total effort. If he was thinking and engaged, that made him feel productive and he ended the day happier, no matter what the result.

Boredom Leads to Overtrading

Other traders react differently to sideways or uneventful markets. Boredom signaled them to overtrade. In this instance, the line I hear frequently is, "My job is to trade, so not trading just feels wrong. Sitting on my hands doesn't make sense." This is typically caused by a subtle fear that makes boredom a threat to your trading operation. Or it's driven by a need for action that comes from overconfidence or mild desperation.

If boredom cues your mind to overtrade, you need to dig into the reason why. Does your mind go into overdrive? Are you worried about how long this market will last, why you're the only one not making money, or how it will affect your goals or your bonus? If boredom brings up these types of questions, it's not a discipline problem. It's linked to fear, and you'll find the answers in the Fear chapter.

Overtrading can also come from overconfidence. The illusion that you can control your results and force profits, as well as a need to always have positions on, is a sign of desperation or lack of confidence. Review chapter 7.

You can also use periods of boredom to correct the weaker parts of your decision-making process that lead to mistakes like overtrading.

Figure out the specific ways that your decision-making process changes, and when you become bored, train the correction. For example, thinking about the context of the market as a whole. If that's a consideration you don't think about when bored, training to do so will allow you to eventually think about it instinctively.

I'm not suggesting that you can automatically have a perfect understanding of the market as a whole, or that you're automating your decisions. I'm suggesting that you can upgrade the process for *how* you make decisions, by training yourself to consider factors that you fail to see when you're bored. The net result is that it becomes easier to avoid overtrading.

Believing There's Nothing to Learn

Boredom can also signal a perceived lack of opportunity to learn and develop. But guess what? There's always an opportunity to learn. In these moments you just lack the clarity for what that means. It's easy to lose sight of what you're trying to improve on and to be too lax in adapting your strategy to a market like this. Boredom happens because you're not challenged.

Trading in a market like this may be easy for you. In that case, boredom is a signal that you have extra mental bandwidth that could be used productively. You could use it as an opportunity to look at aspects of trading that you wanted to work on, but put off.

The dynamics in trading are varied and constantly changing, and that's a big reason many of you love it—every day is unique. There are always new areas in which to develop an edge; trading is always evolving, and there's always more to learn. Figure out how to use your extra bandwidth.

Bored When Burned Out

Boredom might be a signal that you're burned out, and if you are, the only correction is an extended break. Burnout can be easy to miss. You may think that you're being lazy, or making excuses for why you don't have the energy you usually do.

What you need is a way of distinguishing burnout from these other discipline problems, like laziness, by finding some key markers. You can't just blindly keep pushing yourself. Burnout is a bit like a burn to your skin; there are matters of degree, and the worse it is, the longer it takes to recover.

One of the biggest indicators of true burnout is being tired of the repetitive nature of trading—where it just feels like a chore. You've lost the excitement and interest you usually have for it. Whereas if you're being lazy, you're more likely to make excuses and spend your time elsewhere. For example, when you're lazy, you have no problem trading—that's still exciting—but the idea of researching or analyzing trades sounds painful. But when you're burned out, the whole thing is just overwhelming—or seems boring.

To be clear, burnout is not permanent, and it's not bad. I'm actually a fan of pushing yourself to the point of mild burnout because it means you have hit your own limitations. If you never get burned out, you don't know how much more capacity you have left on the table. Being able to recognize the signs of burnout—like boredom—is an important skill. It allows you to work as hard as you possibly can and then know when to back off.

BEING OVERLY RESULTS-ORIENTED

Obviously, results are important. But problems arise when an excessive focus on results causes your process to break—you end up focusing too much on intraday profit, locking in winners too early, looking for outsized profits, ignoring your own rules, and/or trading outside your system or strategy. Usually there's an emotional reason for this, but from a discipline standpoint, you may just believe that results are all that matter.

Ultimately your success is determined by the amount of money you make, and when your results dominate your intraday focus, it's easy to lose sight of how you make money. It's a distraction. You're distracted by the shiny object that's your PnL. You disregard elements of your decision-making process, like risk management, and take trades with a smaller edge, or even no edge at all. You jump into new markets without considering your lack of experience. You ignore the process.

Result and process goals work together. Result goals are the end point; process goals determine how you'll get there. A terrific example of how they work together is how the United States came to land on the moon in 1969.[9] Against a backdrop of tremendous political tension between the U.S. and the Soviet Union, President Kennedy sought a challenging but achievable "win" that the U.S. had a solid chance of completing first.

In 1961, he set the goal of landing on the moon before the end of the decade. Prior to his announcement, most scientists doubted it was feasible. But with the stakes raised, the scientific community, government, and private industry needed to figure out how to make it happen.

How do you build a spacecraft capable of landing on the moon and returning to Earth? How do you train astronauts to navigate in space? How do you get the 400,000 people who eventually worked on the project to work together? These and thousands of other steps, or process-oriented goals, paved the way to get mankind to the moon and back.

Elevate your focus on process and how you'll attain the lofty goals (albeit less lofty than Kennedy's) you want to attain in trading. If you're overly results-oriented, one reason could be that you lack clarity around the process by which you'll attain them; for example, nailing down a consistent decision-making process, creating a strong pre- and post-market routine, and reducing tilt. These types of goals allow you to shift your focus from the ups and downs of your results, or your daily PnL, to the processes that produce it.

To be clear, you're not eliminating result goals. I don't want you to stop focusing on results. I want you to drive toward them in a more disciplined way. Making money remains the dominant focus long term, but how you make money is your dominant focus short term. The way to do that is to elevate the importance of process goals.

You already show up every day with the goal of making money, but none of you would ever choose to do it by relying on getting lucky after having made a series of bad decisions. Whether you realize it or not, you place a high value on the quality of your process. Elevate your process-oriented goals, and your focus won't be dominated by results. Think of this as goal diversification. This is particularly important in trading, since you can control whether you achieve your process goals in the short term.

These process-oriented goals can become even more specific and detailed as you determine how to achieve each one. Take the goal of improving discipline. Define how you'll do it; for example, by working to create a clear map of your discipline A- to C-games, improving recognition of early signs that discipline is falling, and actively working to correct it in real time. Then, even when you're tired or in a drawdown—two things that normally make it harder to maintain discipline—you can see progress that a sole focus on results would have missed.

Ultimately, the energy you put into achieving your process goals is fueled by your strong desire to reach your result goals. And the stronger your desire to achieve your result goals, the harder you'll work on your process goals.

Process-based goals are especially important in industries like trading, where the variance makes it difficult to have full control over your monetary results. If, at the end of the day, you don't hit your monetary goal but you're now able to focus for five hours without getting distracted, execute your strategy, and consistently follow your routine, at least you'll know you've improved and controlled what you could.

DISTRACTIBILITY

There's a shocking level of distractibility in today's world, and traders are not immune. In fact, in some ways, you're particularly exposed to it. You must sift through streams of data from multiple sources in order to interpret and capitalize on opportunities.

But as you interface with these data streams, it's easy to allow information that's irrelevant to your trading decisions to flow in. You've got the charts open, but you're trying to do something on the side, and you end up making a subpar trade because you weren't focused enough to make a proper judgment.

You may think such distractions don't affect you. But here's a quick way to demonstrate what happens when the mind attempts to do two things simultaneously: While reading the next several lines, focus on the sensation of your legs against your chair or the feeling of your feet on the ground. Force yourself to feel the sensation of your legs or feet, while paying close attention to what you're reading. See if you can notice the shift that your mind makes between reading and sensing your legs or feet.

Do you notice how each time your attention switches, you lose information from the other point of focus? Your eyes may continue to scan the page, but you no longer pick up every word, and you may even have to reread them. And every time you focus only on reading, you lose awareness of the sensation in your legs and feet.

Imagine this happening while trading. Every time you focus on Twitter, a text message, or an unrelated discussion, you may fail to pick up data relevant to your trading decisions.

Focus can be broken down into two parts: attention and concentration. While people often use these terms synonymously in terms of focus, there is an important distinction. **Attention is the direction of your focus**, determined by your goals, needs, motives, interests, priorities, and values. **Concentration is the amount of focus** you have, which is ultimately determined by your level of energy.

If these subtle differences are unclear, think about the way in which people talk about focus. When someone says, "Pay attention," they're telling you *where* to focus. When they say, "Concentrate," they want you to increase your *level* of focus. This distinction is important because it illustrates the two ways of improving focus—give it better direction and increase the amount of it.

Attention

Imagine that you're in a dark room. Hidden in the darkness are all the areas in your life fighting for your attention: Trading, family, Twitter, cat videos, click bait, exercising, a good meal, your next trip, picking up the dry cleaning, etc. Literally everything that you could be interested in is represented on the floor, ceiling, and walls. You can't see them right now because the room is dark, but they're there.

Now, imagine you turn on a flashlight, much like how you first open your eyes and start your day. You shine the light around to get your bearings and understand all of your options. Then it's time to choose. You decide to trade. You shine the flashlight in that direction, and all of the things that are integral to your success are illuminated: your routine, your pre-market checklist, and trade journal are all there.

Immediately you know exactly where to focus, because it's lit up by the flashlight, and just as importantly, everything unrelated remains hidden, in the dark—there are no other options illuminated by the beam of light. Trading becomes your entire world because every other option is invisible.

That's the power of your goals: To point your focus in the right direction and block out all of the other things that don't matter. Guided by your goals or motives, focus is your tool for gathering the information needed to make decisions.

Yet what does your focus actually look like during the trading day? Does it stay in the right place for an hour or so, and then fade like the batteries are dying? Is it a wide beam that casts light across many things at once? Or is it a narrow beam that jumps around? If your goals aren't up to date, if they lack deep personal meaning, if they're too far away to feel real, or they lack clear details, your focus will never reach the level that's truly possible. Moreover, every strategy that you'd use to fix your focus will only be a Band-Aid.

You want your focus to be completely consumed by what you want to focus on. The question is: Why does it get pointed at something less relevant, or even irrelevant, when you're trading? Saying you're distracted is too simple.

When you look closely at the motives or reasons behind why you would choose to have your attention drift elsewhere, you'll find a conflict. Consciously you might know that trading should consume all of your attention, but your strength to hold your focus in the right place has been compromised by the desire to shine the flashlight onto something else.

For example, let's say that you find yourself unable to stop paying attention to the trade ideas from other traders on Twitter or those of a trading group. Why is that? Perhaps you want to be entertained, or social. In order to get yourself to consistently focus on your charts and be disciplined in your focus, you need to resolve the reason you seek diversion during the trading day. Use the Mental Hand History to get at the root of the conflict.

This perspective was particularly helpful for Brian, from Canada. Remember him from chapter 3? His Inchworm was too wide, and the idea of sucking less, along with a framework to achieve his lofty goals, helped him to swiftly identify and correct greed and fear. Yet while those problems had been addressed, his focus still needed work.

For a long time, the way he had dealt with the emotion was to procrastinate, lose focus, and think about the future. His mind would frequently wander to sports, finances, or imagining an ideal life. With the greed and fear removed, we took aim at improving his focus by first applying a strategy of taking defined, five-minute breaks throughout the day whenever he felt very distracted. When this had happened previously, he would disappear for a lot longer than five minutes, often the rest of the day. He didn't understand how to reliably get back in front of the charts.

At first, he set the five-minute breaks to occur every 25 minutes, following the Pomodoro Technique of time management. During the break, he would first note what was on his mind, then give himself a few minutes to relax before reemphasizing process, focus, and execution for the next 25-minute block. This really helped him to reset and refocus.

Throughout the day, I also had him log every distraction to make him account for every instance his focus wasn't optimal. These distractions ranged from something as simple as a thought about sports to as large as getting lost in social media, or imagining his future.

Lastly, we found that his focus issues were connected to his experience in school and in his prior corporate job. An intelligent hard worker, he naturally thrived in both environments and was very successful. H expected to have the same results in trading, despite the environmen being very different. The uncertainty and lack of structure expose weaknesses in his focus that had begun in school, because he hadn needed to fully focus to get straight A's.

His Mental Hand History revealed the underlying issues:

1. **What's the problem:** I have very high expectations about the amount of money that I want to make and what I want to achieve. And I frequently envision a future income level and lifestyle, which includes traveling the world and living in the Caribbean.

2. **Why does the problem exist:** Trading is my source of income to fund that lifestyle, but it's hard, and can be a real struggle. These thoughts are an easy escape from the struggle and the work I must put in today, in order to eventually get there. Effectively I'm choosing comfort and ease in the short term.

3. **What is flawed:** Thinking that I can achieve the outcome that I want without actually putting in the work. I know what I had to do in school and in my previous corporate jobs, and I'm expecting my intellect to get me what I want without having to work for it. My past experience gave me a false sense of certainty that I can expect to be as successful in trading as I was previously.

4. **What's the correction:** I need to grow beyond my expectations from the past. I don't have guarantees here. I have a lot of belief and a lot of desire. I've gotten this far by half-assing it. Just think of what I could do if I put my full effort into doing the work needed right now! I must embrace the discomfort and put in the focus needed to pursue my goals.

5. **What logic confirms that correction:** I've faced uncertainty successfully before; I just didn't appreciate it. I need to take trading head on, with a process that allows me to get where I want to be. If I feel comfortable, I'm doing it wrong. Take the risk. It's ok to fail. It's ok to have trades lose. If I escape, I stop myself from learning and take away the chance to attain my dreams.

Taken together, he worked the process day after day, and over time he naturally progressed beyond the 25-minute blocks. Now he focuses until he hits a point where his distractions become disruptive. Sometimes his focus can last as long as several hours, or as little as 20 minutes, at which point he follows the five-minute break routine to reset and start again.

Concentration

With your goals set, attention directed where it needs to be, and any conflicts removed, the next part of the equation is concentration. Increasing concentration is no different than the overall idea of increasing discipline. There's an endurance component to it that requires energy. Many of you start with sufficient energy, but quickly lose it because you lack a strong connection to your goals. Ideally you want your goals to be so well known, they're like the back of your hand.

On the other hand, some of you lack endurance: you're like an out-of-shape athlete. To build your endurance, you must design an exercise program to increase the duration of high-quality focus. Much as there's tremendous diversity in how athletes train, there's considerable diversity in how traders operate, so much so that it's tough to create a defined workout for everyone. Ultimately, you must do what works best for you.

That said, the general advice that has worked well for my clients is to strive for around an increase of concentrated time by 10%, week over week, combined with a week with no increase every four to six weeks. That may sound low, but the key is finding a way to achieve sustainable growth, not temporary progress fueled by inspiration.

Having mapped your discipline problems earlier in the chapter, you can now go deeper into detail on the specific ways your focus becomes divided. Follow these steps:

1. List all of the things you focus on that are low value, or that you'd consider a distraction; for example, trading group banter, daily PnL, positions, or divergent moves in related markets.

2. Determine when they tend to arise. For example, are they more present at the beginning, middle, or end of a session?

3. Rank the severity of the distraction as minor, moderate, or severe.

4. Select one or two from the most severe category.

5. When the urge to engage in those distractions appears, push yourself to focus for an amount of time that's doable, but not overwhelming—5, 10, or 20 minutes.

Too often, traders try to fix all their distractions at once, and think that it's easy to improve just by keeping it in mind. The urge to engage in those distractions is strong, and the more you avoid it, the stronger the urge gets. That's expected in the short term. You're battling to build discipline around your focus. That takes repetition and experience.

Work hard to maintain focus for 5, 10, or 20 minutes and then either do it again or take a short break before doing it again. Trying to focus for three, four, or five-plus hours at a time can feel overwhelming. But chopping up the time makes it easier and feels more like a workout.

Another thing you can try is something I call "Prepare for Perfect." This is an experiment that can be good for those who are easily distracted, or if emotional problems previously affected your focus. It can also be useful if you haven't been in the zone for a while and have forgotten what it's like to even be there.

Your goal with this experiment is to create the best possible conditions to reach a peak level of focus for trading. Imagine your next trading session was the most important of your entire life. What steps would you take to ensure your focus was perfect? This is just an experiment, so really go for it and don't worry about whether it's practical to do on a regular basis.

Identify everything you need in order to be at your best—getting proper sleep, planning and eating an optimal diet, getting a moderately intense workout, avoiding social media for 24 hours, etc. Then actually do whatever you think it'll take, even if it means setting aside a few days to properly prepare for the session.

The purpose of this experiment is to experience optimal focus. From there you'll gain insight into what it takes to be at your peak, and perhaps most importantly, recognize more easily when your focus is poor, and why, which will feed your ability to push yourself to increase the duration of your focus for 5, 10, or 20 minutes at a time.

Lastly, everything I've talked about in this section was framed around improving intraday focus, but all of the concepts and strategies also apply to work outside of trading hours.

LAZINESS

Calling yourself lazy is actually lazy. Rather than analyzing why you lack the motivation to do what you ought to be doing, you conclude that you're just lazy and treat it as an incurable disease, or an immovable part of your character. Laziness seeks this kind of comfort. Believing laziness is something you can't change is easy. Laziness loves doing the minimum.

If you believe deep down that laziness is permanent, even if it's just a small part of your character, it would be illogical for you to try to do anything to change it. However, laziness is not a fixed trait. Breaking out of this ailment takes some work, but this section can make that task easier.

You might equate laziness with having zero motivation. But it's actually impossible to have no motivation. Instead, think of being lazy as having a strong motivation to sleep for hours, watch TV, or mindlessly surf the Internet. While that might seem like I am just changing around words, stating it that way is important for understanding and fixing the problem.

Laziness is actually a skill that, for better or worse, has been learned. You've learned the skill of doing something other than what you ought to be doing. Instead of learning how to be productive, you've learned how to be lazy—and you're quite good at it.

In trading, laziness is more likely to show up for the tasks around trading, like reviewing previous trades, developing new trade ideas, and reading research, vs. the desire to get into the action and trade. The intensity of trading gives you the rush that makes it fun and exciting. Research, on the other hand, can be tedious and boring. You have to generate the intensity to make it valuable. Why do the research or analyze your trades when it's easier to do something mindless?

Laziness can develop for many reasons. Perhaps it started early in your life, if you weren't pushed to excel, or if the environment wasn't that challenging for you. I'm not saying all people who are lazy are smart, but I've seen many people who *are* very smart develop poor work habits when their educational environment didn't challenge them. They did enough to meet their goals, either to get A's quite easily or to get by without trying very hard and still get into a good college.

In comparison to the standard provided to them, they weren't lazy. However, relative to their potential, they were incredibly lazy. But their potential wasn't the benchmark, externally or internally. The habits that formed during that time continue today.

People also become lazy when the structure they're used to having in their lives is gone. When living with family, going to school, or working for someone else, you don't have to think much about what to do; you just have to do it. The value of having that structure provided for you often goes unrecognized until it's gone. Now you have to do both—decide what to do and actually do it. That extra layer may not seem like much, but it makes life, or trading, more challenging and can lead to laziness.

Or maybe after you started making good money and had some success, you no longer felt any urgency. Perhaps you were incredibly motivated for much of your life and trading career. But, having reached the goals you'd dreamed of—whether being able to quit your job to trade full-time or feeling financially secure enough to not worry about money for years—laziness has unexpectedly popped up.

The issue here is that now you're either coasting on your previous success, expecting to easily continue, or you've simply failed to set a new goal or determine new things to challenge you. In this way, laziness is just signaling a lack of direction that drives you.

Finally, trading is an enterprise that attracts people with the fantasy of easy money. They lacked the right work ethic prior to trading and, as a trader, struggle to put in real work. Trading is enjoyable and doesn't have to feel like work. But it's easy to lose sight of how to become successful. Choosing productive activities and having a more rigorous work ethic may not seem fun at first, but it's definitely more fun than failing, having an ordinary job, or proving your doubters right.

Success is also gratifying, and makes the mundane tasks that are necessary to achieve it less painful. This doesn't mean that putting in extra hours of work is more fun than going out with friends, or taking time off to travel. But those decisions take on a different context when they give you a greater chance of reaching your goals.

To begin correcting this problem, you need to change the way you view yourself. You're not lazy. You're highly motivated to do those other things, rather than what you ought to do. Motivation is simply the energy you have behind your goals. And when you look more closely at the specific habits you avoid and the ones you choose to do instead, you gain insight into the reasons behind your preference for unproductive activities.

You may be changing the flawed idea that laziness is a character trait, breaking out of the mold where your potential is defined by other people, learning to hold yourself accountable to your own structure, or breaking the illusion that money in trading comes easily. Find the motivation to drive toward your own vision. Redefine your goals, as a trader or for your career.

Then zero in on the day-to-day micro decisions. There's a list of things you should be doing, and there's a list of things you're doing instead. To consistently choose more of the things you ought to be doing, uncover the reasons behind your laziness and build the skill to make better choices:

1. Write the excuses you make for choosing the lazy things you do
2. Write why each of those excuses is flawed or wrong
3. List of all the productive things you can do instead, and the value of each activity

Then when those moments arise, think of the short- and long-term value of the productive habits compared with the low-value, immediate-gratification lazy ones. Doing what's less fun now means you can have much more fun in the future. Work harder when it's hard and eventually it'll become easy. Don't hide behind your potential. See how good you can actually become.

Laziness seeks comfort, but you can no longer delude yourself into thinking that laziness is something that you can't change. You can no longer lazily call yourself lazy. Maybe that will compel you to dive into the reasons you formed these habits, patterns, or skills and develop new ones.

PROCRASTINATION

Constantly putting off what's important defines the skill of procrastination. Sure, there's a lot you could be doing, such as reviewing your trade journal, researching a new strategy, or upgrading your chart-reading skills. But it's easier to delay that work until tomorrow. The problem is that tomorrow—for those of you who are highly skilled procrastinators—is a fantasy that will never be realized.

You're a master at delaying today's work. But when tomorrow becomes today, you're not skilled at getting work done—you're skilled, once again, at delaying it until tomorrow. The fantasy is that you'll actually do the work tomorrow, but what I just described is why that won't happen, so the pattern continues.

Eventually, you finally become fed up with your antics, realize you need to make some money, worry you might get fired, or there's some other reason that makes you feel like your back is against the wall. Being in that position triggers a rush of inspiration. You put your nose to the grindstone and rip through all the things you've been delaying and avoiding.

Unfortunately, when you successfully avoid the worst case, you're more likely to slip back into that habit again. There's no real consequence other than some wasted time and opportunity, and that's a business expense you're willing to take. Your behavior has seemingly been rewarded and there's no reason for you to change. And yet here you are. Which means you know procrastination is causing some kind of damage, and it's time for a change.

If you want to stop procrastinating, you first must eliminate the belief that "there's always tomorrow," and develop the skill of doing the work that you would ordinarily delay. That means learning how to work when you're not under intense pressure or stress. Working with your back against the wall is easy—you have no choice but to get it done. Procrastination took away your options, but it also created a lot of stress or pressure in order to focus and motivate you.

To break that cycle, you need the strength and willpower to remove delaying as an option. Remember, today is when improvement happens, not just in your trading but also in reducing procrastination. Today is your only opportunity to improve. Tomorrow is a fantasy.

One of the problems with procrastination is that the value of work you end up doing under intense pressure gives you a false sense of strength and mastery. Obviously, this is different if you're studying for an exam related to work. But if we're talking about upgrading the competency that defines you as a trader, in these periods of intense work you're mostly expanding capacity at the front end of your Inchworm. You're not permanently upgrading your C-game.

Instead, you end up with a wide range and all of the problems associated with it. Correcting procrastination helps to narrow your range and build your competence in a more stable and consistent way.

Building the skill to work consistently doesn't happen overnight. As I've discussed before, start with what you can guarantee you can do regularly, even if that means working on it for just 5 to 10 minutes a day. Of course you can do more, but you can't sustain that output consistently yet.

As 5 to 10 minutes becomes easier, you can scale up the time, and eventually build toward what's optimal. In the end, you'll find this to be a much more sustainable way of developing competence than delaying and cramming.

In this chapter we've looked at how to tell when you're dealing with an emotional vs. actual discipline problem, the many signs of discipline problems, and ways that issues with discipline might manifest. You've also learned multiple tactics for addressing challenges with discipline, from focus tracking and time-management tips to using the Mental Hand History. You should be well on your way to enhancing your discipline—or at least knowing what steps you need to take to improve it.

Early in the book I talked about how control isn't a solution—resolution is. Resolution frees you from having to constantly fight greed, fear, tilt, overconfidence, lack of confidence, and poor discipline. Instead, when you permanently correct the performance flaws that cause those problems, your mind is freed up to focus on trading and figuring out how to make more money. We've been steadily working toward resolution throughout the book.

Now that we've explored the many ways that emotions and discipline problems can hijack performance, how to recognize them, and identify the root cause, you're ready to take the final step. I'll get deeper into how the brain works, so you can correct your problems in real time, while avoiding the brain's tendency to commandeer your good intentions.

CHAPTER 9

CORRECT YOUR PROBLEM

"Give a man a fish, and you feed him for a day.
Teach a man to fish, and you feed him for a lifetime."

—origin unknown

You realize by now just how detrimental your mental game problems are. Envision them gone. That's what resolution can do, and it's an outcome worth the hard work it takes to get there.

I imagine some of you are overwhelmed by what you've read thus far and others are optimistic about what this system can do. Rest assured that at this point, you have the foundation for how to recognize your problems and correct your reactions. Now, you should be firmly focused on the work needed to resolve them. Resolution is your ultimate goal because that's how you can truly take your performance to another level.

For many of you, the road to resolution isn't a straight line and looks different than you expected. Having been a coach for over 15 years, I've learned a lot about the process involved with resolving problems. I've crafted this chapter to make that process easier and faster, regardless of your starting point.

Traders often assume that their mistakes, especially mental and emotional ones, should be easy to fix. You know what the mistake is. So just don't do it anymore, right? Seems like a simple enough strategy. But in the heat of the moment it's not that simple. Mistakes continue to happen, and you either get pissed off, feel pressure, lose confidence, lose motivation, become distracted as a form of denial, blame something random, make excuses, or any combination of the above.

You know the definition of insanity is doing the same thing over and over, expecting a different result, yet you tenaciously believe the problem should be fixed easily and still don't work on it. Plus, since now you're even more aware of it, you think, *There's no way I'll make that mistake again.*

And when it doesn't show up for a few days, a week, or even a month, it gives you a false sense of confidence. But eventually the mistake happens again, and your emotional reaction is even stronger this time.

This chapter is your way out of that cycle of chaos. You'll dive a bit more into how your brain works and how it can trip you up, so that you can avoid the problems it might be causing. You'll learn how to correct your problems in real time, as well as how to build your strategies into a daily habit, since repetition is the biggest factor in reaching resolution. Finally, you'll understand how to evaluate your progress and avoid common reasons progress can get derailed.

Let's get started by looking at a few key ways your mind might be hijacking your good intentions.

MALFUNCTIONING MIND

We could spend years talking about the intricacies of the human brain. Untold numbers of books and papers have been written to decipher how it works, and that research will continue. But all you really need to know are a few key principles.

The brain is organized in a hierarchy. The first level is where all of the most important functions of the brain are stored, such as heart rate, breathing, balance, and sleep and wake cycles. Skills you have mastered, like riding a bike or inputting an order, are also there.

The second level of the brain is the emotional system, and the third is the mental level, containing all of the higher brain functions such as thinking, planning, self-awareness, organization, and emotional control. But the hierarchy has a catch.

And it's a big one: **When the emotional system becomes overactive, it shuts down higher brain functions.**

This is why you make poor decisions when your emotions run too high. The brain prevents you from being able to process information correctly. When emotions are overactive, the loss of higher brain functions is something that no one can control.

Both positive and negative emotions can cause this breakdown in mental functioning. For example, you learned in chapter 7 that while having confidence is important to performance, too much of it can be a problem. When you're overconfident, the excessive amount of emotion flooding your mind compromises your decision-making. This could lead you to overlook some factors or overestimate the accuracy of your opinion, and that alters your evaluation of risk.

Regardless of the emotion, the following can also happen:

- When emotions are at their highest level—shock, euphoria, blind rage—your mind goes completely blank and you stop thinking altogether.
- Your mind moves so fast that you miss key pieces of data, so your decision-making process is incomplete.
- You overweight the importance of some factors and fail to consider relevant ones.
- You know the right answer, but can't access it—as if your head is in a fog.
- You fall back into bad habits that you're surprised to find you're still doing.
- You're aware that what you're doing is wrong, but you can't stop yourself; it's like you're compelled to trade bigger and take excessive risks.
- Your focus narrows and you tunnel into one of your indicators and ignore others that you typically use.
- You've identified a juicy trade, but can't execute it.

Take a minute to let the way that overactive emotions shut down your higher brain sink in. If your strategy doesn't take this into account, you have very little chance, aside from pure luck, of fixing anything.

There's even a scientific principle that describes the relationship between emotion and performance. The Yerkes-Dodson law states that your performance improves as your emotions rise, but only to a certain point.[10]

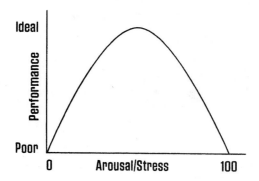

As this law defines it, your threshold is the tipping point on the right side of the curve, where emotions start to become overpowering. At this point, performance declines, because the emotional system begins to shut down higher brain functions, like thinking, decision-making, and emotional control. When that happens, you lose access to the knowledge and skills you're currently learning in proportion to the intensity of the emotion.

The further you pass your emotional threshold, the more knowledge you lose. Things that are brand new are the first to go. Skills that are much better known, and close to being mastered, are the last to disappear.

You know your emotion has crossed your threshold and become overactive when it's begun to impair your thoughts, actions, perspective, and decision-making process. Of course, everyone's threshold is different. It's a very personal metric. Keep an eye out for when your biases start to pop up more, your decision-making ability starts to change, and your access to certain information starts to shrink.

On the left side of the curve, the opposite happens. When you don't have enough energy or emotion to think, as occurs when you're tired, bored, burned out, or lacking discipline, you need to build up enough emotion to kick the thinking part of your brain into gear. Emotion is essential for performance. Problems only start when there's too much or too little. The mental game strategy outlined in this chapter is designed to keep your emotional level at the top of the curve, so your performance can be at its highest level more often.

On the surface this concept may seem simple, but it has massive implications for how to address emotional problems. While you can't control the fact that the emotional system has the power to shut down your ability to think, you're not powerless—you just have to work within this limitation.

You must start trying to control your emotions before they have gone too far past your emotional threshold. Timing matters a lot. If you don't catch the rise of emotion early, and it becomes too intense, you'll be in an uphill battle for control.

The prefrontal cortex is the area of the brain responsible for emotional control, which is one of the higher brain functions weakened as emotions rise.[11] At the exact moment when you most need this part of the brain, it can't respond as well, because of that emotional intensity. Simply put, emotion has the power to weaken your ability to control it. And the further your emotions rise past your threshold, the lower the odds that you'll be able to regain control. Too often, traders begin trying to control their emotions *after* their ability to think has weakened. That's like bringing a water pistol to a gunfight.

Whether the loss of higher brain functions is caused by overconfidence, anger, or fear, the consequences are significant for traders. You rely on higher brain functions to make money—this is some of the most valuable territory in the brain. This is where you think and weigh information from multiple sources, such as prior knowledge, experience, actions, and, of course, real-time market data.

Understanding how your brain can malfunction gives you another tool that takes you closer to achieving resolution. Now, let's get into a real-time strategy that brings the battle for progress to the front lines.

REAL-TIME STRATEGY

So how *do* you resolve a mental game problem? You must get to the point where you can correct your reaction *as it happens.*

Once you've learned to recognize when your performance flaws have been triggered, that's your cue to fight back with a correction that, in real time, quickly gives you greater mental and emotional control. What makes this system powerful is that when you use the correction in real time, you also gain repetitions needed to eventually reach resolution: two benefits from one action.

Correcting your reaction is a combination of having the right logic and ensuring the logic is so clearly defined in your mind that it's strong enough to stop the pattern in its tracks.

From your work in chapters 4 through 8, mapping your pattern and using the Mental Hand History, you've identified the correction—now it's time to use it. To do that, you use a four-step process that I explain below. The amount of detail needed for the explanation might seem overwhelming, but once you get the hang of it, you'll find you can complete this process in a matter of seconds.

Learning to correct your reaction is where a lot of the hard work in the system lies. First you find the flaw. Then you come up with a correction. But to truly change flaws, biases, wishes, and illusions, you must repeat the correction over and over, and over again. You become like professional athletes who spend dedicated and focused time to hone their technique, so it's strong enough to compete.

Here you're learning a technique for the mind. In this way you're mastering the correction so that it upgrades and permanently corrects the flaw. Once permanently corrected, you've reached resolution. The old way of reacting is disabled, and you automatically have the presence of mind needed to trade at your highest level.

I liken this process to chopping down a tree. You may want a chainsaw, but you get an ax. For some of you, the tree is large, you're weak, and the ax has a blunt edge. Over time, as you work the process, you get stronger, and learn how to sharpen your ax. Just like becoming a skilled trader, you have to put in a lot of work. There's no other way.

Step 1: Recognizing a Problem Has Been Triggered

This is where mapping your pattern really helps. As I said at the outset of chapter 2, you can't stop or correct a problem that you can't see. Now is your chance to use the map of your pattern to identify the signals that a problem has been triggered.

Eventually, you want to get to the point where your map is internalized, so you can easily recall it under intense emotional situations. Until that point, keep it nearby so you can quickly reference it.

Once you recognize a signal, that's your cue to move on to Step 2.

Step 2: Disrupting Momentum

Newton's first law of motion tells us that an object in motion stays in motion until acted upon by an outside force. Your pattern is like an object in motion. There's an unmistakable momentum to your emotional reactions as they barrel toward the same terrible conclusion, unless you become the force to challenge it. The best way to do that is to disrupt the momentum of the pattern as soon as you recognize it.

The primary purpose of disruption is to create separation between the reaction and the correction, which increases the odds of the correction having an impact. As soon as you recognize your pattern has been triggered, use one of the following four methods of disruption:

- **Take a deep breath.** This is not some esoteric kumbaya kind of thing. A singular deep breath can produce a distinct effect while being simple enough that you don't have to step away from your desk. Take a deep breath that fills your stomach, not your chest. This is called diaphragmatic breathing and it cues the body to relax. (Google it.)

  Also, focus intently on your breath. The strength of your focus is in large part where the disruptive power comes from. If this is new to you, take some time to train yourself in the process. Several times a day, or once an hour, imagine that some emotion you're struggling with was triggered.

Practice taking one diaphragmatic breath while strengthening your focus on your breath. Over time you'll notice a distinct improvement in the strength that breath has to stop the problem in its tracks.

- **Write.** Take a few moments to write down your thoughts, emotions, or whatever is on your mind in that moment. You can type or handwrite your notes. It's a personal preference, so do whatever works for you.
- **Stand up or take a walk.** In heated moments, traders often naturally stand up from their desk or take a short walk to make sense of what's happening. You may also try combining this by going for a walk and then writing down your thoughts when you get back.
- **Talk.** Some traders prefer to vent to a colleague in their office, in an online forum, or to other trading friends.

You already do these things instinctively. The idea is to turn them into deliberate techniques and strengthen their effectiveness. If you find there's one you already do, it makes sense to start there. You can also use a combination when the reaction is more severe. For example, a deep breath only works when the emotional intensity is low, so write and then stand up to disrupt the pattern when the intensity is higher.

Traders who only make a few trades per week have the luxury of having time to disrupt their pattern. The risk of missing out on a profitable trade is low. However, it's clearly suboptimal to have extended or recurring periods where you're more focused on managing your emotions in this way. Over time, the goal is to shrink the amount of time you're away from your desk.

On the other hand, traders who make several trades per hour must develop a quick process to disrupt their pattern. Their goal is speed, and that often requires spending extra time to train the process to the point where you can easily apply one of the four options above.

Step 3: Injecting Logic

Injecting Logic is the real-time antidote for the emotions causing errors in your execution. Leveraged in the right way, it's one of the strongest tools you have to reach resolution. Injecting Logic builds on what people tend to do naturally when facing a mental game problem—talk themselves through it—and turns it into a technique that can be trained.

Thinking is your primary tool to fight against your pattern, and the benefit of what psychologists call "self-talk" has been well established in performance research.[12] The key is to apply it when emotions are still small and to use logic that you have trained.

The goal is to craft a bite-sized statement or phrase that you have written out, rehearsed, and reviewed prior to each trading session. This makes it strong enough in your mind to have an immediate impact on your emotional state, prevent secondary emotion, and work toward a lasting correction to your underlying flaw. Here are a few examples:

- **FOMO:** The market is a constant stream of opportunities—I will not capture all of them.
- **Fear of failure:** Sometimes, the risk from staying on the sidelines is the greater risk.
- **Hating to lose:** I'll win some and I'll lose some—losses are inevitable—but as long as I control my emotions when the losses occur and continue trading within my strategy, I will profit over the long term.
- **Mistake tilt:** Hating mistakes is like hating to learn; if I actually learn from it, the money lost is an investment in developing a bigger edge.
- **Injustice tilt:** I get good luck too. Look for it and stick to my strategy. That's how I make money long term.
- **Lacking confidence:** I spent a thousand hours on this plan. Am I really going to let one trade change it?
- **Overconfidence:** My head is in the clouds. Fantasizing about what I want to make from the trade doesn't mean that's what I'm going to make. Do your job!

- **Boredom:** If I go looking for action for the sake of action, that makes me a gambler, not a trader.
- **Focus:** Trading is a job. Run it like a serious business that demands my best. When the session is over, I can focus on other things. Not now!

For your logic statement to be effective, it must be potent. It must represent what you uncovered in the Mental Hand History and accurately address both the underlying flaw and your understanding of why it's flawed.

When you have the right logic, it has a noticeable effect in reducing your emotions in the moment. Early in the process, the decrease in emotion will be small, but distinct. Eventually, you'll reach a point where the logic is so potent that you immediately feel a significant change.

To figure out the correct logic to inject, take what you wrote in Steps 2 through 5 of the Mental Hand History to craft your statement or phrase. At the start, it's ok for it to be based on negative language, such as "You can't be perfect, and expecting to be is a recipe for pain." Positive language can sometimes lack potency—don't get hung up on the idea that negative thinking is bad.

Also, don't get hung up on trying to craft the perfect statement right away. Just try something out and give it a few days to see if it has any impact on your emotional state. The standard of improvement is to suck less. Remember, you don't get a chainsaw. Start wielding that ax and get some feedback.

Early in the process, to some degree it doesn't matter what you say—which means you're at risk for a placebo effect. Sometimes just saying something reasonable can stop your pattern. This is fine at the start, but remember that managing a problem isn't the same as resolving it.

Take, for instance, not closing out a losing position because you hope it will come back. You know it's wrong to hope a position will come back, so you say, "Hope isn't a strategy; close it and move on to the next one." While that's reasonable and gets you to close out the position, you're not addressing *why* you were so reluctant to close it.

The same could be said for any of the logic examples above. If your emotions continue to reoccur and cause the same problems without any sign of progress, you haven't gone deep enough. Injecting Logic becomes no different than any of the other strategies designed to temporarily control such emotions as denial, avoidance, distraction, or desensitization. Don't make this mistake. Dig deeper into your problem, reevaluate what you wrote in the Mental Hand History, and devise a new Injecting Logic statement.

If you have the right logic and use it at the right time, it will have an effect. Leverage this tool. And remember, one of the major benefits of Injecting Logic is that it simultaneously has an effect on the current emotion, as well as moves you closer to resolution by upgrading the faulty logic, biases, and illusions. But the latter takes time. You must repeat the process again and again and again, like the tree you're chopping down.

Regardless of what logic you settle on, train it. This is how you create logic that's strong enough to cut through and decrease fear, greed, or a loss of confidence in real time. Spend time outside of trading hours to review your Mental Hand History and your logic statement. Commit them to memory. Test yourself.

When you practice your deep breathing, pair it with your logic statement so the two steps become tightly linked. Memorize not just the actual words of your logic statement but the intent. You should be so fluent in this logic that you can recite it in any situation, under intense stress. The stronger the logic becomes in your mind, the more potent the injection.

Sometimes the correct logic is simply an idea you already know well but haven't trained or applied in the right way. When emotions have caused your mind to malfunction, those ideas are gone. They're either too weak to be remembered or don't have the desired impact on your emotional state.

Here are some ideas for how best to use your Injecting Logic statement:

1. **Use your own language.** The statement or phrase needs to reflect the way you actually talk and think. Make sure you use logic that

truly fits. The perfect statement is the one that does the job for you, not the one that sounds best or works for others.

2. **Take an expanded view.** Some clients like to write an entire paragraph that expands on the themes and ideas surrounding the correction and flaw. Then at the start of each trading day, they review the paragraph and pull out a line, phrase, or a word to inject that day. For them, potency comes from having an expanded or deeper view of the problem and correction.

3. **Write down your phrase or statement.** Put it on a note card, sticky note, word document, cell phone, or whatever you find most convenient. This way, you don't have to dig it out of your memory at a time when your mind is malfunctioning.

4. **Adjust if you need an auditory or multimedia approach.** Consider making a voice recording of your statement, or pair it with a picture, song, or movie clip.

5. **Review the logic hourly.** If you have difficulty avoiding severe mistakes, consider preemptively reviewing your logic every hour, half hour, or on a schedule with some regular frequency. This way you'll be more likely to catch the emotion, prevent a significant buildup, gain control more quickly, and minimize the damage.

6. **Avoid these common mistakes.** If Injecting Logic doesn't work, usually it's because:

   - You began using it after your emotions were already too strong and had crossed your emotional threshold. At that point it's too hard think clearly. Injecting Logic is really just thinking. Therefore, if your emotions have weakened your ability to think, trying to inject logic is like attempting to run on a sprained or broken ankle. You must start Injecting Logic when your emotions are small. That may require you to revisit your pattern, and look for earlier signals to map.

   - Your statement wasn't tailored enough to the performance flaw. Go back to the Mental Hand History and complete Steps 2 and 3 again. There's more you need to understand about the underlying cause in order to create a potent statement.

- Accumulated emotion instantly flooded your mind and you didn't even have a chance to use it.
- Something new threw you off. Either the existing problem changed and you didn't recognize it was triggered, or you're dealing with a new problem entirely.
- You need to study it more. The logic is not strong enough yet.

Finally, make sure to hone your ability to know when to use Injecting Logic. Become skilled at identifying the key moments when you need to disrupt the pattern, so that instead of acting on emotion, you're actively fighting to correct it.

Inject logic when emotions have been triggered, and you have to fight to maintain the right perspective—for example when you're taking heavy or consecutive losses, missing opportunities, or likely to move your profit target. All the work you're doing to make the logic strong is for these moments, so you can increase the odds that you can correct your reaction and prevent mistakes.

Early on, you're going to fail when tilt, fear, or greed shut down higher brain functions. The key is working hard to lengthen the time that it takes to fail and to minimize the execution errors when you do. As you gain more experience and repetition, the stronger your logic becomes, and it remains in use at times it previously would have failed.

Momentum is in your favor. Whereas previously emotions got the better of you because you didn't know enough to avoid them, now that only happens when trying to apply the correction in new or challenging situations.

Step 4: Use a Strategic Reminder

Up to this point the strategy has focused on correcting your emotional reaction so that you're less likely to make a mistake. But greater emotional stability doesn't guarantee that. As soon as the malfunctioning mind is in play, strategic and technical aspects of your trading also disappear from your mind, potentially leading you to trade outside your plan or strategy.

A Strategic Reminder can protect your decision-making process and increase the odds of improved execution.

Giving yourself a simple reminder can go a long way toward improving real-time execution, as well as training the weaker aspects of your decision-making process. When mapping your pattern, you already identified the ways that your decision-making process gets altered, flagged the types of errors you typically make, the factors that you ignore, and the changes to your perspective on the market or price. Now, use this information to protect yourself at a time when the risk of making a mistake is high.

To create your Strategic Reminder, think about what happens when emotions are present and select one of the following options. Write it down and keep it with your Injecting Logic statement. You have several options:

- **Option 1: Write down your most common mistakes.** Keeping a list of these mistakes handy reminds you of what to avoid. This goes back to the power that recognition can have in the short term to create some immediate improvement. For some traders, the corrections to these mistakes are obvious, but they don't realize it until after they make them.

- **Option 2: Write down your entire decision-making process.** While some traders see this as tedious, others like having all of this detail. They embrace the opportunity to articulate their entire decision-making process and ensure they're training like an athlete and perfecting their technique.

- **Option 3: Write down only the technical factors or data you fail to consider.** If you think Option 2 is too tedious, here's the shortcut. Rather than reminding yourself of your entire decision-making process, focus only on what goes missing and force yourself to consider it.

The aim is to establish higher levels of execution and decision-making. That requires a one–two combo of Injecting Logic for the mental and emotional side, and using a Strategic Reminder for the technical and strategic side. Adding a Strategic Reminder is different than the emotional and mental work that's the main focus of this book, but it directly fits into the system because it's a critical piece that can minimize mistakes.

Some of you, like the scalpers out there, don't have time to use a Strategic Reminder. That doesn't mean you can't benefit from the exercise of nailing one down, even if you can't use it in real time. Instead, it can be a helpful tool to have as part of your pre-market routine, reinforcing the key elements of quality execution that you're trying to make when emotions pop up.

To recap, the complete real-time strategy is:

1. Recognize that your pattern has been triggered.
2. Disrupt the momentum of that pattern.
3. Use Injecting Logic to correct the flaw.
4. Use the Strategic Reminder to improve your execution.

Again, with practice, these four steps can be completed in seconds. As you get better and better at recognizing and disrupting your pattern and injecting these corrections, your ability to recover will change from hours or days to seconds and minutes. Like any other skill, it may feel clunky at the beginning, but it will eventually get smoother and faster.

Rinse and Repeat

Until the problem is resolved, it's going to keep coming back, like a fly that won't leave you alone. Be prepared to go through the four steps again and again. On some days, you'll need to repeat these steps more than on other days. No two days in trading are exactly the same.

As you go deeper into the day and become mentally fatigued, it often becomes more difficult for you to use strategies correctly and adjust your reaction. It's easy to think that you would build on your success earlier in the day, but that doesn't always happen.

Building the mental strength to control and correct your emotional reactions is a lot like weight lifting: Start with the amount of weight you can lift and then steadily increase it. Rather than just expecting yourself to continue trading at a time when you typically would quit, push yourself to avoid a big mistake for just 5 or 10 more minutes. Then, as you get mentally stronger, add another 5 to 10 minutes.

Sure, 5 to 10 minutes can seem insignificant, but so would the amount of weight you'd be able to lift on your first trip to the gym. Start small, and then push yourself to maintain control longer and longer. Eventually, the severity of the patterning that's triggered will decrease in intensity—an indication that you're moving toward resolution—and you'll be able to avoid severe reactions for hours, even during some very difficult times.

Use Quitting as a Short-Term Strategy

As long as you have a clear plan to resolve your mental game problems, quitting can be a viable short-term strategy while you work toward resolution. There isn't a hard-and-fast rule to determine when the best time is to quit; sometimes you need to push yourself, while other times you need to quit to avoid a big step back, mentally or emotionally.

Part of this skill is knowing when a mental game issue is too severe to carry on and you need to take a break, or quit. Of course, sometimes you don't know the limits of your capacity until you hit a brick wall. My advice is to err on the side of caution in the short term.

By following the system laid out in this book, your capacity will increase over time, provided that you don't continually push yourself too far beyond the point of failure. Like someone in physical therapy rehabbing an injury, if you overdo it, you risk getting reinjured.

BUILD A PRODUCTIVE ROUTINE

Once you have identified the problem to resolve, you need to work the problem with a consistent routine and rigorous focus. When you have a routine that prepares you properly, you're more likely to execute well and make improvements.

On the other hand, if you do fail, you're more likely to understand why, and to learn from it, which ultimately leads to progress in the future. Essentially, you create a cycle of improvement that allows you to make the most of each trading session.

Take Time for a Warmup

The value of a warmup is widely understood within sports and most areas of performance. While the idea of warming up before playing poker was surprisingly novel when I first entered the poker world, that's not the case in trading. What may be novel, however, is the idea of a warmup, or pre-market routine, being used not only to put you in the right state of mind for trading but to better prepare you to correct the range of problems you're likely to face.

In practical terms, this means your warmup should include reviewing the maps you have created for each problem area. This increases the likelihood that you spot the real-time signals of a problem. You should also reread the Mental Hand History and Injecting Logic statements to strengthen your understanding of the cause and correction of the problems that you'll face.

You might think back to a few recent scenarios that were troublesome. Envision yourself going through the process of seeing the signals of the problem, taking a deep breath or standing up, and then using Injecting Logic and a Strategic Reminder.

Basically, you're mentally rehearsing the actions you'll take to control or correct your problems. If all your materials are already prepared, the whole process takes 3 to 5 minutes. Be sure to focus intently and bring a sense of priority. Never just go through the motions.

Take Time for a Cooldown

Just like the warmup is an implicit part of most performance arenas, especially for athletes, cooling down is as well. For athletes it tends to be more focused on physical recovery—getting treatment, icing down muscles, etc.—to help the body to heal and recover. The cooldown is essentially preparation to be able to do it all again tomorrow.

As a trader, your cooldown may include logging trades into your journal, analyzing them, and checking PnL. But you need to also focus on recovery from a mental and emotional standpoint. For example, add details to your map, write and vent about your emotions to prevent accumulation, and analyze your progress.

Your mind has captured so much data, including the emotions, thoughts, and actions that surround each problem. If you're diligent about capturing those details and working through them, you'll find the 5 to 15 minutes you spend will be incredibly valuable the following day.

Since this time is so valuable, here are a few suggestions for adjustments you can make to your cooldown, depending on the type of day you've had.

On a day **when your emotions stay relatively stable**, where problems may pop up but you handle them with relative ease, it's unlikely there will be many new things to note. Instead, reinforce your progress by thinking or writing about what improved. Don't just focus on the negatives. Emphasize instances where your attempts to correct anger, for example, were successful, especially if it took a lot of mental effort.

On a day **when emotions are high**, vent your emotions by writing them down, and then either reread an existing Mental Hand History on this topic or complete a new one. This will help you to prevent accumulated emotions and reinforce the correction.

You don't need to start immediately after the trading day is over. But I strongly recommend you start within 30 minutes, while the ideas are fresh in your mind and the emotion is raw. That's the good stuff. Not only do you not want to lose those critical details but this is also a prime opportunity to generate new insights.

On a day **when emotions are super high**, you probably want to just go blow off steam, wallow in self-pity, or enjoy the rush of a euphoric day, and one of the last things you want to do is sit down and write. But your goals are recovery and getting in good shape for the next day. The best thing you can do is dump as many thoughts down as you can. In part, because when your problems are the biggest, you get a better glimpse into the root of the problem.

You don't have to do a Mental Hand History. Just be a detective and grab the data. If you just rush off, you might lose details that could be critical to solving the problem.

Take Time to Work the Problem

You can't show up right before a trading session and map your pattern, complete a Mental Hand History, define Injecting Logic statements, or finish an A- to C-game Analysis. Before a session, you only have time to review or revise existing materials, not generate them from scratch. To work efficiently toward resolution, these are tools that need to be worked on at the times when you would normally be doing research, learning new concepts, or other things to improve your trading.

I realize that I'm adding more responsibilities, and there's only so much time in the day. Perhaps now that you're working aggressively on your mental game, you'll prioritize this work. Then as the materials are created, and you have a strong overall strategy, you can reduce the time spent to an amount you can consistently maintain. In general, you want to be sure you continually work the problems, even if that means just reviewing or updating existing materials.

Evaluate Progress

If you want to reach resolution as efficiently as possible, you need to know whether you're making progress or not. That's not so simple, because of both the unpredictable nature of trading and the complexities of evaluating your own mental and emotional state.

A common mistake I see traders make is relying on emotions as a measuring stick for progress. Even when you're making progress, you may not feel the difference emotionally. For example, you might feel just as fearful entering a trade today as you did several months ago. But if you look closely, you notice your thoughts are less pessimistic, you hesitate less, and you no longer open a one-minute chart with your eyes glued to every tick. Those indications of progress aren't evident from your emotions—you have to look at changes to other signals on your map.

Identifying whether or not you've made progress is critical. You could incorrectly think nothing has improved—when it has—and lose confidence or motivation in a strategy that's actually working. Or, if you aren't improving, you need to know this, so you can figure out what's not working. The following are some general indications your mental game is improving.

Are you increasingly able to recognize your pattern, including being able to spot signals before you reach your threshold? While you may not have established the ability to control or correct your emotions in real time yet, you're better at seeing what's happening. While this may seem insignificant, increased recognition is a critical first step. The remainder of the real-time strategy doesn't work without it.

The next big marker of progress is being **able to control or correct your emotions.** Look for those moments when greed, tilt, or fear is *about* to cause a mistake, but you catch yourself and use Injecting Logic. It's not so much that you don't react as that you don't let the reaction carry you away in the manner it used to. That, in turn, reduces your emotions and improves your decision-making and execution. While you may have to battle for that progress, you win the battle more often.

At first, your mental and emotional state may improve by only a fraction of a percent. That's still something to build on, because you're simultaneously training the long-term solution. Over time, the correction becomes more potent, cutting through the emotional reaction faster, so you can minimize the damage and recover more quickly. You also don't need to take bigger chunks of time off during the trading day.

Eventually, you will clearly have **less emotion to battle,** and you'll see that resolution has begun. Resolution isn't a light switch, especially with intense emotions. Think of it more like a volume knob that you dial down. For example, you still feel that immediate reflex of greed or the impulse to revenge trade, but, apples to apples, it's 10% less intense.

As progress continues and you resolve more of the problem, you automatically generate less and less emotion. That means your emotions are naturally more stable, and whatever fear, anger, or overconfidence remains is much easier to chop through. Eventually, the triggers no longer produce emotion and the problem is resolved.

The biggest problem in recognizing resolution is that you won't know when you've crossed the finish line. It's not like running a race where the end is marked. But there are clues that indicate you've arrived. Here are some signals of resolution:

- You remain competent, even under intense pressure or extreme fatigue. To see how far you've come, compare your current worst to your prior worst and see how much your decision-making process has improved.
- In your B-game, the impulse to make mistakes caused by emotion disappears. There's less interference or noise in your B-game. It feels qualitatively different.
- At times when your emotional reactions were previously intense, they're now less severe, automatically and without conscious effort.
- You have increased mental clarity or bandwidth to improve your A-game. Mental space has been freed up through backend mastery, and that makes you more creative, willing to innovate, or open to learning new things.
- You have a greater desire to tackle projects or concepts that you had previously been introduced to, but didn't feel like you were able to begin.

Another indication of resolution is **evolution in your mental game.** As the back end of your range progresses, your C-game changes—either with previous problems becoming smaller versions of themselves or entirely new ones popping up. Perhaps you got rid of your issues with low confidence, but you swung too far in the other direction and now, at times, become overconfident. Or improvements in your perfectionism lowered the fear of loss and you began to enter more trades, but now you tilt from losing.

You must see these new problems as evidence of progress. You graduated to a new C-game, and that means you have the potential to reach an even greater A-game . . . perhaps you've already seen it.

Or, despite your best efforts, unfortunately your mental game hasn't improved. You've worked hard using the system, but you haven't been able to sustain a change of any significance. In the next and final chapter, you'll be able to troubleshoot common causes that stall progress or create significant setbacks, and learn what to do about them.

CHAPTER 10

TROUBLESHOOTING A LACK OF PROGRESS

"The most important thing to do if you
find yourself in a hole is to stop digging."

—Warren Buffett

At the end of the last chapter I talked about evaluating your progress. But what if you're not making progress? While there's too much diversity to troubleshoot all of the potential causes of a lack of progress, in this chapter we'll drill into six common ones.

DIFFICULTY RECOGNIZING YOUR PATTERN

Your reactions come swiftly and arise, seemingly, out of nowhere. Problems continue to happen, but you can't spot how they start. You see the evidence in the aftermath of mistakes and losses, but you can't recognize the preceding signals that are critical to stopping your emotions from escalating or keeping your discipline from breaking down.

In my experience, there are two common scenarios why you can't recognize your pattern. In scenario one, you haven't really done the work. Be honest with yourself. Did you just read through the book, expecting the changes to come through osmosis, or did you actually put in the time and effort to map your patterns as I suggested?

If you didn't do the work, you need to. There's no way around it. To make it easier, try talking with a mentor or another trader. Maybe in the early stages you need someone to brainstorm with and bounce ideas off.

In scenario two, you did the work, but you're so skilled at suppressing your emotional issues day to day that you didn't find anything. Then, out of nowhere, you have these big blowup days, and you can't recognize what prompts them. The key here is to become more attuned to the signals of suppression. What are the actions you take or the thoughts you have that you use to manage emotions or keep them at bay?

These are currently your automatic responses to the presence of greed, fear, or anger. For example, you might immediately talk with another trader about what happened, or you might be hyper-logical in your assertions that a loss didn't affect you. Those responses are the signals of a low-level problem, and you can begin mapping from there.

You should also complete a deep dive after your next blowout day to try to get to the roots of the issue. Use the different sections of the book to complete a Mental Hand History, and then take those ideas and bring them to your day-to-day attempts to recognize their presence.

For example, let's say you figure out that you have an illusion of control. That's what causes the mixture of greed and overconfidence that's part of the blowup. Now look day to day and ask yourself: How am I over-controlling? For example, you're overly focused on keeping your R-factor high and you've set your stops too tight because you think price will move in your favor. These become additional signs of where greed or anger can begin, and you've got a starting point for Injecting Logic and to begin to correct the illusion of control.

THINGS GET WORSE BEFORE THEY GET BETTER

Ideally, you'll take the lessons and tools you've gained from this book, put them into action, and immediately make progress. But sometimes, for several reasons, the opposite can happen and problems worsen.

First off, once you start looking more closely, you might find the problems in your mental game are actually worse or more complex than you had originally thought. Essentially you've ripped off the bandage to get a look at the injury and it's not pretty. What you thought was your C-game wasn't—it's more like you have an F-game. But while the truth can hurt, at least now you know what you're dealing with, and can plan how to proceed.

Being more aware of your emotions can also feel like you're taking steps backward. Greed, fear, or tilt can feel more intense when you pay closer attention to them. These are not actual steps back. Rather, you're becoming aware of what had previously been ignored.

All the new information about your mental game can be overwhelming. You've learned a lot of new theories about learning and emotion, found out about numerous problems you might face, and discovered their causes and corrections—all while trying to understand the details of your problems.

There's a lot more that you're aware of now. So you're figuratively tripping over all this new information while you work toward developing greater competence. This isn't uncommon, especially if you read the book all in one pass.

If this sounds familiar, focus on the low-hanging fruit that will give you some easy wins and a chance to turn what you learned into a simple strategy you can build on. This way, you'll find some solid ground to stand on, rather than trying to do too much, all at once. Otherwise, you'll feel like you're treading in quicksand, where everything you do makes you sink deeper.

If you have trouble prioritizing, consider this guideline: Try something, and if you're not making progress within two weeks, reevaluate and select something else. At times getting started is the only way to gather the info you need. Some things you can't learn from the sidelines.

Finally, another reason you might have gotten off on the wrong foot is the variance in market. Sometimes the timing as to when you start to implement these new mental game strategies coincides with a shift in the market, or a streak of losses that is out of your hands. Don't overreact to circumstances you can't control.

Instead, think of the opportunity another way—getting beaten up early allows you to get to the true bottom of your range that much faster. Then, as market conditions or results turn in your favor, you're apt to have fewer surprises down the road. Sure, it would be great to see progress immediately, but if the opposite happens, take advantage of the opportunity it provides.

BURNOUT

Burnout is common among traders. The markets don't care about your need to take time off. And if you're trading markets that are open 24/7, it feels as though you never get a break. In the back of your mind are constant thoughts and awareness about trading.

There's also a high demand for precision with every single decision, which makes you more like an athlete than an employee in a secure nine-to-five job. Plus, when you're trading your own money, in a drawdown, or struggling to get a feel for the market, the constant stress can burn you out.

As it relates to your mental game, burnout intensifies your problems and limits your ability to improve them, even if you have correctly identified the root cause. Your mind is in a weakened state, so you lack the strength, clarity, and poise to execute your strategy and fight for progress. Emotional volatility is higher, and emotions accumulate at a faster rate, which means you have more emotion to handle and less mental strength or willpower to battle it.

The correction for burnout is simple: rest. There's no other way around it. The problem is that the kind of rest that you need to recover from burnout is costly. You don't make money when your trading business is closed, and for some of you it makes sense to push yourself through these times, like an injured athlete in the playoffs who has to stick it out because giving up isn't an option.

There comes a point, however, where burnout is too significant. Much like the classifications for physical burns to the skin, there are different levels of severity to burnout. The more severe it is, the worse your decisions become and the longer it takes you to recover.

To prevent a severe burnout, you need to figure out the one or two signs that indicate you're *nearing* that point. The signs could be emotional—you no longer have any control over tilt or greed. Or it could be evident in your discipline. Maybe you can't follow your own rules to make proper entries and exists.

You might notice a distinct change in your motivation. For example, mild burnout is signaled by a lack of interest in completing thorough research. On the other hand, not wanting to trade at all indicates severe burnout.

The best time to research your signs of burnout and identify the key factor is after each occurrence of burnout. Think of it like mapping any other problem I've described in this book. Take good notes, and the next time around, use what you've found to spot the early indicators of burnout. Then you can take steps just prior to reaching that point. For example, if you find that 15 days of breakeven trading during an intense market is your limit, then, after day 10, take extra steps to help you reset daily.

Prioritize your cooldown, diet, exercise, and sleep. Be social, engage in your hobbies, read for enjoyment and not development, or do something fun and not overly mentally stimulating. This will help to not only delay the onset of burnout but possibly prevent it entirely—you stay right at the edge, without quite going over it.

BLOATED BRAIN

Previously I discussed how focus is your tool to gather the data you need to make decisions. But when you gather too much data, a subtle problem emerges that few traders know about, one that I call "bloated brain." Even though it's not commonly identified, I do believe it's commonly experienced, as I have seen through years of working directly with clients.

Think about those trading days where you were intensely focused for so long that you stopped being able to properly analyze the market and missed opportunities, or forced poor setups. Or how about the times when you were researching, studying new methods, or back-testing for large chunks of time and reached a point where your brain just shut off—you couldn't focus any longer and new information no longer made any sense.

At those times, your mind is so full of data that you don't have the room to hold any more. You're like a soaked sponge unable to absorb any more water. You have a hard time concentrating, miss key information, and feel mentally exhausted—like your head is in a fog. You most likely assume that you're just tired, and that it's a natural consequence of a long day, or the intensive focus of researching and learning. And, to some degree, that's true. But fatigue doesn't tell the full story.

The other side of the story is that your brain is full of data. The deluge of information crammed into it creates the drop in clarity, thinking, and execution during the trading day, and can make it hard to segregate trading from your life. You try to have dinner with your family, watch a ballgame with a friend, or whatever you do to relax, but your mind won't stop. You're there, but not totally there. Thoughts continue to pop up.

Then when you're tired and ready to go to bed, your mind is active and won't settle. You replay mistakes and missed opportunities, reconsider the exit strategy on a profitable position, or mull over new research that you were thinking about earlier. This can go on for hours. Other times, you fall asleep right away, but wake up early to thoughts about trades or research.

In some ways, you might not consider it a problem. You like the constant focus and innovative thoughts, and you view the loss of sleep or lack of presence with family and friends as a cost of this business. But you also know what it feels like when your mind is sharp—fresh, energized, focused—and you don't have it as often as in the past.

When there's too much data being absorbed, it can also carry over day to day. Accumulated data is very much like accumulated emotion, and in a subtle way it can limit your ability to think clearly and process information the following day. When you're driven to optimize your performance and learning, a cluttered mind is a hidden danger. The good news is that it's fairly easy to address by adding simple habits into your daily routine.

The brain has a natural process for digesting information and converting it into valuable knowledge, just as the body's digestive system extracts nutrients from food. You can make that process more efficient.

During the trading day, or during a long period of researching or studying, take breaks before your brain shuts off. Taking just a few minutes, where you stop consuming new data, can give your brain an opportunity to digest more of what you've absorbed.

In that time, take some notes, go for a short walk, or meditate. You may not feel like you're completely reset, but in some ways that doesn't matter. You're looking to just delay the drop-off in your performance until the end of the trading day or duration of research, so you can maximize the effectiveness of your working time.

Then, after trading or researching, help your brain digest the data by writing, or talking and then taking notes, whichever you prefer. You don't even have to review what you write to experience a benefit. The mental clarity you achieve from getting the data out of your head is valuable on its own. However, I recommend that you review a few of the key takeaways from your writing as part of your warmup before the next time you trade.

This creates a cycle where you regularly focus on improving specific parts of your tactical and mental game, before, during, and after you trade. That kind of repetition is key to accelerating improvement.

Writing is also a good tool when you can't sleep. Rather than trying to go to sleep when your mind is full, write about what's in your head. Note down details of a difficult decision, mistakes that you made, or modifications to your strategy. Do it until you have nothing left to write about, or up to 30 minutes, and then try to go to sleep. You may not fall asleep without any thoughts the first time you try it, but with practice you'll train your mind and eventually fall asleep faster.

Clients who follow this advice tell me that by regularly dumping out the data that accumulates in their mind, they feel mentally refreshed at times when they previous assumed they were tired. They also can better separate trading from their lives, and go on with their day without the same need to mentally reset by blowing off steam, drinking, or an intense workout. They sleep better, and they have more mental clarity while trading.

Try it yourself for 7 to 10 days and see what you find. The space in your mind is valuable real estate. Keep it clear and you'll see an improvement in your execution.

WHEN LIFE BLEEDS INTO TRADING

Sometimes your mind is consumed by emotional and energy-draining personal concerns that affect your progress. For example, an illness in the family, conflict with your significant other, or major decisions or tasks, such as moving or renovating a home, can be all-consuming.

When life bleeds into your day, it can take away from the enjoyment, the challenge, and the curiosity you ordinarily bring to trading. Execution and performance drop, and suddenly the weight of the outside factors seems even greater because you're losing money too. Not only does trading suffer but you go right from the trading session back to the personal dealings. You don't get a break, and things can quickly spiral out of control.

The goal is to protect your progress and execution by keeping all the personal thoughts, tasks, and emotions out of trading. Essentially, you create a bubble around trading that keeps your life out of it. In addition, keeping your personal life separate gives you a much-needed break and allows you to attend to the personal stuff with a clearer mind. Trading becomes like a mini-vacation from your personal life.

Here are the steps to create a bubble around your trading:

- **Step 1:** An hour before the trading day starts, write down everything on your mind on that particular topic. It could be how you feel, specific thoughts, a practical to-do list, or things you want to say to people. Spend up to 20 minutes doing this.
- **Step 2:** After completing that initial writing task, draw a mental line in the sand, where from that moment until the end of the

trading day, you don't allow yourself to think about your personal concerns.

- **Step 3:** Now, around 40 minutes before the trading day, you should use the time as you would normally. The timing isn't arbitrary. Writing up to 20 minutes allows you to release the thoughts without being consumed. It also builds in a buffer of time. If you have additional thoughts about that personal stuff that you can't get out of your head, you have a chance to capture them and reaffirm the idea that you're not thinking about this until the end of the trading day.

    Then, whenever you have momentary thoughts, use the Injecting Logic of "Not now." And if they don't go away, take a few moments to write them down and reaffirm the bubble.

Of course, sometimes you have practical things that must be attended to during the trading day; for example, 11:00 a.m. is the only time the doctor or contractor can talk. Once these tasks have been concluded, repeat Step 3 and get back into the bubble.

When Trading Exposes Personal Problems

When you have unresolved issues in your personal life, even ones you didn't know were a problem, they can spill out into trading. Having these issues appear in trading can often be confusing, because you don't experience anything like them outside of trading. In the rest of your life, you're confident, decisive, and emotionally balanced. It doesn't seem to make sense why these emotions come out in trading.

Trading is a unique test that can bring out your deepest fears, unresolved rage, and personal insecurities. These problems directly affect your execution and profitability, compelling you to take on too much risk, lock up profit prematurely, or chase losses, but they have nothing to do with trading. Rather, investing so much of your time, energy, money, future, confidence, and identity into trading eventually just brings out these deeper personal issues.

Some of you have a need for trades to work out to confirm a sense of personal competence, purpose, and success. When you fail in trading, you feel like a failure in life. Or maybe you get so angry when you get stopped out that you're compelled to immediately reenter. Perhaps as a kid you hated losing and were relentless until you won.

Maybe you can't seem to make a move, even when you want to. Maybe your parents expected perfection and overreacted to any mistakes you made. Now, fear of a mistake keeps you on the sidelines, and you get pissed off when you miss entries—either way you can't win.

The good news is that once you get to the root of the problem, you have a chance to cross-train and improve both your personal life and trading at the same time.

Digging through personal issues can be tough. If you want to try tackling them on your own, use the Mental Hand History as your tool to organize your work. Look closely at the cause of your trading problems and identify the personal equivalent. Then, use what you find as Step 1 and complete the remaining four steps. If the problems you have are particularly severe, consider working with a therapist.

To give you an example of what this can look like, here's a story about my client Will. After retiring from senior-level roles in corporate America, Will took up trading as a part-time occupation that would, hopefully, add to his retirement income. In his previous career Will was known as an even-keeled guy who got things done. But when he began trading, he tapped into a vein of anger he didn't realize existed.

Trading stocks and equities, Will's general goal was to trade for an hour or two in the morning, freeing up the rest of the day for other pursuits. The problem was, he would make some money, then take a loss and end up giving it all back in a death spiral. He would get angrier and angrier, until he was in a full-blown rage. He would scream, cuss, break things, and literally fling himself to the floor and pound on it in frustration. He had no control over his reactions and had turned into a person he didn't recognize.

Will described days when he'd be yelling, "Kill the trade!" but feeling like his arms were frozen. He couldn't get out. He actually videotaped himself so he could watch what it was like and was astounded. "It was like aliens had taken over my body," he said. "I watched myself acting like a five-year-old—I was throwing a temper tantrum!" Will hadn't experienced this level of anger before, in either his personal life or his former career, which made the problem harder to comprehend. It was, at that time, inexplicable to him.

Will began extensive research. He read books and applied their advice. He produced volumes of material, trying to understand and address his anger. Will was one of the most meticulous clients I have had in my entire career when it came to the amount of content he produced by journaling, mapping his patterns, and working through his problems.

As we dug through that material, we soon realized that he had problems with an illusion of control, perfectionism, and a fear of failure, all of which were rooted in childhood trauma he needed to come to terms with.

As Will worked through the personal trauma outside of trading, it was important for him to recognize, while he was trading, that his emotions were related to those old issues. The urge to, for example, add to a loser, oversize trades, or avoid setting protective stops was a signal that his personal problems were seeping into his trading.

In those moments Will began Injecting Logic that incorporated corrections he had found on the personal side. That allowed him, for the first time, to stabilize his emotions enough to take losses and avoid a major blowup.

We continued to work through each step of my system, using many of the strategies outlined in the Desperation section of this book to establish clean layers of control, catalog his accomplishments to date, and identify the roots of his technical errors using the Mental Hand History. Over time, Will's anger lessened, and that allowed him to become more aware of when it started so he could quickly correct it.

He focused on the probabilistic nature of trading and got himself more comfortable with the overall risk and the role of variance. He learned to remind himself that if price didn't move in the direction he wanted, he wasn't responsible for that result unless he held on to it, against his plan. Eventually, Will could make a mistake and think, *Well that was a boneheaded move*, and quickly reset, rather than pounding the table and losing control.

I caught up with Will after not talking for a couple of years. He told me that today, about 98% of that initial anger is gone. He no longer breaks keyboards in half, throws the computer mouse across the room, or has tantrums (though he admits he still cusses a bit). As we caught up, Will wondered why the childhood trauma had come out in trading and not before.

I explained his situation to him with an analogy related to war. It was as if Will had experienced war crimes during deployment and couldn't process them until he was safe at home. In his case, the "crimes" were trauma from his childhood, and being retired with a firm financial future felt like being "home safe." Trading just happened to be what he was doing when the layers of trauma started to emerge, and due to the intense nature of trading, those wounds were ripped open and laid bare.

Having healed a majority of his personal trauma and the trading mistakes that were caused by it, the problems Will deals with now are the normal ones covered in this book. He's graduated. The key for him, going forward, is to remember that the system worked, and to use it again on the more typical performance problems so he can continue to improve.

As you've no doubt realized by now, continuing to improve is a core theme of the mental game.

FINAL THOUGHTS

"In any given moment we have two options:
to step forward into growth or to step back into safety."
—Abraham Maslow

You began reading this book knowing that something—or many some-
things—were getting between you and trading at a level you knew was
possible. No doubt you'd already explored your technical skills and
eventually realized the stumbling blocks in your way had to do with
your mental game—and that's why you turned to the system I offer in
this book.

After diving deep into this system and learning about the performance flaws at the root of your problems, you're armed with the strategy and tools to correct them.

The system works if you do the work. To make progress, take what
you have read in these pages and start applying it every day.

Use the descriptions and accounts of other traders to help you
uncover your own patterns and the unique ways your performance
flaws emerge. Map your patterns and develop an A- to C-game Analysis. Complete Mental Hand Histories. Create Injecting Logic statements
using your own words, and a Strategic Reminder that applies best to
your style of trading.

And incorporate other resources, both from within trading and outside of it, that resonate with you, such as books, videos, quotes, or inter-
views. There are many valuable sources of information out there that
you can use within the system to help you achieve resolution.

Be ruthless in identifying and correcting the many mistakes you
make as you go, but find moments to have fun with the process. Like the

market, there will be ups and downs. Some days you'll reach new highs, and other days you'll struggle. Embrace that reality and just keep doing the work.

Permanently correcting or resolving your performance flaws, biases, illusions, or wishes doesn't come quickly. You need a lot of repetition. Most often, you also need a lot of repetition in a lot of different situations. Keep at it.

Continue to use this book as a resource along the way. There's too much to absorb and apply in just one pass. When your mental game progresses beyond the problems that originally brought you here, apply the system to your new problems.

Remember, the system isn't meant for you to use once and set aside. Growth is a constant for those who want it. If you continue to apply the techniques, tactics, and insights, you'll continue to make progress and reap more benefits. You'll be able to keep moving your Inchworm forward and improve your A-, B-, and C-games.

The time to start is now. Literally, right now—even if that means taking just one minute to begin moving forward. No more excuses. Get to work. It's time to turn your potential as a trader into a reality.

If you'd like to stay up on my latest blogs, podcasts, or projects, or to access downloadable worksheets that can, for example, help you map your patterns, complete an A- to C-game Analysis, or fill out a Mental Hand History, go to: https://jaredtendler.com.

Endnotes

CHAPTER 5: FEAR

1 Timothy D. Wilson & Daniel T. Gilbert, *"Affective Forecasting,"* in M. P. Zanna (Ed.), *Advances in experimental social psychology, vol. 35* (pp. 345–411). Elsevier Academic Press, http://wjh-www.harvard .edu/~dtg/Wilson%20&%20Gilbert%20(Advances).pdf.

2 Dan Gilbert, "The surprising science of happiness," TED Talk, February 2004, https://www.ted.com/talks/dan_gilbert_the_surprising _science_of_happiness#t-174602.

CHAPTER 6: TILT

3 Daniel Kahneman & Amos Tversky, "Prospect Theory: An Analysis of Decision under Risk," *Econometrica*, Econometric Society, March 1979, Vol. 47, No. 2, pp. 263–292.

4 Amos Tversky & Daniel Kahneman, "Advances in Prospect Theory: Cumulative Representation of Uncertainty," *Journal of Risk and Uncertainty*, Kluwer Academic Publishers, 1992.

5 Abigail Tucker, "Are Babies Born Good?," *Smithsonian Magazine*, January 2013, https://www.smithsonianmag.com/science-nature/are -babies-born-good-165443013/?c=y&story=fullstory.

6 Benedict Carey, "Payback Time: Why Revenge Tastes So Sweet," *The New York Times*, July 27, 2004.

CHAPTER 7: CONFIDENCE

7 J. Kruger, & D. Dunning, "Unskilled and unaware of it: how difficulties in recognizing one's own incompetence leads to inflated self-assessments," *Journal of personality and social psychology*, December 1999, pp. 1121–1134, https://pubmed.ncbi.nlm.nih.gov/10626367.

CHAPTER 8: **DISCIPLINE**

8 "Ethos of the U.S. Navy SEALs," National Navy UDT–Seal Museum, https://www.navysealmuseum.org/about-navy-seals/ethos-of-the-u-s -navy-seals.

CHAPTER 9: **CORRECT YOUR PROBLEM**

9 Carmine Gallo, "JFK's Twitter Friendly Version," *Forbes*, May 25, 2011, https://www.forbes.com/sites/carminegallo/2011/05/25/jfks-twitter -friendly-vision/#424a6ee568ce; see also "The Decision to Go to the Moon: President John F. Kennedy's May 25, 1961, Speech before a Joint Session of Congress, NASA, https://www.nasa.gov/feature/john-f -kennedy-and-nasa; https://history.nasa.gov/moondec.html.

10 Robert M. Yerkes & John D. Dodson, "The relation of strength of stimulus to rapidity of habit-formation," *Journal of Comparative Neurology and Psychology*, November 1908, Vol. 18, Issue 5, pp. 459–482.

11 Amy Arnsten, Carolyn M. Mazure & Rajita Sinha, "Everyday Stress Can Shut Down the Brain's Chief Command Center," *Scientific American*, April 2012, Vol. 306, No.4, pp. 48–53.

12 David Tod, James Hardy & Emily Oliver, "Effects of self-talk: a systematic review," *Journal of Sport & Exercise Psychology*, October 2011, Vol. 33, pp. 666–687.

Acknowledgments

I'm not a natural writer, so I relied heavily on others for help. I'm deeply appreciative to the many people who helped make this book happen. I could not have completed it on my own.

First and foremost, my writing partner Beth Kupchinsky. Thank you for your incredible expertise and unwavering dedication to this project. Even though the finish line took longer to reach than expected, you were an incredible partner from beginning to end. Your questions, insights, and perspectives helped me to see my material in a new light, and I am forever grateful.

Marcy McDonald, my amazing editor. Thank you for your vision and guidance. You delivered on your promise and brought the book to another level.

To all the clients I've worked with over the years, thank you for helping me to better understand the nuances of trading and the demands of your profession. I particularly want to thank the traders who lent their stories and examples to this book: Alex Raguz, Brendan, Brian Heffernan, Carlos, Chris Duhanci, David Lombard, Frantz Gheller, Giacomo, Goro Kanehara, Gurdeep Gosal, Joseph Abboud, Max Sydney, Michael Whalen, Nick Whitton, Rodrick, Vishal Nathu, Vlad Brykin, and Will Ranney. Your voices helped bring the book to life and for that I'm greatly appreciative.

To my family and friends, thank you for your support and encouragement. Especially my wife Corey and daughter Teddy. No question, 2020 was a challenging year, but you two made it possible for me to complete this book—and enjoy the process. No small feat. Thank you for giving me the space to focus on it. I'm so lucky to have you two in my corner, cheering me on.

About the Author

 Jared Tendler, M.S., LMHC, is an internationally recognized mental game coach. His roster of clients spans 45 countries and includes independent and institutional traders, world champion poker players, entrepreneurs, esports athletes, and several PGA Tour players.

In addition to *The Mental Game of Trading*, Jared is also the author of two best-selling books, *The Mental Game of Poker* and *The Mental Game of Poker 2*. Jared previously served as the Head of Sport Psychology for the esport organization Team Liquid. He was a key driver of many of their championships, including The International 2017 (DOTA2), the Intel Grand Slam (Counter-Strike) and four League Championship Series titles (League of Legends).

His interest in the mental game was born out of personal experience. While playing collegiate golf for Skidmore College, Jared was a three-time All-American and won nine tournaments, yet continually choked in major national events. Driven to find answers, he earned a master's degree in counseling psychology and became a licensed therapist to solve the problems conventional sports psychology couldn't. Since then, Jared's straightforward and practical approach to coaching has helped thousands solve their mental game problems and perform at their highest levels.